LABORATORY Manual

BIOLOGY

CBSE Class XI

Author
Manvi Sirohi

Name...

Class...................... Section...................... Roll No......................

School...

Arihant Prakashan (School Division Series)

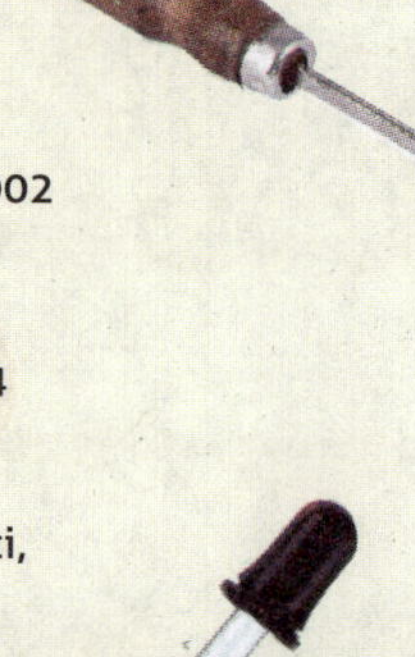

Arihant Prakashan (School Division Series)

卐 Administrative & Production Offices

Regd. Office
'Ramchhaya' 4577/15, Agarwal Road, Darya Ganj, New Delhi -110002
Tele: 011- 47630600, 43518550; Fax: 011- 23280316

Head Office
Kalindi, TP Nagar, Meerut (UP) - 250002, Tel: 0121-7156203, 7156204

卐 Sales & Support Offices

Agra, Ahmedabad, Bengaluru, Bareilly, Chennai, Delhi, Guwahati, Hyderabad, Jaipur, Jhansi, Kolkata, Lucknow, Nagpur & Pune

卐 Price : ₹ 375.00

TXT-29-T071773-7-26

Published by Arihant Publications (India) Ltd.

For further information about the books from Arihant, log on to **www.arihantbooks.com** or email to **info@arihantbooks.com**

Follow us on

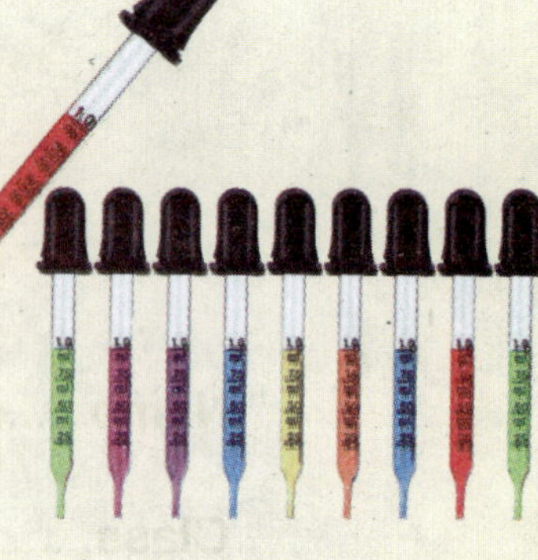

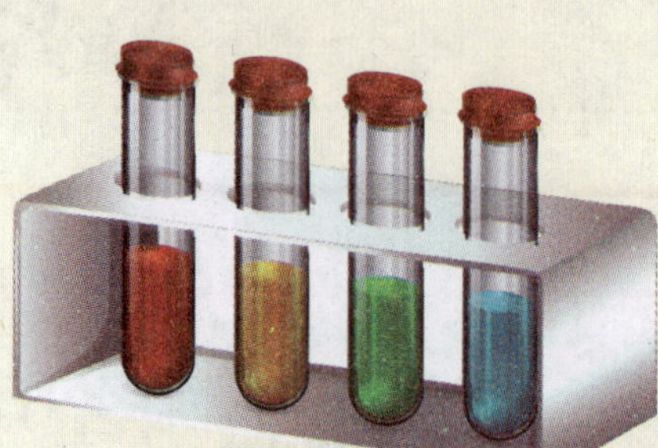

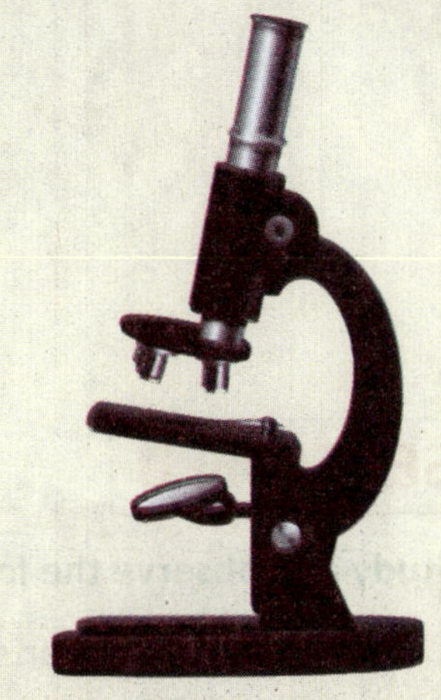

Contents

SECTION B

Study and observe the following (Spotting Experiments)

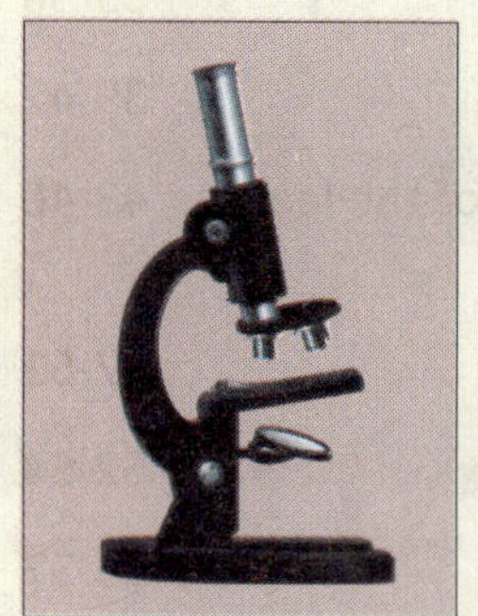
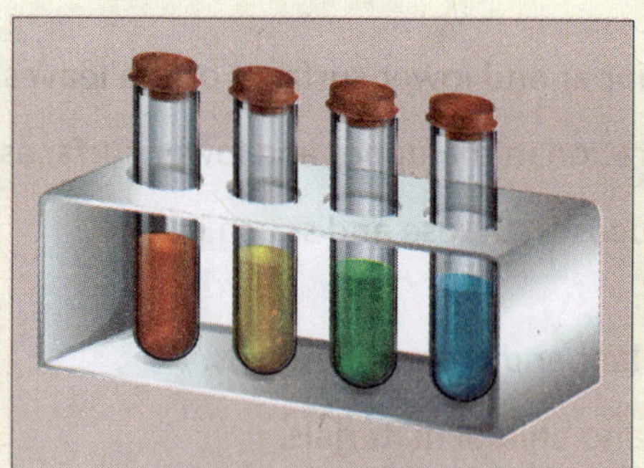

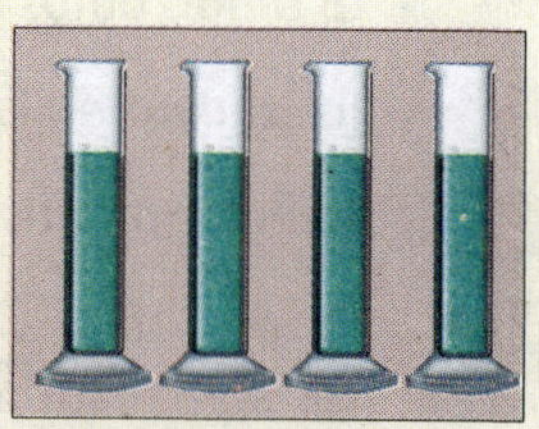
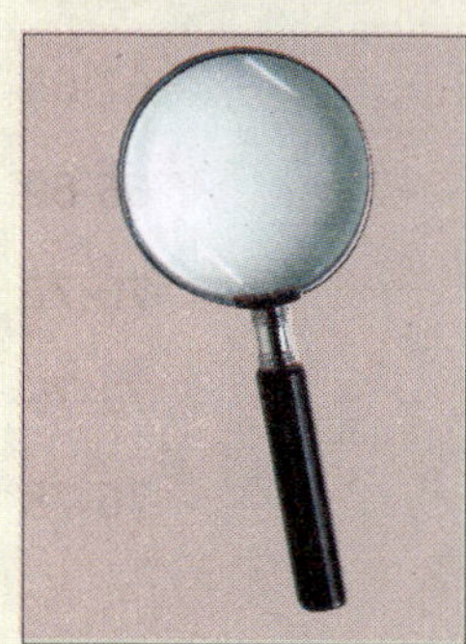
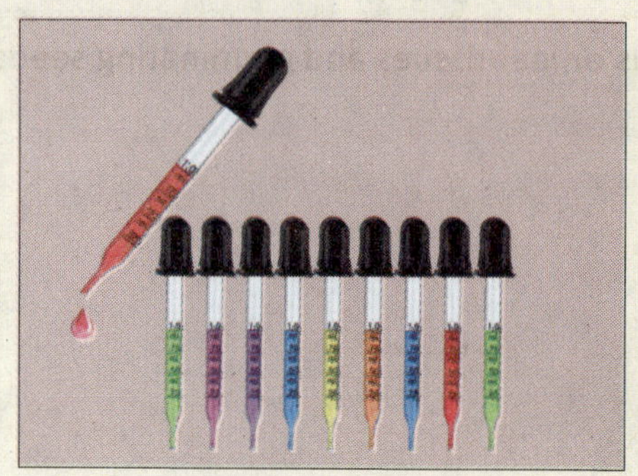
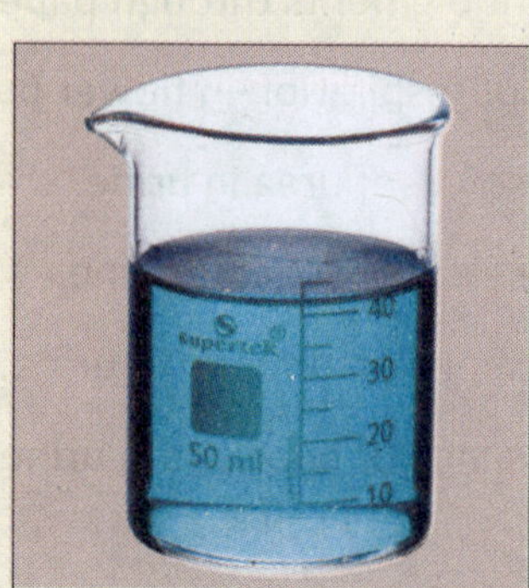

Syllabus

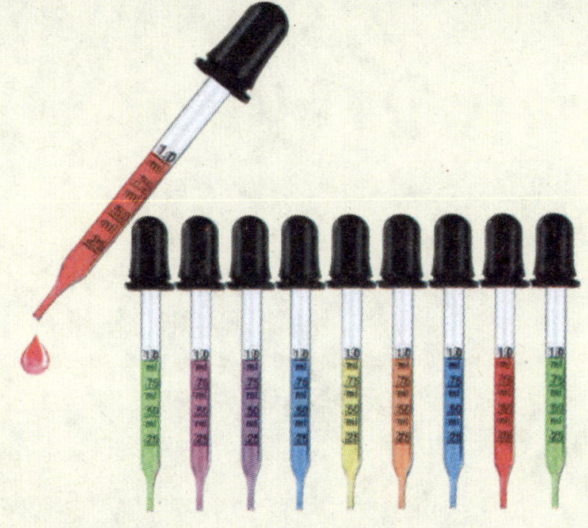

Time allowed : 3 Hours		Max. Marks : 30
Evaluation Scheme		Marks
One Major Experiment Part A (Experiment No- 1,3,7,8)		5 Marks
One Minor Experiment Part A (Experiment No- 6,9,10,11,12,13)		4 Marks
Slide Preparation Part A (Experiment No- 2,4,5)		5 Marks
Spotting Part B		7 Marks
Practical Record + Viva Voce	(Credit to the student's work over the academic session may be given)	4 Marks
Project Record + Viva Voce		5 Marks
Total		30 Marks

PART-A

List of Experiments

1. Study and describe locally available common flowering plants, from family Solanaceae (Poaceae, Asteraceae or Brassicaceae can be substituted in case of particular geographical location) including dissection and display of floral whorls, anther and ovary to show number of chambers (floral formulae and floral diagrams), type of root (tap and adventitious); type of stem (herbaceous and woody); leaf (arrangement, shape, venation, simple and compound).
2. Preparation and study of TS of dicot and monocot roots and stems (primary).
3. Study of osmosis by potato osmometer.
4. Study of plasmolysis in epidermal peels (e.g. *Rhoeo*/lily leaves or flashy scale leaves of onion bulb).
5. Study of distribution of stomata on the upper and lower surfaces of leaves.
6. Comparative study of the rates of transpiration in the upper and lower surfaces of leaves.
7. Test for the presence of sugar, starch, proteins and fats in suitable plant and animal materials.
8. Separation of plant pigments through paper chromatography.
9. Study of the rate of respiration in flower buds/leaf tissue and germinating seeds.
10. Test for presence of urea in urine.
11. Test for presence of sugar in urine.
12. Test for presence of albumin in urine.
13. Test for presence of bile salts in urine.

PART-B

Study and observe the following (spotting)

1. Parts of a compound microscope.
2. Specimens/slides/models and identification with reasons - Bacteria, *Oscillatoria*, *Spirogyra*, *Rhizopus*, mushroom, yeast, liverwort, moss, fern, pine, one monocotyledonous plant, one dicotyledonous plant and one lichen.
3. Virtual specimens/slides/models and identifying features of - *Amoeba*, *Hydra*, liverfluke, *Ascaris*, leech, earthworm, prawn, silkworm, honeybee, snail, starfish, shark, rohu, frog, lizard, pigeon and rabbit.
4. Mitosis in onion root tip cells and animal cells (grasshopper) from permanent slides.
5. Different types of inflorescence (cymose and racemose).
6. Human skeleton and different types of joints with the help of virtual images/models only.

INDEX

S.No.	Name of the Experiment	Page No.	Date	Remarks

INDEX

S.No.	Name of the Experiment	Page No.	Date	Remarks

LABORATORY Manual

BIOLOGY

CERTIFICATE

This is to certify that Experiments recorded in this Practical Notebook have been performed

by ____
(Student's Name)

of __________ of ________________________________
(Class/Section) (School Name)

during academic session ____________________

....
Examiner Signature

....
Principal Signature
(with school stamp)

....
Teacher Signature

Your Laboratory

A biology laboratory is essential for testing ideas and concepts through experiments because it allows student to directly engage with the biological phenomenon.

It provides a unique learning environment where students develop scientific temper, acquire relevant skills and become familiar with various techniques and methodologies of scientific investigation.

A science student cannot truly learn without a laboratory. Learners get exposure to various advanced techniques and tools used in research, preparing them for future endeavours.

Lab Essentials

To perform experiments successfully, a learner needs to enter the biology laboratory well prepared with following essentials:

1. **A Laboratory Record Book** For documenting all the information including data recordings and their interpretations.
2. **A Laboratory Manual** For detailing the experiments and procedures to be followed.
3. **Dissection Box** Required for various tasks such as handling and manipulating living materials, conducting experiments and preparing slides. It includes scissors, scalpels, forceps, dissecting needles, razor, hand lens, dropper, fine brush, etc.
4. **Laboratory Coat** Required to protect the learner against chemical spills and biological contaminants, ensuring safety and hygiene during experiments.
5. **A Hand Towel** For cleanliness and drying hands.

Precautions While Working In the Laboratory

- Carefully listen to the teacher's instruction before performing an experiment.
- Be careful while handling sharp tools like scissors, needles, scalpel, razors and forceps.
- Always follow the safety guidelines written on the instruments and chemical containers.
- Be aware of how to use first-aid kit in case someone gets hurt.

Introduction to Lab Instruments

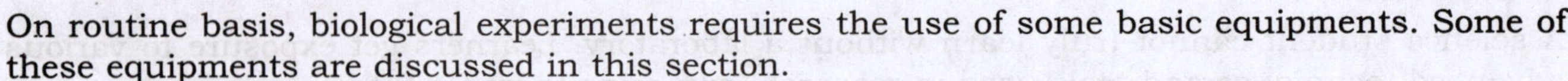

On routine basis, biological experiments requires the use of some basic equipments. Some of these equipments are discussed in this section.

Microscope

Microscope is a widely and extensively used instrument found in all biology labs. It magnifies and resolves the object when seen through it. Microscopes of different powers are used to observe microscopic details of any given sample. Microscope works on the basis of two functions:

- **Magnification** It is refer to how many times larger an object appears when viewed through the microscope compared to its actual size.
- **Resolution** The ability of microscope to distinguish two close points as separate entities.

Microscopes are of two types:

(i) **Light Microscope**

It uses light as a source of illumination. It is of two types:

(a) Dissecting microscope

(b) Compound microscope

(ii) **Electron Microscope**

It uses electrons as a source of illumination for the microscopic field.

a. Dissecting Microscope

It is designed to provide three-dimensional view of objects like insects, plants or larger biological specimens. It is also used to perform dissections of small organisms.

Working

- The object or slide with specimen is placed on the stage of the microscope.
- Lens is moved above the slide with the help of a folded arm.
- Adjustment screws are used in order to move the vertical limb to focus on the slide.

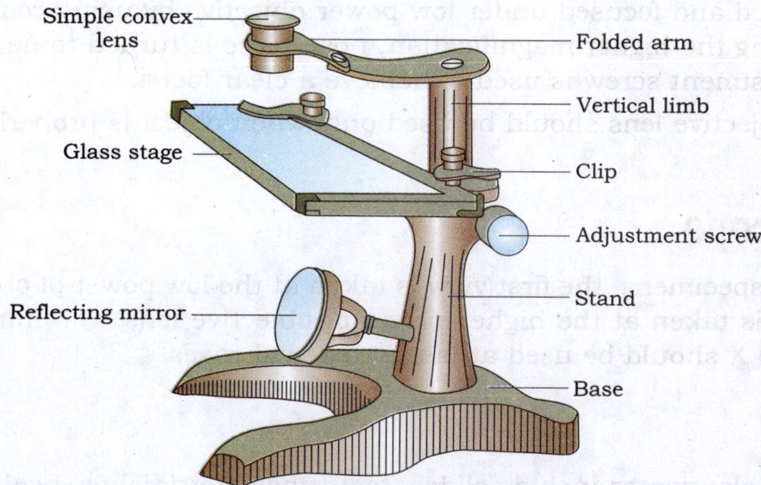

A dissecting microscope

b. Compound Microscope

It is an optical instrument that uses multiple lenses for the magnification of small objects for detailed observations.

Working

- The mirror is adjusted in diffused source of light so that sufficient light enters into the microscope.
- The light entering into microscope should be regulated with the help of diaphragm.
- A clean prepared slide is placed on the centre of the stage such that it lies just under the objective lens and is completely illuminated by diaphragm.

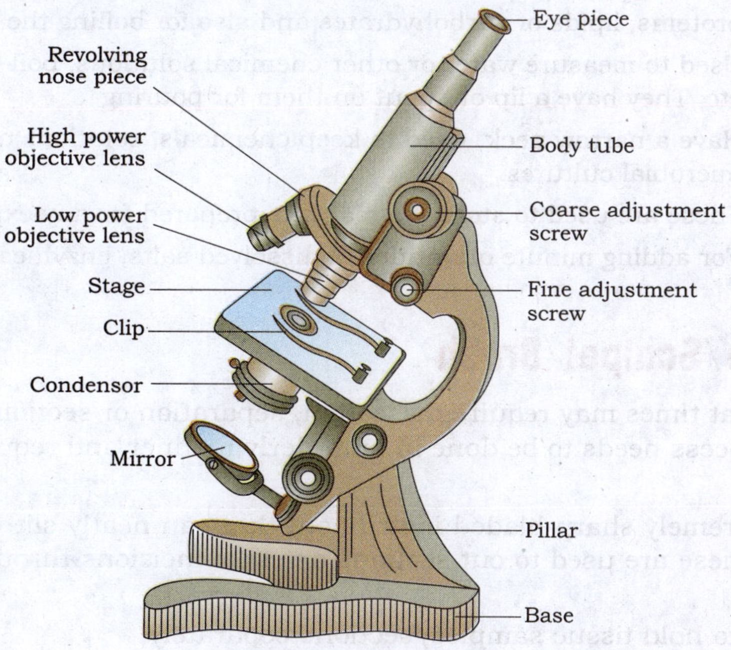

A compound microscope

- The object is located and focused under low power objective by using coarse adjustment screw. For obtaining the higher magnification, nose piece is turned to next higher power lens and fine adjustment screw is used to achieve a clear focus.
- The high power objective lens should be used only when object is properly mounted under coverslip.

Use of Microscope

While observing the specimens, the first view is taken at the low power of objective lens and the second observation is taken at the higher power of objective lens. Oil immersion lens having magnification of 100 X should be used at last for special cases.

Glasswares

The commonly used glasswares include slides, test tubes, petridishes, beakers, flasks, reagent bottles, funnel, etc.

Slides	To view a sample under microscope, a specimen is placed on to a clean glass slide. The sample can be fixed or stained on the slide for undisturbed and clear observation.
Coverslips	Used to cover the section or tissues on the glass slide.
Petridishes	Used to culture the samples (generally microorganism) by placing them on a nutrient agar or broth medium.
Watch glass	Used to keep the fine cut sections in water while preparing the slide. Also used for staining the sections.
Test tube	A sample when requires mixing, addition of solutions, etc. is placed in a clean, dry test tube. It is also used for the biochemical experiments of proteins, lipids or carbohydrates and also for boiling the leaves or tissues.
Beakers	Used to measure water or other chemical solutions, boil or mix the solutions, etc. They have a lip or spout on them for pouring.
Flasks	Have a narrow neck, used to keep chemicals, solutions or nutrient media for microbial cultures.
Reagent bottles	These are used to store the reagents prepared for any experiment.
Glass pipettes	For adding minute quantities of dissolved salts, enzymes or other solutions.

Forceps/Needle/Scalpel/Brush

Biology experiments at times may require dissection, separation or section cutting of animal or plant tissue. This process needs to be done in an orderly manner and requires the use of sharp instruments.

- A **scalpel** is an extremely sharp-bladed instrument that can neatly slit the skin open or cut through tissues. These are used to cut sections or make incisions through muscle and organs.
- **Forceps** are used to hold tissue samples/sections separately.
- **Brush** is used for transferring the sections of specimen from one slide to another slide.

Apparatus and Glasswares Required in Biology Laboratory

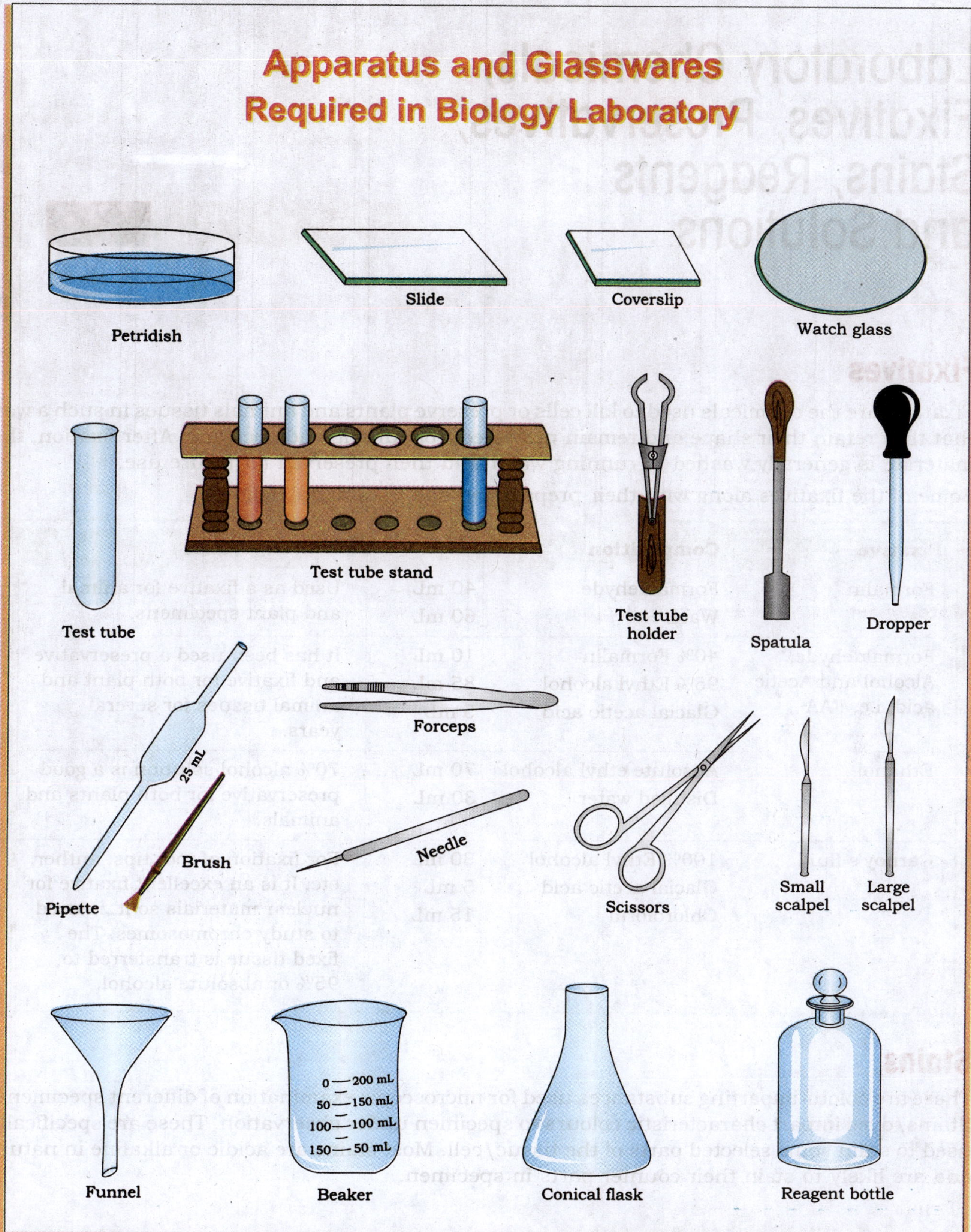

Laboratory Chemicals, Fixatives, Preservatives, Stains, Reagents and Solutions

Fixatives

Fixatives are the chemicals used to kill cells or preserve plants and animals tissues in such a way that they retain their shape and remain protected from drying and decaying. After fixation, the material, is generally washed in running water and then preserved for future use.

Some of the fixatives along with their preparation and uses are as follows:

Fixative	Composition		Uses
Formalin	Formaldehyde Water	40 mL 60 mL	Used as a fixative for animal and plant specimens.
Formaldehyde, Alcohol and Acetic acid, i.e. FAA	40% Formalin 95% Ethyl alcohol Glacial acetic acid	10 mL 85 mL 5 mL	It has been used a preservative and fixative for both plant and animal tissues for several years.
Ethanol	Absolute ethyl alcohol Distilled water	70 mL 30 mL	70% alcohol solution is a good preservative for both plants and animals.
Carnoy's fluid	100% Ethyl alcohol Glacial acetic acid Chloroform	30 mL 5 mL 15 mL	For fixation of root tips, anther, etc. It is an excellent fixative for nuclear materials so it is used to study chromosomes. The fixed tissue is transferred to 95% or absolute alcohol.

Stains

These are colour imparting substances used for microscopic examination of different specimens. Stains/dyes impart characteristic colours to specimen under observation. These are specifically used to stain some selected parts of the tissue/cell. Most stains are acidic or alkaline in nature and are likely to stain their counter parts in specimen.

The most commonly used stains in biology laboratory are discussed below:

Stains	Composition and Preparation		Uses
1. **Acetocarmine**	Carmine powder Glacial acetic acid Distilled water Ferric acetate Dissolve carmine powder in the mixture of acetic acid and water by boiling. Add a few drops of ferric acetate on cooling. Filter and store the solution in a dark bottle.	– 1 g – 45 mL – 55 mL – A few drops	Stains chromosomes dark red. Commonly used to study chromosomes during cell division.
2. **Safranin**	Safranin powder Ethyl alcohol (50%) Dissolve safranin powder to the alcohol and store the solution in a clean bottle.	– 1 g – 100 mL	Used to stain lignified tissues, cutinised tissues and nucleus.
3. **Methylene blue** (Wright's blood stain)	Methylene blue Sodium bicarbonate Distilled water Dissolve sodium bicarbonate in distilled water and add methylene. Boil for one hour then cool, filter and store.	– 0.9 g – 0.5 g – 95 mL	Used for staining blood tissue specimen.
4. **Haematoxylin**	Haematoxylin Ethyl alcohol Saturated aqueous solution of ammonium alum Methyl alcohol Glycerine Dissolve haematoxylin in ethyl alcohol. To this, add saturated aqueous solution of ammonium alum. Expose the solution to light for 48 hours. After this interval, add methyl alcohol and glycerine. Mix these well and keep the solution for 2 months for ripening. Filter and store in stoppered bottles for future use.	– 4 g – 25 mL – 400 mL – 100 mL – 10 mL	Used as a nuclear stain.
5. **Iodine stain** (Lugol's)	Potassium iodide Iodine Distilled water Dissolve potassium iodide in water followed by addition of iodine to the solution while stirring it continuously.	– 10 g – 5 g – 100 mL	Used for staining flagella, cilia and nuclei of the cells.

Stains	Composition and Preparation	Uses
6. **Eosin** (Aqueous)	a. **Aqueous eosin** Eosin powder – 1 g Distilled water – 100 mL Dissolve eosin powder to the distilled water and store it in clean bottle. b. **Alcoholic eosin** Eosin powder – 1 g Ethyl alcohol – 100 mL	Used as a cytoplasmic stain.
7. **Crystal violet**	Crystal violet – 14 g Ethyl alcohol (95%) – 100 mL Dissolve the crystal violet stain in ethyl alcohol and leave it for 2-3 days. Filter and store.	Used to stain bacteria and protozoan.
8. **Basic Fuchsin**	Basic fuchsin – 8 g Ethyl alcohol – 100 mL Dissolve the stain in ethyl alcohol by stirring it continuously. Leave it for three days. Filter and store it.	Used to stain bacteria.
9. **Leishman's stain**	Leishman's stain – 0.15 g (powder) Methyl alcohol – 100 mL Dissolve the stain powder in methyl alcohol and leave it for 48 hours.	Used for staining blood smears. It is used to differentiate and identify leucocytes, malarial parasites and *Trypanosoma*.
10. **Borax carmine**	Borax – 4 g Carmine – 3 g Distilled water – 100 mL Ethyl alcohol (75%) – 100 mL Mix borax powder with carmine powder and dissolve the mixture in distilled water. Now add ethyl alcohol to this mixture. Allow the mixture to stand for three to five days and then filter.	It is generally used to stain cell structure such as nuclei and cytoplasm in tissue sections red.

Mounting Media

These are the chemicals which protect the cell/tissues from being dehydrated. These can fix the cell/tissues or section either temporarily or permanently. Some mounting media are described below.

Mounting media	Preparation and composition	Uses
1. **Glycerine**	Gelatin – 10 g Distilled water – 60 mL Pure glycerine – 70 mL Phenol crystals – 0.25 g Dissolve gelatin in distilled water by heating it. Add glycerine and phenol while the solution is still hot.	• It is used as a temporary mounting media.
2. **Canada balsam**	Canada balsam – 60 g Xylene – 100 mL Dissolve this balsam in xylene in an oven.	• It is a natural resin from balsam fir tree. • Used for permanent slide fixation.
3. **D.P.X**	Distrene 80 – 10 g Dibutyl phthalate – 5 mL Xylene – 35 mL	• It is most commonly used mountant. • Used for permanent slide preparation.
4. **Lactophenol**	Phenol crystals Lactic acid Glycerine Distilled water Cotton blue (For staining fungi) Mix all the mentioned constituents in equal measure.	• It is used as mounting medium and staining agent for fungi.

Biochemical Reagents and Solutions

Some solutions are generally used to test the presence of chemicals in the given samples. The most commonly used biochemical reagents and solutions are listed as follows:

Reagents/ Solutions	Preparations and composition	Uses
1. **Acid water/Acid alcohol**	a. Conc. HCl – 1-2 drops Distilled water – 100 mL b. Conc. HCl – 2 drops 70% Alcohol – 100 mL	It is used to remove excess of aqueous or alcoholic stain from the tissues.

Reagents/ Solutions	Preparations and composition	Uses
2. **Benedict's reagent**	Sodium citrate – 173 g Sodium carbonate (anhydrous) – 100 g Copper sulphate – 17.3 g Distilled water – 1000 mL Dissolve sodium citrate and sodium carbonate in 800 mL water. Dissolve copper sulphate in 100 mL water, mix the two and make it 1000 mL.	• It is used to test the presence of reducing sugars.
3. **Fehling's solution A**	Copper sulphate – 70 g Distilled water – 1000 mL	• It is used to test the presence of reducing sugars.
4. **Fehling's solution B**	Potassium hydroxide – 350 g Potassium sodium tartarate – 350 g Distilled water – 1000 mL ***Note*** Fehling's solution A and B should be mixed in equal volumes, only when needed for use.	• It is used to test the presence of reducing sugars.
5. **Biuret reagent**	3% Copper sulphate – 95 mL 10% Potassium hydroxide – 1000 mL	• It is used to test the presence of proteins in biochemical test.
6. **Millon's reagent**	Mercury – 100 g Nitric acid – 200 mL Distilled water – 600 mL Dissolve mercury in nitric acid and dilute it with water. ***Note*** Never add water to acid. To dilute the concentrated acid, add acid to water slowly and carefully, to avoid bubbling.	• It is used to test the presence of proteins in biochemical test.
7. **Buffer solution**	a. M/15 $Na_2HPO_4 \cdot 12H_2O$ solution $Na_2HPO_4 \cdot 12H_2O$ – 23.88 g Distilled water – 1 L b. M/15 KH_2PO_4 solution KH_2PO_4 – 9.08 g Distilled water – 1 L	• These are used to maintain pH within a range.

Some Common Procedures and Practices

The study of biological parts and processes requires the use of few basic techniques in the laboratory. Some of these skills are mentioned below.

Peeling

- This method requires the removal of an intact section of leaf epidermis layer.
- Separating out a peel from leaf requires a needle and forceps.
- A small part of sample is broken with care, leaving a thin translucent membrane.
- The peel pulled apart is placed on a slide or watch glass in a drop of water and is then stained or mounted for study.

e.g. To study the structure of stomata, a thin peeled section of leaf is required.

Smearing

This technique involves the uniform spreading of cells from a section or sample as a single layer over specific area of slide. The cells get smeared during spreading, which permits a clear study of given process.

- The sample is placed in stain and crushed with scalpel or another slide. By doing this, large pieces are removed.
- The second slide is now placed on the corner and run it over the sample using uniform, but gentle pressure.
- The slide is then gently heated over a flame. It is then covered with coverslip after mounting it with appropriate mounting medium and sealed with melted wax or transparent nail polish.

e.g. Root tips of onion, anthers of *Tradescantia,* blood cells of human, etc are widely used for smear preparations.

Section Cutting

Sections are cut to study the internal structure of an object. It is used for examining the stem, root or leaf. A thin, nearly transparent section is cut with the help of sharp razor or blade in the laboratory.

The section can be cut in two planes

(i) **Transverse Section** (TS) This section passes at a right angle to the longitudinal axis.

(ii) **Longitudinal Section** (LS) This section passes at a right angle to the transverse axis. Sometime, sections are cut in vertical plane. This is known as Vertical Section (V.S.), e.g. section of leaf.

Procedure of Section Cutting

- To cut the section, hold the material between your thumb and first finger or embed it in a pith for better support.
- Now, hold the razor in your right hand and cut several thin sections in a single motion.
- Collect the sample immediately in the watch glass containing water, so as to prevent them from drying or destroying.
- Select a suitable section and place it on the slide with the help of brush for further staining and studying.

Staining

To study the section prepared of plant or animal cells, it is necessary to differentiate them properly. This is achieved by staining the sections using specific stains or dyes.

The stain imparts characteristic colour to different components and helps in distinguishing different tissues, cellular inclusions, etc clearly.

1. **Single Stains** In this, only a single stain is used for the sample to be studied.

   Example – Safranin, aniline blue, etc.

   Filaments of algae, fungi, sections of pollens, spores, etc. can be studied using these stains.

2. **Combination of Stains** In this, two or more stains are employed or used to differentiate or distinguish different tissues, cells or cell inclusions. For this purpose, one acidic dye and one basic dye of contrasting colour are generally used. It is used for the sections of stem, root or leaves.

   The several combination of stains used are:

   (i) Hematoxylin (basic stain) and eosin (acidic stain).
   (ii) Safranin (basic stain) and fast green (acidic stain).
   (iii) Safranin (basic stain) and aniline blue (basic stain).
   (iv) Safranin (basic stain) and crystal violet (basic stain).

Mounting

Mounting is done to protect the section from drying or destroying and to preserve it for longer period of time. Glycerine, DPX or Canada balsam may be used for this purpose.

- When the mounting is done by using glycerine, the slide prepartion is said to be **temporary** while, when mounting is done by using permanent mount like DPX or Canada balsam, the slide preparation is said to be **permanent.**
- Mounting is done by pouring a drop of mounting medium on the section over slide.
- Place a coverslip very gently over it so that no bubble should appear.
- Wipe off the extra mounting medium from the sides of the coverslip with the help of cotton or blotting paper.
- Now, the slide is ready for study.

- In case of permanent slide, prepare a label describing your name and description of material mounted. Fix this label on the glass slide. The description of section (as name of plant and its part) can also be posted on to the slide.

Drawing the Diagram

Make illustrations using pencil only and it should be drawn on the centre of the page. The image drawn on the paper should be proportionate in size with the actual object or specimen or image.

Illustrations should be drawn directly by keeping the object in front and not from the book. All the diagrams or illustrations should be well-labelled. Two lines of labelling should never cross each other. An appropriate caption or heading of the drawing should also be given below it.

Study of Slides

While studying the slides under the microscope, ensure not to disturb the slide once it is set in appropriate position. Draw the diagrams directly from the slide, not from the book.

Study of Specimens/Models

Study the characteristics of the specimen from your text book and try to relate your theoretical knowledge with the practical view of the organism (model or specimen). Draw well-labelled diagrams neatly in the record book directly from the actual specimen. Avoid shading and write the comments.

How to Record An Experiment?

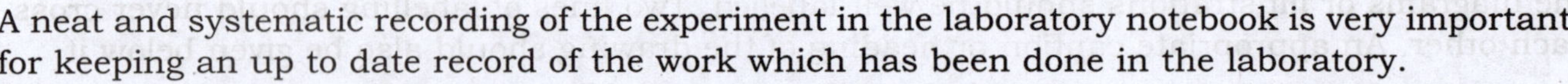

A neat and systematic recording of the experiment in the laboratory notebook is very important for keeping an up to date record of the work which has been done in the laboratory.

Infact, a proper record of the experimental results and conclusions is an indispensable part of scientific work.

The laboratory notebook must be well maintained and protected from mechanical and chemical damage. It should be regularly checked by the teacher.

The experiment should be recorded in the laboratory notebook under the following heads as:

Date......	Experiment No.	Page No. ......
Aim or Objective of the Experiment States the overall purpose of the experiment to be performed.		
Theory or Principle Mention the concept on which the experiment is based in a very brief manner. It also, includes the formula used and clearly explains the symbols involved.		
Apparatus and Materials Required Mention the name of the apparatus and chemicals to be used in the experiment clearly.		
Procedure Mention various steps in the experiment to be followed.		
Chemical Reactions The chemical reactions that take place in the experiment should be written on the left hand side of notebook.		
Diagrams Wherever required, draw the diagrams on the left hand side of the notebook.		
Observations Record the observations or data in a tabular format, avoiding any overwriting.		
Calculations [wherever desirable] For writing the calculations, substitute the observed value in the formula and do the computations systematically and neatly.		
Result State the conclusions drawn from the experimental observations. If the result depends upon the conditions of temperature and pressure, mention these conditions also along with the result.		
Precautions Mention the precautions observed during the setup of the apparatus and while performing the experiment.		
Discussion Under this heading any special inferences or special difficulties faced during the experimentation is been mentioned. These may include points for making the experiment more accurate and for better understanding of the basic principle involved.		

SECTION-A

Experiment 1

AIM

To study and describe flowering plants of family–Solanaceae.

Theory/Principle

The identification of plants is based primarily on morphological features, particularly the floral characters. The angiosperms or flowering plants show a large diversity in external structure called as morphology. The branch of science that deals with identification, nomenclature and classification of organisms is called taxonomy. **Bentham** and **Hooker's** system of classification is an universal classification system used to classify the plants.

Plant body mainly consists of a main axis, which may be branched or unbranched, bearing lateral appendages. The main axis is divided into two major parts, i.e. underground part that develops from radicle called roots and aerial part that develops from plumule, called shoot. The aerial part is comprised of stem, leaves and fruits.

Flower is basically an extended shoot with a condensed axis called thalamus and several parts called floral appendages. A typical flower has four types of floral appendages called sepals, petals, stamens and carpels in distinct whorls known as calyx, corolla, androecium and gynoecium, respectively. The flower arises on the mother axis and possesses a stalk called pedicel. The pedicel is borne in the axil of a small leaf-like structure called bract.

Terms Related to Flower

Bracteate A flower having bract at base.

Ebracteate A flower without a bract.

Pedicellate A flower having a stalk or pedicel.

Sessile A flower without a stalk or pedicel.

Complete A flower having all the four whorls.

Incomplete A flower where one or more than one of the whorls are absent.

Actinomorphic A flower that can be divided into two equal halves through any vertical plane, e.g. *Brassica*.

Zygomorphic A flower that can be divided into two equal halves along a single vertical plane only, e.g. *Lathyrus*.

Asymmetrical A flower that cannot be divided into equal halves by any plane, e.g. *Canna*.

Bisexual A flower having both male (stamen) and female (carpel) sex organs.

Unisexual A flower having either male or female reproductive organs.

(i) **Staminate** Flower having only male sex organs.

(ii) **Pistillate** Flower having only female sex organs.

Dimerous Floral leaves of each whorl are in multiple of 2, e.g. poppy.

Trimerous Floral leaves of each whorl are in multiple of 3, e.g. lilies.

Tetramerous Floral leaves of each whorl are in multiple of 4, e.g. mustard.

Pentamerous Floral leaves of each whorl are in multiple of 5, e.g. *Hibiscus*.

Hypogynous A flower where ovary is situated at the highest place on thalamus with the remaining floral structures underneath, so that the ovary is superior and other floral structures are inferior, e.g. mustard and China rose.

Perigynous A flower in which the ovary is placed at the same level as other floral structures, so that the ovary is half superior and half inferior, e.g. rose and peach.

Epigynous A flower in which the ovary is placed lower to other floral structures on the thalamus, so that the ovary is inferior and other floral structures are superior, e.g. ray florets of sunflower.

Floral Appendages

A flower consists of four whorls namely, calyx, corolla, androecium and gynoecium.

Calyx

It is the outermost whorl of flower and is composed of sepals. It is green in colour and can perform photosynthesis. It also protects the flower when the flower is not in fully-developed state.

Forms of Calyx

(a) **Polysepalous** Calyx consists of sepals that are free at their ends, e.g. mustard.

(b) **Gamosepalous** Calyx consists of united sepals, e.g. *Petunia*.

Corolla

It is the second whorl of flower, composed of petals, which are brightly coloured to attract insects for pollination.

Forms of Corolla

(a) **Polypetalous** Flower contains free petals.

(i) **Cruciform** Consists of four, free, regular and clawed petals, arranged in the form of a cross, e.g. *Brassica*.

(ii) **Caryophyllaceous** Consists of five clawed petals in which limbs of the petals are placed at right angle to the claws, e.g. *Dianthus*.

(iii) **Rosaceous** Consists of five or more sessile petals or with very short claws and their limbs are spread outwards, e.g. rose.

(b) **Gamopetalous** Corolla is composed of fused petals.

Aestivation

The mode of arrangement of sepals or petals in the floral bud, with respect to the other members of the same whorl is called aestivation. The pattern of aestivation is an important feature in the classification of plants.

Forms of Aestivation

(a) **Valvate** Sepals and petals are close to each other by their edges but do not overlap, e.g. *Calotropis*.

(b) **Twisted** Regular overlapping of one margin of each petal or sepal by the next petal/sepal member and the other margin is overlapped by the previous petal or sepal, e.g. *Hibiscus* or China rose.

(c) **Imbricate** Five sepals/petals are arranged in such a way that one sepal/petal is completely external and another sepal/petal is completely internal, while three petals are partially external and partially internal, e.g. *Cassia*.

(d) **Vexillary** When the largest of the five sepals/petals overlaps the two lateral sepals/petals, which in turn, overlap the two small anterior sepals/petals (keel), e.g. pea. It is also known as descending imbricate.

(e) **Quincuncial** Out of five sepals/petals two are completely internal, two external and one has one margin external and the other margin internal, e.g. guava.

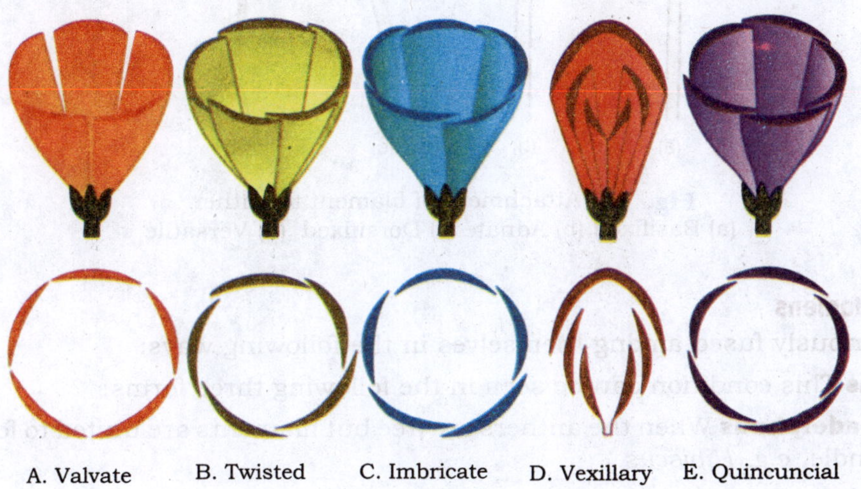

Fig. 1.1 Aestivation in flowers

Androecium

It is the third whorl of flower, which is composed of stamens. Stamens represents the male reproductive organ and consists of a stalk or filament and an anther.

Forms of Androecium

(a) **Polyandrous** Stamens are free, not attached to any whorl, e.g. lotus.

(b) **Epipetalous** When stamens are attached to the petals by their filament, e.g. sunflower and brinjal.

(c) **Epiphyllous** When stamens are attached to the perianth by their filament, e.g. lily.

(d) **Didynamous** Out of four stamens, two are long and two are short, e.g. *Ocimum*.

(e) **Tetradynamous** Out of six stamens in two whorls, the two outer ones are short and four inner ones are long, e.g. *Brassica*.

I. Fixation of Filament to Anther

The attachment of filament to anther can be of following types:

(a) **Basifixed** When the filament is attached to the base of anther, e.g. mustard.

(b) **Dorsifixed** When the filament is attached on the dorsal surface of anther, e.g. passion flower.

(c) **Adnate** When the filament is attached along the whole length of anther, e.g. *Magnolia*.

(d) **Versatile** When the filament is attached to the middle of connective, so that anther lobes can swing in air, e.g. grasses.

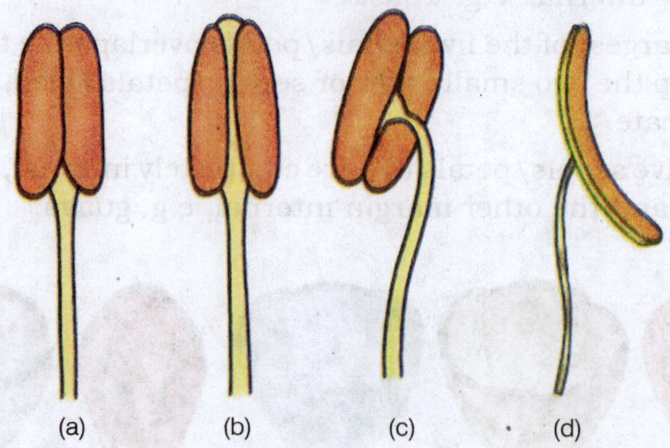

Fig. 1.2 Attachment of filament to anther
(a) Basifixed (b) Adnate (c) Dorsifixed (d) Versatile

II. Cohesion of Stamens

Stamens are variously fused among themselves in the following ways:

(a) **Adelphous** This condition can be seen in the following three forms:

(i) **Monoadelphous** When the anthers are free but filaments are united to form one bunch or bundle, e.g. *Hibiscus*.

(ii) **Diadelphous** Anthers are free but filaments are fused to form two bundles, e.g. *Lathyrus*.

(iii) **Polyadelphous** Anthers are free but filaments are fused into more than two bundles, e.g. *Citrus*.

(b) **Syngenesious** Anthers are fused but filaments are free, e.g. sunflower.

(c) **Synandrous** Stamens are fused in both the regions, i.e. anther lobe and filament, e.g. *Cucurbita*.

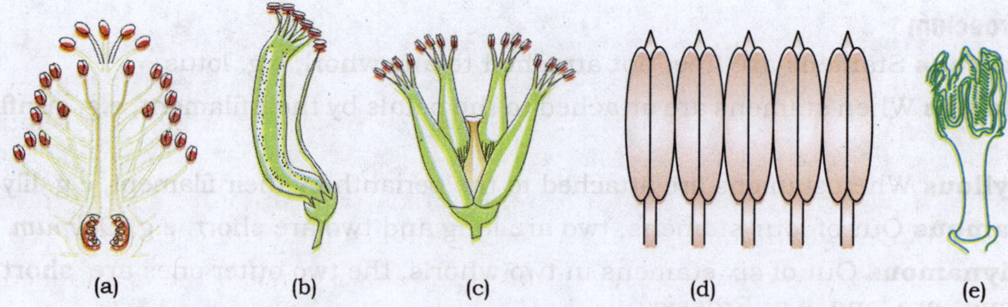

Fig. 1.3 Cohesion of stamen: (a) Monadelphous (b) Diadelphous
(c) Polyadelphous (d) Syngenesious (e) Synandrous

Gynoecium

Gynoecium is the female reproductive part of flower and is made up of one or more carpels. It is the innermost whorl, consisting of stigma, style and ovary.

I. Forms of Gynoecium

(a) **Monocarpellary** Gynoecium contains one carpel, e.g. pea.

(b) **Bicarpellary** Gynoecium contains two carpels, e.g. *Petunia*.

(c) **Pentacarpellary or Polycarpellary** Gynoecium contains five or many carpels, e.g. China rose.

II. Fusion of Carpels

Depending upon fusion, the carpels are of two types:

(a) **Apocarpous** A pistil has two or more carpels that are free from each other, e.g. lotus and rose.

(b) **Syncarpous** A pistil with two or more carpels which are fused with each other, e.g. China rose and tomato.

III. Locules in Ovary

The cavity enclosed by ovary wall is called locule. The number of locules in the ovary corresponds to the number of carpels in the gynoecium. Depending on the number of chambered locules in the ovary, ovaries are of following types:

(a) **Unilocular** Ovary with one locule or chamber, e.g. pea.

(b) **Bilocular** Ovary with two locules or chambers, e.g. *Datura*.

(c) **Multilocular** Ovary with many locules, e.g. lady finger and China rose.

IV. Placentation in Ovary

The arrangement of ovules within the ovary is known as placentation. The placentae is a tissue by which ovules are attached to the inner wall of the ovary. The placentation can be of following different types :

(a) **Marginal** The placenta forms a ridge along the ventral suture of the ovary and the ovules are borne on this ridge forming two rows, e.g. pea.

(b) **Axile** The ovary is partitioned into several chambers or locules and the placentae are borne along the septa of the ovary, e.g. China rose, tomato and lemon.

(c) **Parietal** Ovule develops on the inner wall of ovary or on peripheral part of the ovary and is single chambered. It becomes two chambered due to the formation of a false septum during maturation, e.g. mustard and *Argemone*.

(d) **Free central** Ovules are borne on the central axis and septa are absent and the ovary contains only one chamber (unilocular), e.g. *Dianthus* and primrose.

(e) **Basal** Placenta develops at the base of the ovary and a single ovule is attached to it, e.g. sunflower, marigold, etc.

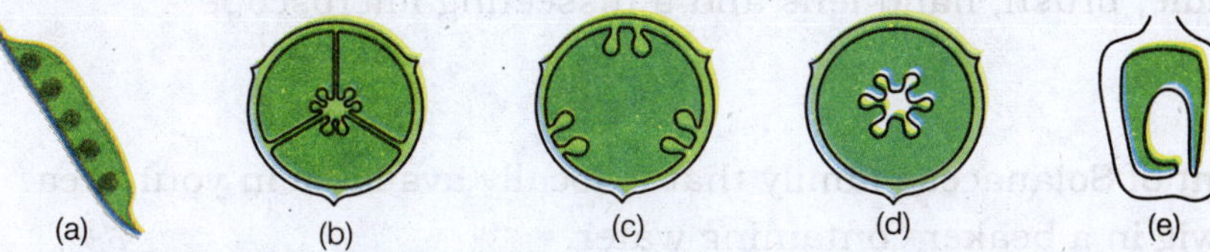

Fig. 1.4 Placentation in ovary: (a) Marginal, (b) Axile, (c) Parietal, (d) Free central, (e) Basal

Floral Diagram

It is a graphical or diagrammatic representation of transverse section and ground plan of a floral bud in relation to the mother axis.

A floral diagram provides the information about the number of floral parts, their arrangement and the relation they have with one another. It depicts following characters of the flower:

(i) The presence or absence of bract and bracteoles.
(ii) Number and arrangement of floral leaves in relation to one another.
(iii) Aestivation of sepals and petals.
(iv) Symmetry of flower.
(v) Types of placentation, etc.

In the floral diagram, the position of the mother axis with respect to the flower is represented by a dot on the top of the floral diagram. Calyx, corolla, androecium and gynoecium are drawn in successive whorls, calyx being the outermost and gynoecium being in the centre.

Floral Formula

The symbolic representation of floral characters is called floral formula. The various symbols used in a floral formula are shown in the table below.

Symbols	Descriptions	Symbols	Descriptions
⊕	Actinomorphic	♂	Unisexual staminate flower
P	Perianth	K	Calyx
A	Androecium	G	Gynoecium
%	Zygomorphic	♀	Unisexual pistillate flower
Br	Bracteate	C	Corolla
$A_{(n)}$	No. of fused stamens	$\underline{G}_n$	Superior ovary with free carpels
⚥	Bisexual flower	Epi	Epicalyx
Ebr	Ebracteate	$C_{(n)}$	No. of fused petals
$\widehat{C\ A}$	Epipetalous stamen	$\overline{G}_{(n)}$	Inferior ovary with fused carpels

Requirements

Locally available plant specimens of Solanaceae family. Each plant should have at least a small branch with few internodes, leaves, flowers and fruits, glass slides, water, beaker, petridish, razor, blade, needle, brush, hand lens and a dissecting microscope.

Procedure

1. Take a plant of Solanaceae family that is locally available in your area.
2. Keep the twig in a beaker containing water.
3. Study the habit of plant, its root system, stem and leaf morphology, inflorescence and flowers.

4. Describe the floral features and vegetative parts of the plant.
5. Observe the flower bud under dissection microscope or a hand lens and note down the aestivation patterns of calyx and corolla, number of sepals and petals and number of stamens.
6. Cut LS of the flower, place it on a slide and observe under the dissecting microscope to study position of stamens, number of carpels and position of ovary.
7. Mount a stamen on a slide and study the attachment of filament to anther, dehiscence pattern of anther and number of anther lobes.
8. Mount the pistil and study the ovary, style and stigma.
9. With the help of a sharp blade, cut a TS of the ovary and observe the type of placentation and number of locules.
10. Draw the well-labelled diagram of specimen and its parts as well as write down the floral formula and comments in your notebook based on the observation made.

Observation

Family– Solanaceae

It is a very large family, commonly called as the potato family. It is widely distributed in tropics, sub-tropics and even temperate zone. *Solanum nigrum* (makoi), *Petunia alba, Solanum tuberosum* (potato), *Solanum melongena* (brinjal), etc. are some plants belonging to this family.

Classification (*Solanum nigrum*)

Division – Angiospermae
Class – Dicotyledonae
Order – Solanales
Family – Solanaceae
Genus – *Solanum*
Species – *nigrum*

Habit Annual herb.

Root Usually branched tap root system.

Stem Herbaceous, erect, cylindrical, branched and green.

Leaves Alternate along the stem, simple, petiolate or sessile and reticulate venation.

Inflorescence Cymose

Flower Ebracteate, pedicellate, actinomorphic, complete, bisexual, pentamerous and hypogynous.

Calyx Five sepals, united or gamosepalous, valvate aestivation, persistent and green coloured.

Corolla Five petals, united or gamopetalous, valvate aestivation and white coloured.

Androecium Five stamens, epipetalous, polyandrous, anthers dithecous and dehisence by apical pores.

Gynoecium Bicarpellary, syncarpous, ovary superior, obliquely placed, bilocular with many ovules in each locule, axile placentation and, swollen placenta.

Gynoecium Bicarpellary, syncarpous, ovary superior, obliquely placed, bilocular with many ovules in each locule, axile placentation and, swollen placenta.

Fruits Berry

Seeds Endospermic and dicotyledonous.

Floral formula $Ebr \oplus ⚥\ K_{(5)}\ \overset{\frown}{C_{(5)}\ A_5}\ \underline{G}_{(2)}$

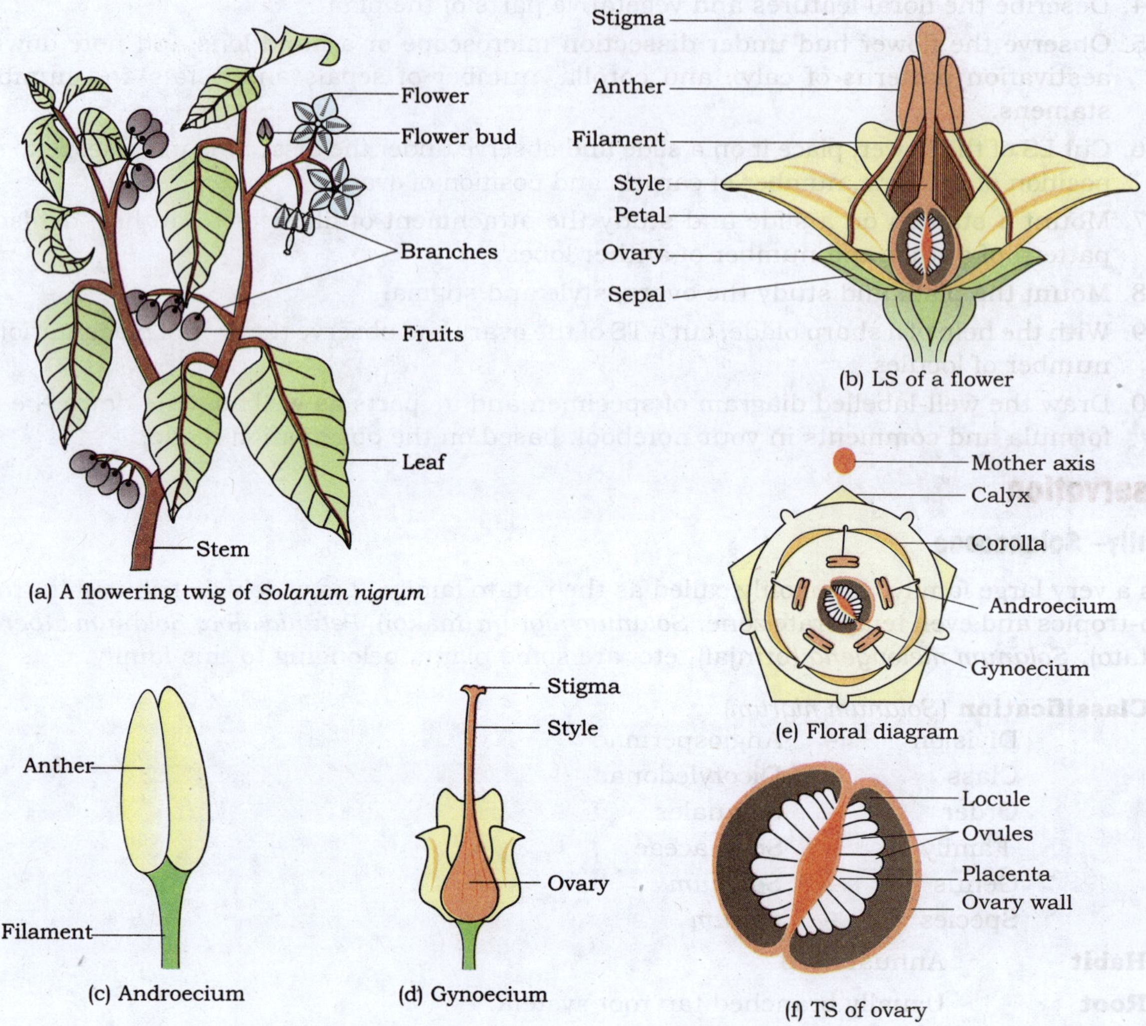

Fig. 1.5 Description of *Solanum nigrum* (family-Solanaceae)

PRECAUTIONS

- *Plant should be taken carefully so that root, stem, leaves and fruits are not damaged.*
- *The flower should be dissected carefully and each whorl should be placed separately for proper study of each part.*
- *The study of flower should be done immediately after dissection because it may get dried.*

Viva-Voce

Q.1 In which type of placentation would the ovary be always unilocular? NCERT

Ans In free central placentation, ovary contains only one chamber (unilocular) and the placenta bears ovule that arises from the central axis, e.g. *Dianthus*.

Q.2 If a flower is epigynous, what is the position of its floral parts? NCERT

Ans In an epigynous flower, the innermost whorl, i.e. gynoecium is covered by the elongated margins of thalamus. The other floral parts are borne at the top of the fused thalamus and ovary. The ovary is inferior, e.g. ray floret of sunflower.

Q.3 When is the ovary said to be superior?

Ans When the gynoecium or ovary develops at the top and the stamens, petals and sepals are borne successively below it, the ovary is said to be superior and this condition is called hypogynous condition, e.g. *Brassica*.

Q.4 What is the difference between apocarpous and syncarpous ovary?

Ans Apocarpous ovary has two or more free carpels, e.g. lotus and rose, while syncarpous ovary has two or more fused carpels, e.g. China rose and tomato.

Q.5 What is aestivation?

Ans The arrangement of different floral leaves (both petals and sepals) of a whorl in relation to each other in a flower is called aestivation.

Q.6 What is a floral formula?

Ans Floral formula is the symbolic representation of floral characteristics of a flower.

Q.7 Define floral diagram.

Ans Floral diagram is the diagrammatic or graphical representation of transverse section and ground plan of a floral bud in relation to the mother axis.

Q.8 Where is the mother axis drawn in a floral diagram?

Ans Mother axis is drawn at the top in a floral diagram.

Q.9 What is gamopetalous condition?

Ans When the corolla or petals are fused in a flower, it is said to be in gamopetalous condition.

Q.10 Define locule.

Ans Each chamber in an ovary is called a locule.

Q.11 Define the term 'flower'.

Ans Flower is the modified shoot and is a reproductive part of a plant that contains male and female structures.

Q.12 Name five plants of Solanaceae family.

Ans
(i) *Solanum tuberosum* (Potato)
(ii) *Nicotiana tabacum* (Tobacco)
(iii) *Cestrum nocturnum* (Night-blooming jasmine)
(iv) *Solanum melongena* (Brinjal)
(v) *Solanum xanthocarpum* (Yellow fruit nightshade)

Q.13 What in the fruit is equivalent to the ovule of the ovary? NCERT

Ans Seeds are equivalent to the ovule of the ovary.

Q.14 What are the essential and non-essential whorls of a flower?

Ans Androecium and gynoecium are the essential whorls of the flower, while calyx and corolla are non-essential whorls of the flower.

Q.15 What is the function of calyx and corolla?

Ans Calyx is green in colour and can perform photosynthesis. It also protects the flower when it is not in fully-developed state. Corolla is the colourful part of flower, which attracts insects for pollination.

Q.16 What is the function of a stamen?

Ans Stamen contains anther lobes which produce pollen grains or male gametophytes. Pollen grains carry two male nuclei, which are essential for reproduction in plants.

Q.17 Give the name of fruits that have persistent calyx.

Ans Tomato, brinjal, etc. are the fruits that have persistent calyx.

Q.18 Draw the floral diagram and write the floral formula from the below given description of a flower.

Bisexual, actinomorphic, hypogynous, sepals 5, gamosepalous, petals 5, free, imbricate aestivation, stamens 6, arrange in 2 whorls, ovary superior, trilocular, axile placentation. NCERT

Ans

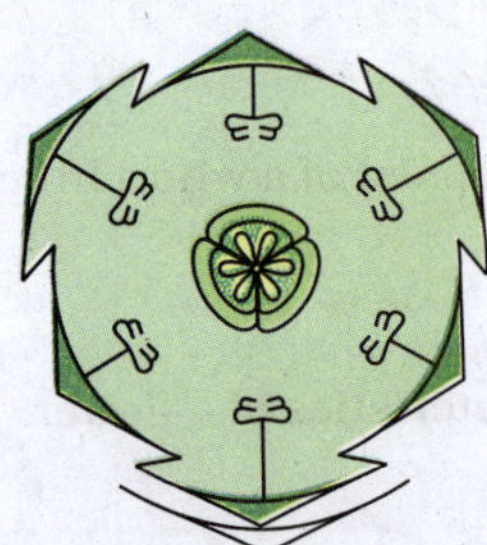

Floral diagram

Floral formula : Ebr ⊕ ⚥ $K_{(5)}\ C_5\ A_{3+3}\ \underline{G}_{(3)}$

Experiment 2

AIM

To prepare and study the TS of dicot and monocot roots and stems (primary).

Theory/Principle

The study of internal structures such as the cells of various tissues in an organ of living body is called anatomy.

A tissue is a group of cells having a common origin and usually perform a common function. Plant body is made up of different kinds of tissues which help in proper functioning by allowing division of labour. In plants, tissues can be categorised as meristematic or permanent on the basis of their ability to divide. These tissues may be simple that contains only one type of cells, like **parenchyma**, **sclerenchyma** and **collenchyma** or may be complex (containing more than one type of cells) like **xylem** and **phloem**. Different types of cells in a tissue differ in their structure, shape, size, function and wall composition. The internal organisation of these tissues differs in roots, stems and leaves.

Requirements

Sample of stems and roots of sunflower, *Cucurbita*, maize or any other locally available monocot and dicot plants, potato or raw papaya, sharp blade, watch glass, petridish, brush, needles, water, beakers, forceps, safranin stain, glycerine, cover slip, dilute acid water, glass slides, blotting paper and microscope.

Procedure

Sectioning of Different Tissues

1. Take 2-3 cm long pieces of root and stem of monocot and dicot plants, preferably of the thickness of a tooth-pick.
2. Use pith of potato or raw papaya for embedding the material to be sectioned. Fix the piece in the pith properly.
3. Now, hold it properly between thumb and index finger of left hand in such a way that the tip of finger and outer smooth surface of material lie in a line. While the tip of the thumb is just a few mm below the upper surface of the material.
4. Wet the surfaces of blade and cut the section of root with the help of it. Carefully move the blade horizontally over the surface of material in quick succession in a manner that a very thin and complete slice of the material is cut and obtained over the surface of razor.
5. Cut the section of shoot in the same manner and transfer all the cut pieces into a watch glass containing water.
6. Select a thin, uniform and complete section and transfer it to the glass slide having a drop of water, with the help of needle and brush.

Staining of Tissues

1. Put 2-3 drops of safranin over the section on the glass slide and allow it to stand for two minutes.
2. With the help of a brush gently transfer the section into a watch glass containing water to remove excess of safranin stain. Now, transfer the section into a watch glass containing a few drops of dilute acid in water to remove excess stain.
3. Transfer the section onto a glass slide and put a drop of glycerine as mounting medium over it. Cover the section with the coverslip.
4. Observe the section under the microscope.

Observation

TS of Dicot Root

TS of a dicot root shows the following features:

All the lignified tissues such as sclerenchyma, collenchyma are stained red with safranin.

Epidermis It is a single, outermost layer of thin walled, compactly arranged parenchymatous cells. Some cells have an outward extension and form the unicellular **root hair** that increases the area of absorption of water and mineral salts from soil. It lacks stomata and cuticle.

Cortex Below the layer of epidermis lies many layers of cortex formed with simple thin-walled parenchymatous cells with intercellular spaces. These may contain leucoplasts and passage cells.

Endodermis It is the innermost layer of cortex. It is a single, circular layer of compactly arranged, barrel-shaped cells. There are no intercellular spaces between the cells. This layer separates the cortex with vascular tissues. Sometimes, a band of thickening, called **casparian strip**, is found on the radial and inner walls of endodermis.

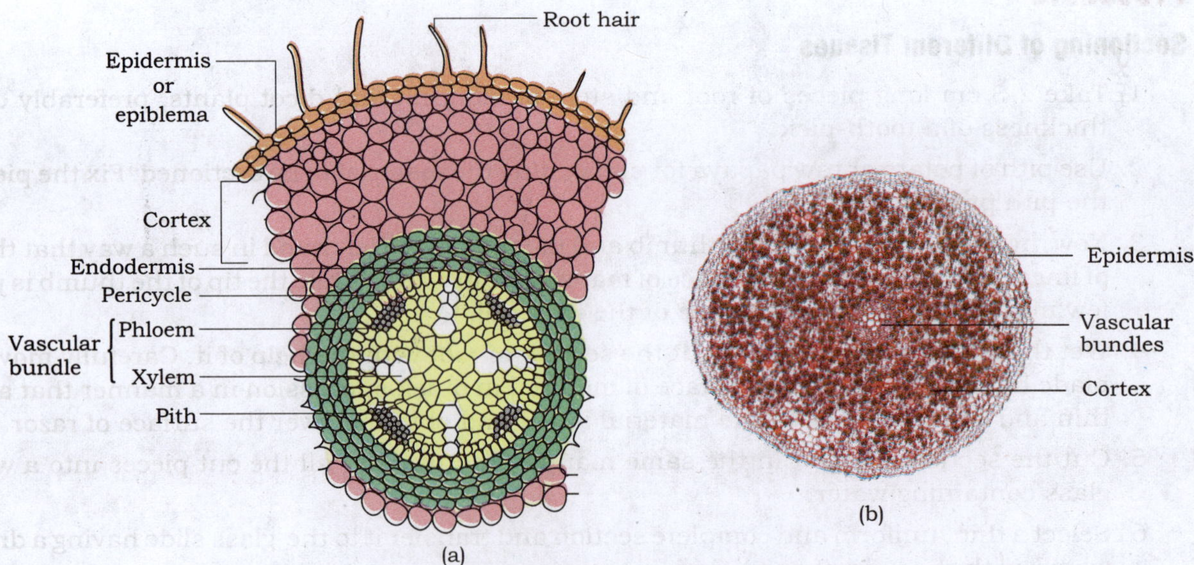

Fig. 2.1 (a) TS of a dicot root, (b) Microscopic view of TS of dicot root

Pericycle It is a single circular layer of cells that lies internal to the endodermis. These are thin walled parenchymatous cells with abundant protoplasm and compact arrangement.

Vascular Bundle In a dicot root, vascular bundles are arranged in a ring. The bundles are radial and there are equal number of separate bundles of xylem and phloem. Xylem bundle shows exarch condition, i.e. protoxylem lies towards the periphery and metaxylem towards the centre. Xylem vessels are polygonal in outline.

Conjunctive Tissues Xylem and phloem bundles are separated from each other by the parenchymatous cells called **conjunctive tissues.**

Pith It occupies the central area and is either poorly developed or absent in a dicot root. It consists of parenchymatous cells with intercellular spaces.

Examples of Dicot Root *Phaseolus radiatus, Ranuculus, Cicer, Ficus.*

TS of Monocot Root

The anatomical structure of a monocot root is similar to that of a dicot root except for a few key differences.

Vascular Bundles In monocot root, more than 6 (8 or more) alternate bundles of xylem and phloem are present, this condition is called **polyarch**. Vascular bundles are radial, i.e. **xylem** and **phloem** lie on different radii. Exarch xylem condition is seen, i.e. protoxylem lies towards the outer side and metaxylem towards the centre. Xylem vessels are rounded or oval in shape and phloem consists of sieve tubes, companion cells and phloem parenchyma.

Pith The central part of monocot root is occupied by well developed pith formed of parenchymatous cells with intercellular spaces. It is large in size.

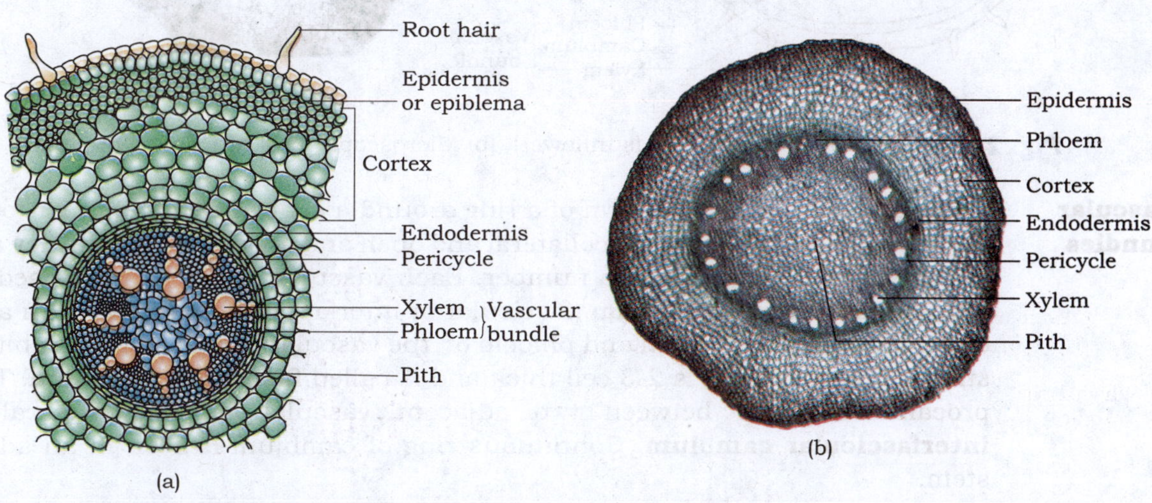

Fig. 2.2 (a) TS of a monocot root, (b) Microscopic view of TS of monocot root

Examples of Monocot Root *Canna, Zea mays, Smilax, Allium cepa.*

TS of Dicot Stem

TS of a dicot stem show following features.

Epidermis It is composed of parenchymatous rectangular cells. Multicellular **trichomes** or epidermal hairs are present.It is covered with a thin layer of cuticle and bears few stomata.

Hypodermis It lies just below the epidermis and consists of 3-4 layers of collenchymatous cells. It primarily gives mechanical strength to the stem.

Cortex It is composed of thin-walled, oval or rounded parenchyma cells possessing prominent intercellular spaces.

Endodermis It is the innermost layer of the cortex consisting of a single layered barrel-shaped cells which is devoid of intercellular spaces. Casparian strips are absent, cell of endodermis are rich in starch therefore, the layer is also called as **starch sheath**.

Pericycle It is multilayered and alternating bands of parenchyma and sclerenchyma cells are present. It lies in between the endodermis and the vascular bundles.

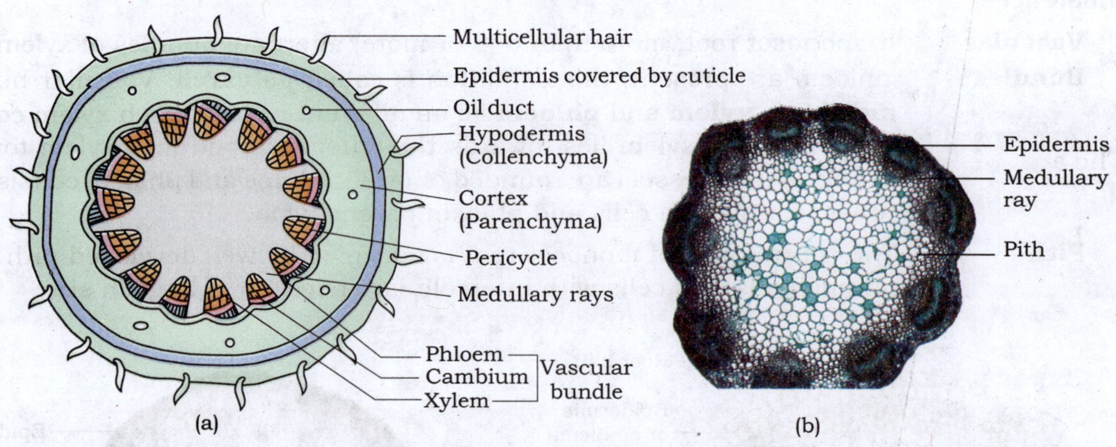

Fig. 2.3 (a) Anatomy of dicot stem (sunflower), (b) Microscopic view of TS of dicot stem

Vascular Bundles These are arranged in the form of a ring around a central pith and inner to pericycle. These are conjoint, collateral and open and are equal in size. They are wedge-shaped and definite in number. Each vascular bundle is composed of **phloem**, **xylem** and **cambium** (fascicular or interfascicular) and are open and endarch. In between xylem and phloem of the vascular bundle, a procambium strip is present which is 2-3 cell thick and is called **fascicular cambium**. The procambium lying between two adjacent vascular bundles are called **interfascicular cambium**. Continuous ring of cambium is seen in an adult stem.

Medullary Rays These are also called as pith rays. These are non-vascular areas present in between the vascular bundles. The medullary rays connect the pith with pericycle and cortex. They help in the radial conduction of food and water. These also transport gases from pith to cortex and *vice versa*.

Pith It is also called as medulla. It forms the central part of the stem and consists of rounded, oval or polygonal parenchymatous cells. Intercellular spaces are present between them and these cells store food material.

Examples of Dicot Stem *Helianthus, Tinospora, Ricinus, Xanthium.*

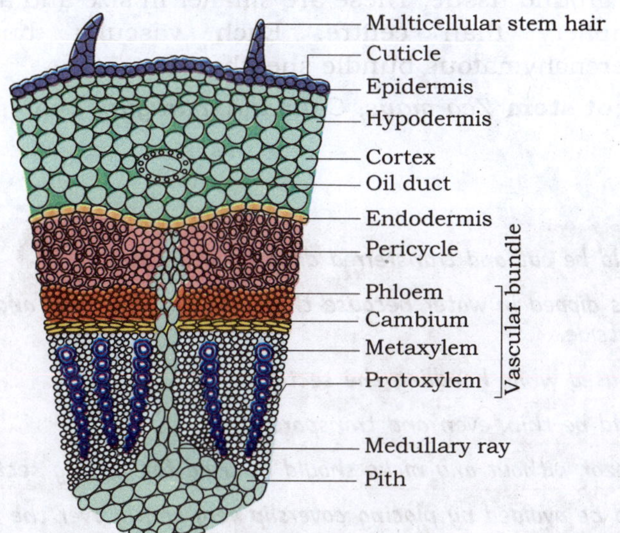

Fig. 2.4 TS of dicot stem (sunflower)

TS of Monocot Stem

The anatomical structure of a monocot stem is similar to that of dicot stem except for a few key differences.

Epidermis It is the single outermost layer of thin-walled, compactly arranged, barrel-shaped, parenchymatous cells. It is uniseriate and covered with a thick cuticle. Epidermal hairs are absent and stomata are present at few places in the epidermis.

Hypodermis It is 2-3 layered, lignified and consists of sclerenchymatous cells which lie just below the epidermis and provide mechanical strength to the stem.

Ground Tissue It lies below the hypodermis (except the vascular bundles). The ground tissue is made up of rounded parenchymatous cells with distinct intercellular spaces.

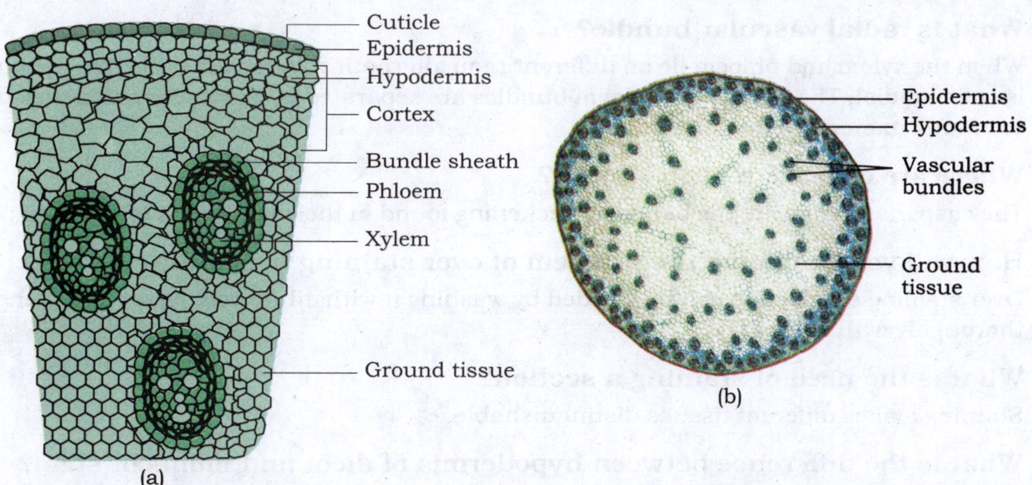

Fig. 2.5 (a) TS of monocot stem (maize), (b) Microscopic view of TS of monocot stem

Vascular System In monocots, a large number of vascular bundles lie scattered throughout the ground tissue. These are smaller in size and are more in number towards periphery than centre. Each vascular bundle is surrounded by sclerenchymatous bundle sheath.

Examples of monocot stem *Zea mays, Canna, Asparagus*, Doob grass.

PRECAUTIONS

- *The section should be cut and transferred directly into water.*
- *Keep the sections dipped in water because they may get dried out and cells will not be visualised clearly if kept outside.*
- *Brush should be used while handling the section.*
- *The section should be thin, even and transparent.*
- *Sharp blade or razor without any nicks should be used for cutting section.*
- *Air bubble should be avoided by placing coverslip very gently over the stained section.*
- *Extra glycerine and stains should be avoided by wiping it gently with the help of a filter paper.*

Q.1 Which type of xylem arrangement would be seen in TS of root of lily plant? NCERT

Ans TS of root of lily (monocotyledonous plant) shows exarch condition, i.e. protoxylem lies towards outer side and metaxylem towards centre or pith.

Q.2 Which part of a dicot stem is meristematic? NCERT

Ans The cambium present in between xylem and phloem in vascular bundle has the ability to divide rapidly, hence it is the meristematic tissue in a dicot stem.

Q.3 Where do we find the scattered vascular bundle?

Ans Scattered vascular bundle are the characteristic feature of monocot stem.

Q.4 What is radial vascular bundle?

Ans When the xylem and phloem lie on different radii alternating with each other, the vascular bundle is called radial. The xylem and phloem bundles are separated by parenchymatous tissues. These are found in monocot and dicot roots.

Q.5 Where are casparian strips found?

Ans The casparian strips are the bands of thickening found in the endodermis of vascular plants.

Q.6 How will you overcome the problem of over staining of section?

Ans Over staining of a section can be avoided by washing it with dilute acid water and then thoroughly with water.

Q.7 What is the need of staining a section?

Ans Staining makes different tissues distinguishable.

Q.8 What is the difference between hypodermis of dicot and monocot stem?

Ans In a dicot stem, hypodermis is composed of a few layers of collenchymatous cells, while it is made up of sclerenchymatous cells in a monocot stem.

Q.9 Why is the endodermis of sunflower stem (dicot) also called starch sheath?

Ans The endodermis of a sunflower stem is rich in starch grains, therefore these are called starch sheath.

Q.10 Mention the characteristic features of a monocot stem.

Ans The major characteristic features of a monocot stem are as follows:
Conjoint, collateral, closed, scattered vascular bundle with sclerenchymatous bundle sheath.

Q.11 Mention one feature in which a monocot root differs from a dicot root.

Ans Monocot root possesses well developed pith, while dicot root either does not possess pith or it is present in a very reduced form.

Q.12 How can you identify whether a given slide is of a root or a shoot?

Ans In a slide having section of root, the vascular bundle will appear radial with exarch xylem and epidermis will have unicellular hair while in a slide having a section of shoot the collateral vascular bundles with endarch xylem will be observed.

Q.13 Arrange the following sequentially as you would see in a TS of a dicot stem-pericycle, epidermis, pith, cortex, xylem and phloem. NCERT

Ans The correct sequence of tissues in TS of a dicot stem is as follows:
Epidermis, cortex, pericycle, phloem, xylem and pith.

Q.14 Where do you find radial, conjoint, collateral and open vascular bundles? NCERT

Ans Radial vascular bundles are found in dicot root and monocot root, whereas, conjoint, collateral and open (cambium present) vascular bundles are arranged in rings in a dicot stem.

Q.15 Give the role of xylem and phloem in vascular bundle.

Ans Xylem is responsible for the conduction of water and minerals from soil to various plant parts, while phloem helps in the transport of prepared food from the leaves to other parts of plant.

Q.16 Why is safranin used in staining the section?

Ans Safranin can stain the lignified tissues and cell walls giving them the red or pink colour for better identification therefore, it is used for staining the sections.

Q.17 What is the role of glycerine in mounting the section?

Ans Glycerine is used as a mounting medium in section cutting and slide preparations because it does not allow the plant material to dry and prevents dehydration of section.

Q.18 What is the use of pith for section cutting?

Ans Pith keeps the soft material firm in a place and produces better, thin and uniform section.

Q.19 Why only thin and uniform sections must be used for the study of anatomy of root and stem?

Ans Thin and uniform sections must be used for the study of anatomy of root and stem because light can pass easily through a thin section making various tissues clearly visible.

Q.20 What are collateral vascular bundles?

Ans Collateral vascular bundle is a type of conjoint vascular bundle where xylem is placed towards inside and phloem towards outside facing cortex.

Experiment 3

AIM

To study the process of osmosis by potato osmometer.

Theory / Principle

Osmosis

Osmosis can be defined as the net movement of water molecules or solvent molecules through a differentially permeable or selectively permeable membrane from the region of low solute concentration to the region of high solute concentration, till a state of equilibrium is reached.

Osmosis depends on the **permeability** of the separating membrane. Permeability is the ability of a membrane to allow passage of gases, liquids and dissolved substances through it. The membrane that allows passage of all types of substances through it, is called **permeable membrane**, while the membrane that allows passage of only certain molecules or ions through it is called **semipermeable membrane.**

Osmosis in a Cell

Osmosis is a common physical process observed in living cells and tissues of all organisms.

The living cells contain an osmotically active cell sap. The sap is surrounded by semipermeable membrane called **tonoplast**, which encloses the vacuole, and **plasma membrane**, which encloses the cytoplasm. Thus, living cells show osmosis when placed in water or solutions having concentration lower than cell sap.

Reverse osmosis is expulsion of pure water from a solution through a semipermeable membrane under the influence of external pressure, higher than the osmotic pressure of solution.

Requirements

A fresh large sized potato, peeler, scooper, 10-20% sugar solution (or conc. salt solution), petridish, blade, beaker, water and pins or needles marked with ink (waterproof).

Procedure

1. Cut the potato into two equal halves with blade. Peel off the outer skin of potato and shape the two halves into squares to give it a flat and even base.
2. Make a square or circular-shaped cavity in the centre of the potato by scooping the soft parenchyma with the help of a peeler or scooper. The cavity prepared by scooping should have minimum thickness at the bottom.
3. Place the potato on its flat cut end in a petridish half-filled with water, in such a way that 2/3rd of the potato is dipped in water.
4. Fill half the cavity of the potato with 10-20% sugar solution and mark the level of sugar solution inside the cavity with the help of a pin or needle. This prepared apparatus works as an osmometer.
5. Leave this osmometer undisturbed for about 1 hour.

6. Observe the level of sugar solution in the osmometer at the end of experiment.
7. Repeat this experiment using water in potato cavity and sugar solution in petridish.

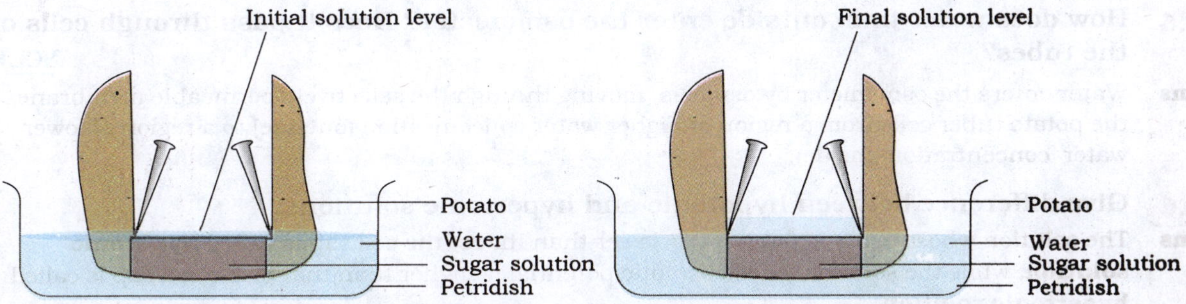

Fig.3.1 Demonstration of osmosis by potato osmometer or osmoscope

Observation

The level of sugar solution in the potato cavity (which acted as an osmometer or osmoscope) rises after sometime due to the entry of water from the petridish into the potato cavity as a result of endosmosis.

Result/Conclusion

A water potential gradient is established between sucrose solution in the potato cavity and the external water. The cell membrane enclosing the cells of potato acts as a selectively permeable membrane for the movement of water and osmosis takes place successfully.

PRECAUTIONS

- *The potato cavity should be deep enough to keep only a thin layer of tissues at the base.*
- *The potato block should be flat at the lower end to keep it stable in the petridish.*
- *Sugar solution should be highly concentrated, as compared to the cell sap of potato cells for osmosis to take place.*

Viva-Voce

Q.1 What is meant by permeability?

Ans Permeability is the ability of a membrane to allow passage of gases, liquids and dissolved substances through it.

Q.2 Define the following terms:

(i) Exosmosis (ii) Endosmosis

Ans (i) **Exosmosis** The outward movement of water from the cell when kept in a hypertonic solution is called exosmosis.

(ii) **Endosmosis** The inward movement of water inside the cell when kept in a hypotonic solution is called endosmosis.

Q.3 Why is the experimental setup called an osmoscope or osmometer?

Ans The discussed experimental setup is called as an osmoscope or osmometer because the difference in initial and final levels of solution in the potato cavity is due to osmosis that occurs from the region of lower osmotic potential to the region of higher osmotic potential.

Q.4 **Why only living cells can act as an osmometer?**

Ans Since, living cells contain an osmotically active cell sap and are surrounded by semipermeable membrane, they can act as osmometer. Dead cells do not have active cell sap.

Q.5 **How does water from outside enter the osmometer? Does it pass through cells of the tubes?** NCERT

Ans Water enters the osmometer by osmosis, moving through the selectively permeable membranes of the potato tuber cells from a region of higher water concentration (outside) to a region of lower water concentration (inside).

Q.6 **Give difference between hypotonic and hypertonic solutions.**

Ans The solution whose osmotic potential is lower than that of the cell sap is called **hypotonic solution,** while the solution whose osmotic potential is higher than that of the cell sap is called **hypertonic solution**.

Q.7 **What do you mean by osmotic pressure?**

Ans It is the pressure which has to be applied to prevent the flow of pure water into concentrated solution under ideal osmotic condition.

Q.8 **Why do we use potato for making an osmometer or osmoscope?**

Ans Potato is an easily available living material and can be handled easily, therefore it is used as an osmometer or osmoscope.

Q.9 **Why is the potato peeled off while making it as an osmometer?**

Ans The skin of potato is thick and makes it impermeable for the movement of water. Therefore, it must be peeled off before making it as an osmometer.

Q.10 **What will happen if we use boiled potato for making an osmometer?**

Ans If we use boiled potato for making an osmometer, the living cells of potato will be killed by boiling and osmosis cannot be demonstrated.

Q.11 **Can we use salt solution instead of sugar solution to demonstrate the process of osmosis?**

Ans Yes, salt solution can also be used instead of sugar solution but it must be concentrated.

Q.12 **Is there any difference in water potential of sugar solution and water?** NCERT

Ans Yes, there is difference between the water potential of sugar solution and water. The water potential of pure water or distilled water is higher than that of sugar solution. Therefore, water moves from the region of higher water concentration (i.e. pure water) to the region of lower water concentration (i.e. sugar solution) during osmosis.

Q.13 **Why is the water potential of sugar solution more negative?** NCERT

Ans The water potential of pure water is zero. As solute is added, the value for water potential becomes more negative because the solute molecules hinders the movement of water molecules. This explains why sugar solution has more negative water potential.

Q.14 **What will be the rate of osmosis if we use 5% sugar solution in the osmometer?** NCERT

Ans If we use 5% sugar solution in the osmometer, the rate of osmosis will decrease. Because the osmosis is driven by the difference in free energy between the solvent in the solution and pure water.

Experiment 4

AIM

To study the process of plasmolysis in epidermal peels of *Rhoeo*/lily leaves or fleshy scale leaves of onion bulb.

Theory/Principle

Plasmolysis is a vital phenomenon, which explains the process of osmosis. It helps in determining the osmotic pressure of a cell and indicates whether a particular cell is living or dead.

It is a process in which shrinkage of protoplasmic contents of the plant cell takes place due to the movement of water out of cell when placed in hypertonic solution of sucrose or salt. This phenomenon is called **exosmosis**.

Hypertonic, Hypotonic and Isotonic Solutions

Based on the concentrations, there are three types of solutions, i.e. hypertonic, hypotonic and isotonic. When a plant cell is placed in a ***hypertonic solution****, water escapes from the vacuoles of the cell by exosmosis. When this plasmolysed cell is again placed in water or* ***hypotonic solution****, it absorbs water due to endosmosis and protoplast restores its original shape. This process is called* ***deplasmolysis****. When a cell is placed in an* ***isotonic solution****, there is no net movement of water molecules.*

Requirements

Leaves of coloured plants like *Rhoeo*, forceps, glass slides, coverslips, beaker, needle, brush, microscope, sucrose solution (20%) and petridish.

Procedure

1. Take a *Rhoeo* leaf and with the help of forcep, gently pull a thin peel from it. Mark this peel as *A*.
2. Keep this peel *A* in a petridish containing water to avoid dehydration.
3. Repeat the above two steps with four other leaves of the same plant. Label them as *B*, *C*, *D* and *E*.
4. Transfer the peels *B*, *C*, *D* and *E* into 20% sucrose solution.
5. Now, transfer the peel *A* carefully with the help of needle and brush on a clean glass slide.
6. Mount peel *A* in a drop of water and put a coverslip over it.
7. Examine the slide under microscope. Make a sketch of the cell particularly showing the cell wall and cell membrane.
8. Repeat the steps 6th, 7th and 8th with the peels labelled *B*, *C*, *D* and *E* at intervals of 5, 15, 20 and 30 minutes, respectively. Make the sketch of the cell particularly showing the cell wall and cell membrane of each peel.
9. Draw the cell observed under microscope and also record the observation in the table.

Observation

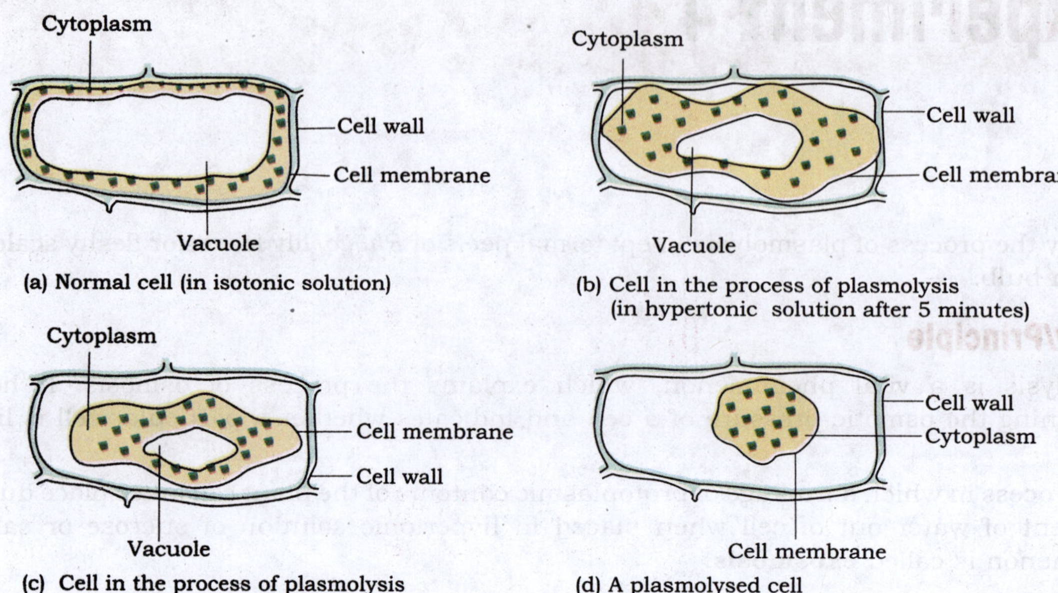

(a) Normal cell (in isotonic solution)

(b) Cell in the process of plasmolysis (in hypertonic solution after 5 minutes)

(c) Cell in the process of plasmolysis (in hypertonic solution after 15 minutes)

(d) A plasmolysed cell (in hypertonic solution after 20 minutes)

Fig. 4.1 Different stages of plasmolysis in a plant cell

	Time (minutes)	**Total no. of cells in a field of microscope** (M)	**No. of cells showing plasmolysis** (N)	**% of plasmolysis** $\left(\frac{N}{M}\times 100\right)$
Peel *A* (control)	5 15 20 30			
Peel *B*	5			
Peel *C*	15			
Peel *D*	20			
Peel *E*	30			

Result

The cells get plasmolysed in hypertonic solution. When observed after 5 minutes the plasma membrane has started to shrink and has become completely plasmolysed after 20 minutes.

PRECAUTIONS

- *The peel should be of proper size and should not be exposed to dry environment.*
- *Fresh and active plant material must be used.*
- *Different slides should be used for viewing different peels.*
- *Slides must be kept dry by removing extra solution with a blotting paper.*
- *The cells must be kept undisturbed in hypertonic solution, so that sufficient exosmosis may take place.*

Viva-Voce

Q.1 Why is the plasma membrane also called semipermeable membrane?

Ans Plasma membrane allows only few substances to pass through it, therefore it is called semipermeable membrane.

Q.2 When the plasmolysed cell is placed in water, it regains its original size. Why?

Ans When the plasmolysed cell is placed in water, it regains its original size due to endosmosis. This makes the cell turgid due to deplasmolysis.

Q.3 Name the hypertonic and hypotonic solutions used in the experiment. NCERT

Ans Hypertonic solution used in the experiment is the salt solution, while hypotonic solution is water.

Q.4 Why is plasmolysis observed in cells of peels kept in salt solution?

Ans When the peel is kept in the salt solution the cells become plasmolysed due to exosmosis. Water from the cells comes out to maintain the concentration of both the regions, i.e. to attain equilibrium.

Q.5 Why do cells of peel *A* kept in water remain turgid? NCERT

Ans The peel *A* is kept in water or isotonic solution, that has a similar concentration as the cell sap. Therefore, no change occurs in the cells of peel *A* and it remains turgid.

Q.6 What is the significance of plasmolysis?

Ans The significance of plasmolysis are as follows

1. Weeds can be killed in a playground by adding excessive salts in their roots.
2. Meat, fish, vegetables, etc. are dried and salted to protect against spoilage by bacteria and fungi.
3. Plants growing in the walls, foundations of buildings are killed by adding large quantities of salts in their roots. The root cells of such plants are killed due to plasmolysis.

Q.7 Why is salt or sugar added to jams and pickles?

Ans Excess of salt/sugar kills microbes due to plasmolysis of their cells. Therefore, addition of salt or sugar to jams and pickles, prevent their decay by the microbes.

Q.8 What do you mean by incipient plasmolysis?

Ans The stage at which the process of plasmolysis has just begun is known as incipient plasmolysis.

Q.9 Does animal cell show plasmolysis? Why?

Ans No, animal cells do not show plasmolysis as they do not have cell walls.

Q.10 Why is plasmolysis observed in cells of peels kept in sucrose solution? NCERT

Ans Sucrose solution is a hypertonic solution in comparison to the cell sap. Therefore, when cells of peels are kept in sucrose solution, they show plasmolysis.

Q.11 What will happen if the plasmolysed peels are transferred to water? NCERT

Ans If the plasmolysed peel is immediately transferred to the water, the cells will absorb water by the process of endosmosis and cells again will become turgid, because protoplasm will attain its original shape, but if it is not immersed in water immediately, the protoplasm will be damaged permanently.

Q.12 Why are *Rhoeo* leaves preferred for study of plasmolysis?

Ans The leaves of *Rhoeo* are preferrably used to study plasmolysis because the red colour of leaf cell will make plasmolysis and plasma membrane clearly visible.

Experiment 5

AIM

To study the distribution of stomata on the upper and lower surfaces of the leaves.

Theory/Principle

Stomata are the minute pores present in the epidermal layer of the leaves of all the flowering plants. It performs two important functions; that of transpiration and exchange of gases. A stoma (sing.) is surrounded by two specialised epidermal cells called **guard cells,** which enclose an aperture in the center called the **stomatal aperture**.

Opening and Closing of Stomata

During normal conditions, stomata open during day time and close during night time. However, under stressful condition like drought, stomata remain closed during the day to conserve water and exchange of gases takes place at night. Opening and closing of stomata occurs due to change in the turgidity of the guard cells, in which inner walls are thick and elastic in nature.

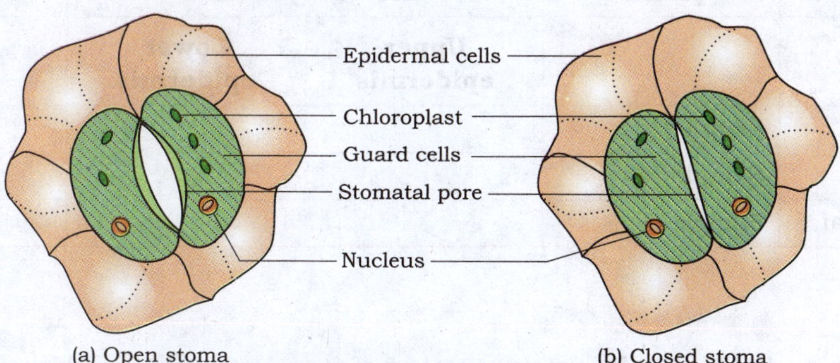

Fig. 5.1 Opening and closing of stomata

Number of Stomata in Plants

The number and distribution of stomata per unit area is variable in leaves of different plants. The number of stomata ranges from a few thousand to over 1,00,000 per cm^2 area of the leaf and occupy 1-2% of the total leaf surface.

Stomatal index is the percentage of number of stomata as compared to all the epidermal cells in a unit area of leaf. It can be calculated as

$$\text{Stomatal index} = \frac{\text{Number of stomata}}{\text{Number of stomata per unit area} + \text{Number of epidermal cells per unit area}} \times 100$$

Requirements

Fresh leaves of one monocot (e.g. lily) and two dicot (e.g. *Petunia* and *Hibiscus*) plants, forceps, needles, blade, blotting paper, brush, watch glasses or petridishes, glass slides, coverslips, safranin, glycerine, water and microscope.

Procedure

1. Take out the epidermal peels from the upper and lower surfaces of leaf of two dicot plants (sample A and sample B) and put them in water in separate watch glasses. The peels can be taken out by tearing the leaf obliquely with a single jerk or scraping it with blade.
2. Now, place the two pieces of peel on the separate watch glasses and stain them with safranin by adding few drops of stain.
3. After few minutes take out the peel and put them on separate slides.
4. Put a drop of glycerine on the slides over the peel and carefully cover the peel with cover slip, so as to avoid air bubbles. Remove extra glycerine by blotting paper.
5. Observe the slides under high power of microscope.
6. Note the absence or presence of stomata. Count the number of stomata in the microscopic field from both sides of the leaf using sample A and sample B.
7. Repeat the experiment with the leaves of the monocot plant (Sample C) and compare your results.

Observation

Record your observations in table given below:

Type of leaf	Name of the plants	No. of stomata in the microscopic field		Shape of guard cell
		Upper epidermis	**Lower epidermis**	
Dicot leaf	Sample *A*			
	Sample *B*			
Monocot leaf	Sample *C*			

Results

Dicot leaf (*Petunia* and *Hibiscus*) has more number of stomata on the lower surface than on upper surface, while, monocot leaf (lily) has equal number of stomata on both the surfaces of leaf.

PRECAUTIONS

- *The peel should immediately be transferred into water else it may get plasmolysed or dried and no structure will then be seen in the peel.*
- *Use brush and needles to transfer the peel from the petridish to the slide.*
- *Curling of peel should be avoided.*
- *Over-staining of peel should also be avoided as it may not give the accurate count of stomata.*
- *Excess glycerine should be removed by using blotting paper.*
- *The slides used for mounting should be cleaned properly.*

Viva-Voce

Q.1 What is meant by the term 'stomata'?

Ans Stomata are the minute pores present on the surface of aerial parts of plants, especially on leaves.

Q.2 Name the specialised cells that are responsible for opening and closing of stomata.

Ans Guard cells are the specialised cells that surround the stomatal pore and are responsible for opening and closing of stomata.

Q.3 What is the role of stomata in plants?

Ans Stomata perform two important functions, i.e. exchange of gases and transpiration in plants.

Q.4 In which type of plants, stomata are present in large number on the lower surface of leaf?

Ans In dicot plants, the stomata are found in large number on the lower surface of leaf.

Q.5 What controls the opening and closing of stomata?

Ans The opening and closing of stomata are controlled by the turgidity of the guard cells.

Q.6 What is stomatal index?

Ans It is the ratio of stomata to the total number of epidermal cells (including stomata) on a leaf, expressed as percentage.

Q.7 Name the processes that will be affected, if stomata were not present in leaves. NCERT

Ans If stomata were not present in the leaves, then the process of transpiration, photosynthesis and respiration exchange will be affected.

Q.8 Is the stomatal distribution same in the upper and lower epidermis of an isobilateral leaf (monocot)?

Ans Yes, the stomatal distribution is typically more uniform in the upper and lower epidermis of an isobilateral leaf (monocot).

Q.9 Name the process by which plants lose water in the form of vapour.

Ans The process of loss of water in the form of vapour from the aerial parts of a plant is called transpiration.

Q.10 Stomata are absent in submerged aquatic plants. Why?

Ans In submerged aquatic plants, gaseous exchange takes place through general surface of the plant by diffusion. Therefore, stomata are absent in these plants.

Q.11 How does transpiration help plants?

Ans Transpiration helps in absorption of water and ascent of sap. Transpiration also provides cooling effect in plant, thus protects it from the harmful effect of sun.

Q.12 **In land plants, stomata are generally more on the lower epidermis than on upper epidermis. What is the advantage?** NCERT

Ans Land plants have more stomata on the lower surface than upper surface of leaves, so as to avoid much water loss due to transpiration as the upper surface of leaf is in direct contact with air and sunlight.

Q.13 **Draw the figure of a stoma you have observed in a monocot leaf and compare it with the shape of stomata in dicot leaf.** NCERT

Ans The guard cells present in monocots are of dumb-bell shape while in dicot, they are bean shaped.

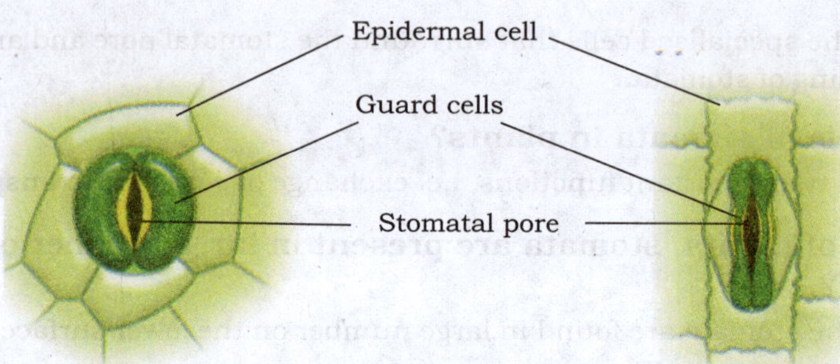

Q.14 **Mention the factors that control the opening and closing of stomata.**

Ans Light, temperature, CO_2 concentration, humidity, etc. are some factors that control the opening and closing of stomata.

Q.15 **How does hypertonic solution affect stomatal opening and closing?**

Ans In a hypertonic solution, water moves out of the plant cell, including the guard cells, which decrease their turgor pressure. This causes the guard cell to become flaccid and results in the closing of stomata to reduce water loss.

Experiment 6

AIM

The comparative study of the rate of transpiration in the upper and lower surfaces of the leaves.

Theory/Principle

Transpiration is the loss of water in the form of water vapour from the aerial parts of a plant. It mainly occurs through the minute pores on the surface of leaves called **stomata** and mostly during day-time when temperature is comparatively high and stomata are open. About 85% of transpiration takes place through stomata and is called **stomatal transpiration**. The number of stomata present on the two surfaces of the leaves differ in most of the plants (especially in dorsiventral leaves). Some amount of water is also lost through cuticles or lenticels and this type of transpiration is called **cuticular transpiration** and **lenticular transpiration** respectively.

Rate of transpiration depends upon several factors, such as:

(i) **Light** The rate of transpiration increases in light as it controls opening of stomata.

(ii) **Temperature** Rate of transpiration increases with the increase in temperature.

(iii) **Wind** Movement of wind helps to remove water vapour over transpiring leaf surface, thus increasing the water vapour gradient and rate of transpiration. However, high wind velocities induce stomatal closure due to rapid water loss from guard cells, thereby, decreasing the rate of transpiration.

(iv) **Humidity** In rainy season, when air is humid, the rate of transpiration decreases. In dry air, the rate of transpiration increases.

(v) **Number and Distribution of Stomata** Number and distribution of stomata on the upper and lower surfaces of leaf varies with plant species. The rate of transpiration increases with an increase in number of stomata.

Transpiration can be easily demonstrated by cobalt chloride paper test. Cobalt chloride is blue coloured in anhydrous (dry) form but turns pink when it comes in contact with water. This property of cobalt chloride is used to demonstrate that water is lost during transpiration.

Requirements

A herbaceous broad leaved potted plant, filter paper, 100 mL measuring cylinder, 5% cobalt chloride solution, blotting sheets, hot plate/oven, forceps, wire gauze, petridish, vaseline, cellotape, dessicator, slides, rubber bands or clips, etc.

Procedure

1. Prepare 100 mL of 5% cobalt chloride solution by dissolving 5 g of cobalt chloride in 100 mL distilled water.
2. Cut small strips of filter paper and immerse them in cobalt chloride solution taken in a petridish for 3-5 minutes.

3. Transfer the soaked strips on a wire gauze with the help of forceps to allow excess $CoCl_2$ solution to drain off.
4. Now, dry the filter paper strip on hot plate or oven but take care that strips should not get burned or charred. These anhydrous cobalt chloride coated strips will appear blue in colour.
5. Store these cobalt chloride coated strips in a dessicator.
6. Select a leaf of a potted plant and blot the leaf dry (if water droplets are seen) from both the sides with the help of blotting sheets.

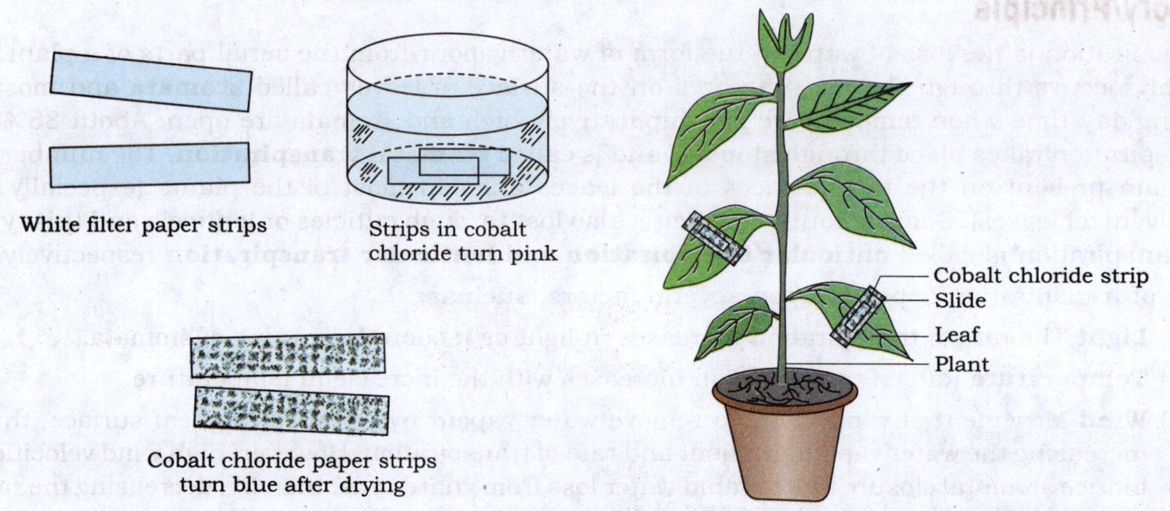

Fig. 6.1 To study the rate of transpiration (loss of water) by cobalt chloride method

7. Keep one dry cobalt chloride paper strip on the upper surface of leaf and stick it with the help of cellotape.
8. Likewise, stick another strip of cobalt chloride ($CoCl_2$) paper on the lower surface of leaf.
9. Hold the leaf in position with the help of two slides and clips or rubber bands. Apply vaseline around the edges of the slide to make it airtight. Now, place the potted plant in sunlight.
10. Observe the colour of cobalt chloride paper attached to both surfaces of leaf at regular intervals, and note down your observations in the table given below.

Observation

Name of the plant		Time taken for change of the colour from blue to pink (in minutes)									
		2	4	6	8	10	12	14	16	18	20
	Upper epidermis										
	Lower epidermis										

Result

Rate of transpiration or rate of loss of water is higher at lower surface of leaf than the upper surface, as the $CoCl_2$ strip attached to the lower surface turns pink much faster than the strip on the upper surface.

PRECAUTIONS

- *A well-watered potted plant should be taken for the experiment.*
- *The cobalt chloride paper should be handled with dry hands or forcep.*
- *The leaf surface must be wiped and dried before putting the cobalt chloride paper.*
- *Equal sized strips should be placed on both the surfaces.*
- *The slides that fix the cobalt chloride strips over leaves should be sealed by vaseline. To ensure that no air or water can enter through the spaces of slide and cobalt chloride.*

Viva-Voce

Q.1 Name the various types of transpiration.

Ans The various types of transpiration are:

(i) Lenticular transpiration (ii) Stomatal transpiration

(iii) Cuticular transpiration

Q.2 Name some external factors which affect the rate of transpiration. NCERT

Ans Light, temperature, wind and humidity are the external factors that affect the rate of transpiration.

Q.3 Which surface of a leaf shows higher rate of transpiration?

Ans Lower surface of leaf shows higher rate of transpiration.

Q.4 What is the reason for the colour change observed in cobalt chloride paper? NCERT

Ans Blue colour of anhydrous cobalt chloride turns pink when it comes in contact with water. This property of cobalt chloride is used to demonstrate that water is lost during transpiration.

Q.5 Why is mid-day or afternoon the ideal time to perform the experiment to study the rate of transpiration? NCERT

Ans The mid-day or afternoon is the ideal time to perform the experiment for studying the rate of transpiration because at noon, the stomata are open and the rate of transpiration is highest at mid-day.

Q.6 Which inorganic ion helps in the process of stomatal opening and closing?

Ans Potassium ion gradient helps in the process of stomatal opening and closing.

Q.7 Why is transpiration said to be a necessary evil?

Ans Transpiration is called as a necessary evil because the water absorbed by the plant is lost by this process after it has been used for photosynthesis. Still, this process is necessary for absorption of water and minerals from soil. It exerts transpirational pull for the ascent of sap and provides cooling effect in plants.

Q.8 **What is the disadvantage of transpiration?**

Ans Very high rate of transpiration causes wilting of leaves in plants. Most of the xerophytes develop structural modifications to check transpiration.

Q.9 **What will happen to the root pressure if plant is transpiring rapidly?**

Ans If plant is transpiring rapidly, root pressure decreases because the increased water demand from the leaves reduces the water availability in the soil for uptake by roots.

Q.10 **Why are the number of stomata greater on the lower surface than the upper surface of a leaf?**

Ans If large number of stomata will occur on upper surface (direct exposure to sunlight), it would lead to great amount of water loss through transpiration. Therefore, in order to avoid excessive transpiration, stomata are present in greater number on the lower surface of leaf.

Q.11 **What will happen to the plant if the rate of transpiration exceeds the amount of water absorbed?**

Ans If the rate of transpiration exceeds the amount of water absorbed, the plant will wilt or may even die if the condition continues for a longer period of time.

Q.12 **How are the plants able to survive under flooded conditions?**

Ans Plants reduce transpiration under flooded conditions by closing stomata to conserve water and prevent further water loss.

Q.13 **Does transpiration take place in aquatic plants?** NCERT

Ans Transpiration does not take place in aquatic plants (completely submerged) because these do not possess stomata on leaf surface and gaseous exchange takes place through diffusion from general surface of the plant.

Q.14 **What result would you observe if the cobalt chloride experiment is carried out in dark conditions?** NCERT

Ans If cobalt chloride experiment is carried out in dark conditions, the cobalt chloride paper will not change its colour because no transpiration or water loss will occur as stomata remain closed.

Q.15 **How is root pressure related to transpiration?**

Ans The positive hydrostatic pressure within the root system due to the active uptake of minerals and water is called root pressure. The root pressure tends to be low when water loss from leaves (transpiration) is high.

Experiment 7.a

AIM

To test the presence of carbohydrates like glucose, sucrose and starch in suitable plant and animal materials.

Theory/Principle

Carbohydrates or **sugars** are the organic compounds made up of carbon, hydrogen and oxygen and are depicted by general formula of carbohydrates, i.e. $C_nH_{2n}O_n$. They act as main source of energy in our body. When present in excess they are converted into fats and get stored in the body. These are also called as **saccharides**.

Classification of Carbohydrates

On the basis of their composition, carbohydrates are classified into three major categories:

Monosaccharides These are the simplest form of carbohydrates, sweet in taste and cannot be hydrolysed into smaller subunits, e.g. glucose, fructose (sweetest natural sugar), etc.

Oligosaccharides These are formed by the polymerisation of few molecules (2-10 units) of monosaccharides, e.g. sucrose (cane sugar), lactose (milk sugar), maltose (malt sugar), etc.

Polysaccharides These are the polymers of several molecules of monosaccharides and are made up of one or more types of monosaccharide units, e.g. starch, cellulose, glycogen, etc.

Carbohydrates can also be classified according to their reducing potentials. This variation in their reducing abilities is used as a means to test the presence of sugar units in a given sample. They are categorised into reducing and non-reducing sugars. Carbohydrates with a free aldehyde or ketone groups (i.e., simple sugars) reduce copper sulphate of Benedict and Fehling's reagent to cuprous oxide forming a yellow or brownish-red coloured precipitate depending on the concentration of sugar.

The various patterns of colour change show following interpretations:

S.No.	Colour change	Approximate amount of reducing sugar
1.	No change in blue colour.	The absence of reducing sugar.
2.	Blue colour changes to green precipitate	0.1- 0.5% of reducing sugar.
3.	Blue colour changes to yellow precipitate.	0.5 -1.0% of reducing sugar.
4.	Blue colour changes to orange-red precipitate.	1.0 - 2.0% of reducing sugar.
5.	Blue colour changes to brick-red precipitate.	More than 2.0% of reducing sugar.

Requirements

Test tubes, funnel, beakers, water bath, test tube holder, test tube stand, droppers, spirit lamp, reagents (Benedict's solution and Fehling's solutions A and B), concentrated HCl, saturated solution of NaOH, dilute iodine solution, fruit juices of apple, grape or banana, extracts of potato, sugarcane juice and rice extract.

Preparation of Reagents

Benedict's Reagent

- Add 173g of sodium citrate and 100g of anhydrous sodium carbonate in 600 mL of water in a beaker and warm gently. The solution formed will be treated as solution A.
- Dissolve 17.3g of hydrated $CuSO_4$ in 100 mL of distilled water. The solution formed will be treated as solution B.
- Add solution B to solution A with constant stirring. Cool the mixed solution and make up the final volume upto 1L with distilled water.

Fehling's Reagent

Reagent A Dissolve 6.93g of copper sulphate in 100 mL of distilled water.

Reagent B Dissolve 20g of KOH and 34.6g of sodium-potassium tartarate (Rochelle's salt) in 100 mL of distilled water.

Procedure and observations

1. Take freshly prepared juices of apples/grapes/banana to detect the presence of glucose and take sugarcane juice to detect the presence of sucrose in different test tubes.
2. Take extract of potato to detect the presence of starch in another test tube.
3. Perform the following tests for detecting the presence of glucose, sucrose and starch and verify your results from the table given ahead.

S.No.	Tests	Observations	Results
1.	**Test for glucose** (monosaccharide)		
(i) **Benedict's test**			
	(a) Take 2 mL of test solution (apple/grape/banana juice) in test tube + 2 mL of Benedict's reagent. (b) Place the test tube in boiling water in a water bath.	The colour changes initially from blue to green and finally to orange or brick red.	Reducing sugar, i.e. glucose is present.
(ii) **Fehling's test**			
	(a) Take 2 mL of test solution in test tube + 2 mL of Fehling's solution A + 2 mL of Fehling's solution B. (b) Place the test tube in boling water in a water bath.	The initial blue colour turns green to yellow and finally a brick red or orange ppt. is formed.	Glucose (reducing sugar) is present.

S.No.	Tests	Observations	Results
2.	**Test for sucrose** (disaccharide)		
(i)	Perform Benedict's and Fehling's test with sugarcane juice.	No change in colour.	Simple sugar (monosaccharides) absent.
	Hydrolysis test		
	(a) Take 10 mL of sugarcane juice and add 2-3 drops of conc. HCl. (b) Boil the test tube gently for 2 minutes. (c) This will result in the hydrolysis of sucrose into glucose and fructose. (d) After cooling, add 4 mL of saturated solution of NaOH or Na_2CO_3 to neutralise the solution and divide the solution into two parts in two different test tubes (*A* and *B*).		
	(e) Perform Benedict's test in test tube *A* containing hydrolysed sample. (f) Perform Fehling's test in test tube *B* containing hydrolysed sample.	Orange or brick red ppt. is observed in the bottom of both the test tubes (*A* and *B*).	Monosaccharides (reducing sugar) are present in the samples.
3.	**Test for starch** (polysaccharide)		
(i)	**Iodine test**		
	(a) Take the extract of potato or rice (2 mL) in a test tube and add few drops of iodine solution in it.	Blue-black colour is observed.	Starch is present in the sample.
(ii)	**Hydrolysis test**		
	(a) Take 2 mL of potato/rice extract + 2-3 drops of HCl. (b) Boil the test tube gently for 2 minutes. (c) After cooling, add 2-3 drops of NaOH to neutralise the solution.		
	(d) Now, perform the Benedict's and Fehling's test with the above hydrolysed sample.	Orange or brick-red ppt. is observed.	Monosaccharides are present in the sample.

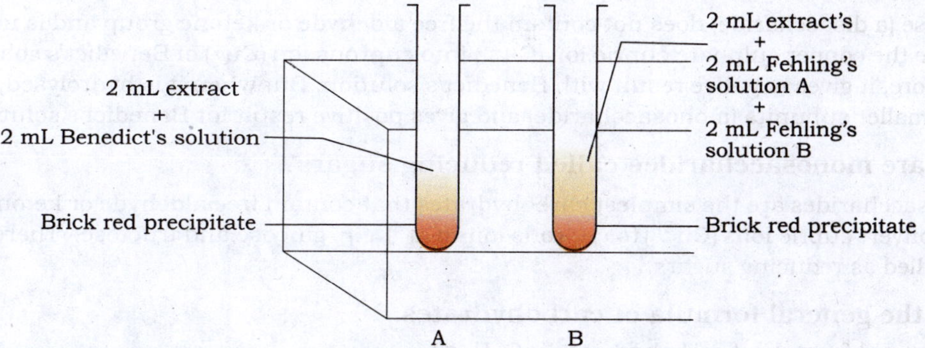

Fig. 7.a.1 Test for glucose A. Benedict's B. Fehling's test

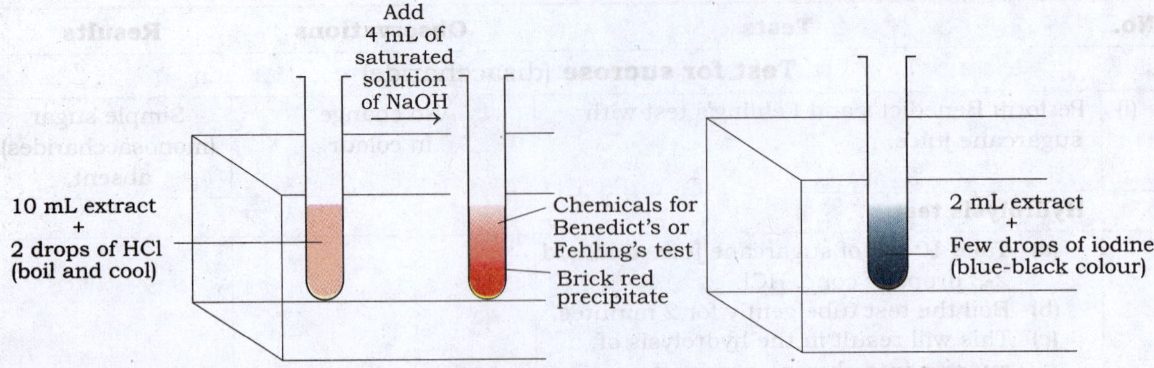

Fig. 7. a. 2 Hydrolysis test for sucrose

Fig. 7. a. 3 Iodine test for starch

PRECAUTIONS

- *Take limited quantities of food extracts and chemicals to avoid wastage.*
- *Wash all the test tubes thoroughly before use.*
- *Use separate droppers for adding different reagents.*
- *Proper care should be taken while heating the samples in test tube.*
- *Keep the mouth of test tube away from yourself and your friends.*
- *Direct heating of test tube should be avoided. The heating should be carried out in water bath.*

Q.1 What is the use of HCl in the test of carbohydrates? NCERT

Ans Sucrose or starch are non-reducing sugars (disaccharide and polysaccharide, respectively) and when they are boiled with HCl, they are converted into their respective monosaccharides or reducing sugars. These monosaccharide units react with different reagents to prove the presence of carbohydrates in the sample extract.

Q.2 Sucrose solution gives a negative result with Benedict's test. Why? NCERT

Ans Sucrose (a disaccharide) does not contain the free aldehyde or ketone group and is unable to reduce the copper sulphate cupric ion (Cu^{2+}) into cuprous ion (Cu^{+}) of Benedict's solution, therefore, it gives negative result with Benedict's solution. But when it is hydrolysed, it breaks into smaller subunits (monosaccharide) and gives positive result for Benedict's solution.

Q.3 Why are monosaccharides called reducing sugars? NCERT

Ans Monosaccharides are the simplest carbohydrates that contain free aldehyde or ketone group and can convert cupric ions (Cu^{2+}) to cuprous ions (Cu^{+}), e.g. glucose and fructose. Therefore, these are called as reducing sugars.

Q.4 Give the general formula of carbohydrates.

Ans The general formula of carbohydrates is $C_nH_{2n}O_n$.

Q.5 **Give the name of the sweetest naturally occurring monosaccharide.**

Ans Fructose or fruit sugar is the sweetest naturally occurring sugar found in honey and fruits.

Q.6 **Give the common names for following sugars:**

(i) Sucrose (ii) Maltose

(iii) Lactose

Ans The other name of the following sugars are as follows :

(i) Sucrose – Cane sugar

(ii) Maltose – Malt sugar

(iii) Lactose – Milk sugar

Q.7 **In which form are the carbohydrates stored in plants and animals?**

Ans Carbohydrates are stored in the form of starch in plants and in the form of glycogen in animals.

Q.8 **Will iodine test give a positive result with glucose, fructose or sucrose solution?** NCERT

Ans No, iodine test will not give a positive result with glucose, fructose or sucrose solution because iodine specifically makes a blue coloured complex with starch.

Q.9 **Name any two disaccharides, along with their constituent monosaccharide subunits.**

Ans The two disaccharides and their constituents are as follows:

Sucrose composed of glucose and fructose.

Maltose composed of glucose only.

Q.10 **Why does the blue colour disappear on boiling and reappear on cooling in the iodine test for starch?** NCERT

Ans Starch is actually a mixture of two components, i.e. water soluble amylose and water insoluble amylopectin. Amylose is a linear chain polymer, which forms crystalline structure in the starch. When amylose comes in contact with iodine molecule, it gives the characteristic blue colour. When the solution of iodine with starch is heated, the crystalline structure gets disrupted forming a random chain and the blue colour disappears. When it is cooled again, amylose refolds into its crystalline form and the blue colour reappears.

Experiment 7.b

AIM

To test the presence of proteins in suitable plant and animal materials.

Theory/Principle

Proteins are the complex biomolecules containing carbon, hydrogen, oxygen, nitrogen and small amount of sulphur and phosphorus.

Proteins respond to various colour reactions due to the presence of one or more radicals or groups of complex protein molecules. Since all proteins do not contain the same amino acids, hence they do not respond in a like-manner to all colour reactions. Nitrogen atom in the peptide chain form a complex (violet colour) with copper ions in the Biuret test. (Biuret test is for peptide bond in the molecule of a protein). Xanthoproteic test is specific for protein containing aromatic amino acids. The benzene ring in the amino acid is nitrated by heating with nitric acid and forms yellow nitro-compounds which turns to orange colour with alkali.

Requirements

Test tubes, spirit lamp, test tube holder, test tube stand, droppers, mortar and pestle, filter paper, funnel, 40% NaOH, 1% $CuSO_4$ solution, concentrated HNO_3, 20% NaOH solution, Millon's reagent (mixture of metallic mercury in nitric acid, followed by addition of water) and milk or albumin of egg or gram seed (protein source).

Procedure

1. Take albumin of egg in a test tube or crush the gram seeds in mortar and pestle and transfer this crushed material in a test tube. Then filter it in another test tube using filter paper and funnel and use this filtrate as test solution.
2. Test for the presence of protein in milk, albumin of egg (animal protein) or gram seed extract (plant protein) by performing the various tests given in the table below.

Observations and Results

Tests	Observations	Results
(i) **Biuret Test**		
(a) Take 2 mL of sample or test solution (milk/egg albumin/gram seed extract) in test tube + 1 mL Biuret reagent (containing 1 mL of 40% sodium hydroxide solution and 1-2 drops of 1% $CuSO_4$ solution).		

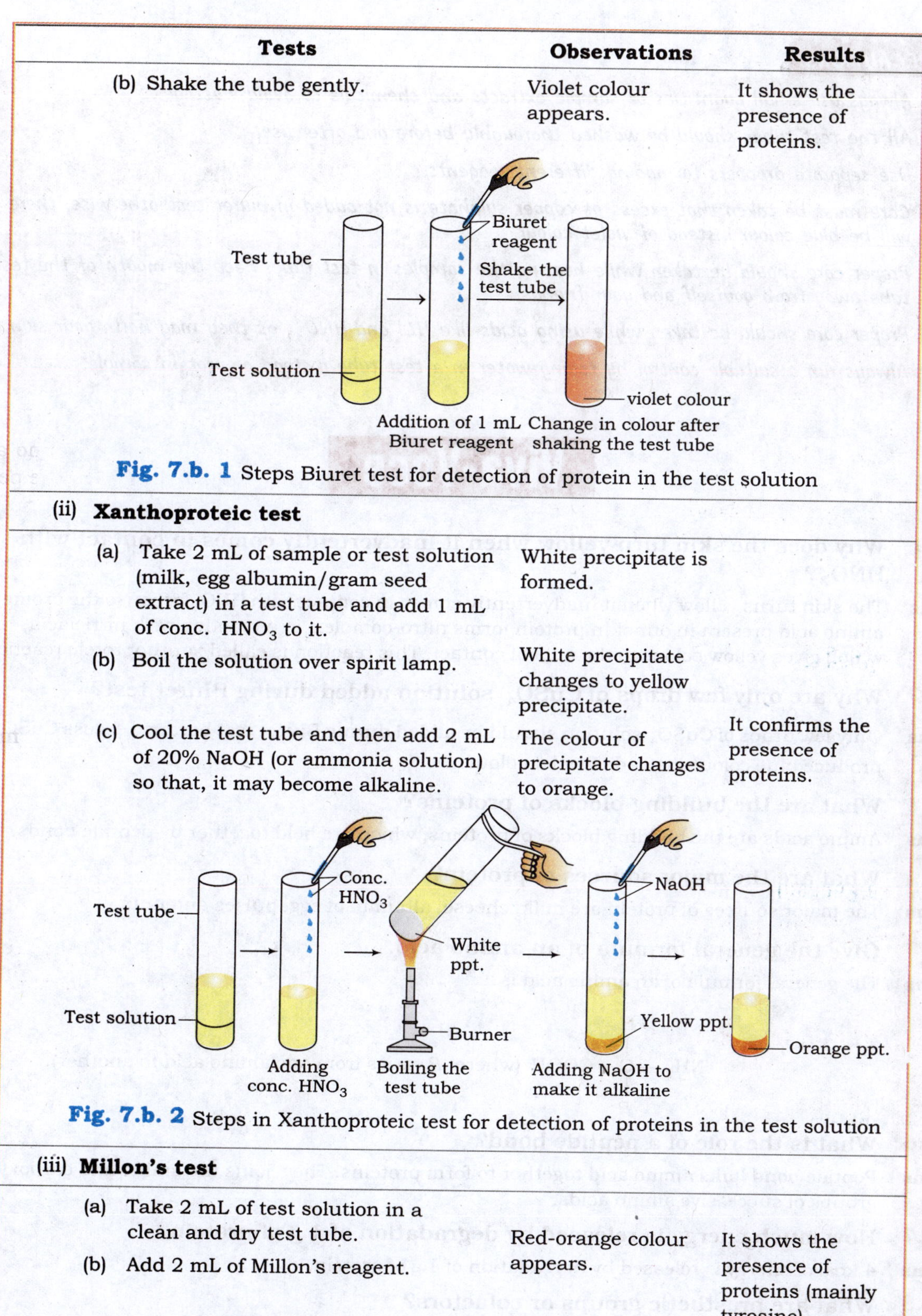

Tests	Observations	Results
(b) Shake the tube gently.	Violet colour appears.	It shows the presence of proteins.

Fig. 7.b. 1 Steps Biuret test for detection of protein in the test solution

(ii) **Xanthoproteic test**

Tests	Observations	Results
(a) Take 2 mL of sample or test solution (milk, egg albumin/gram seed extract) in a test tube and add 1 mL of conc. HNO_3 to it.	White precipitate is formed.	
(b) Boil the solution over spirit lamp.	White precipitate changes to yellow precipitate.	
(c) Cool the test tube and then add 2 mL of 20% NaOH (or ammonia solution) so that, it may become alkaline.	The colour of precipitate changes to orange.	It confirms the presence of proteins.

Fig. 7.b. 2 Steps in Xanthoproteic test for detection of proteins in the test solution

(iii) **Millon's test**

Tests	Observations	Results
(a) Take 2 mL of test solution in a clean and dry test tube. (b) Add 2 mL of Millon's reagent.	Red-orange colour appears.	It shows the presence of proteins (mainly tyrosine).

Note *Millon's test is not specific for proteins as it detects other phenolic compounds as well, therefore, it must be confirmed by performing either biuret test or xanthoproteic test.*

PRECAUTIONS

- *Always use small quantities of sample extracts and chemicals to avoid wastage.*
- *All the test tubes should be washed thoroughly before and after use.*
- *Use separate droppers for adding different reagents.*
- *Care must be taken that excess of copper sulphate is not added in biuret test otherwise, there will be blue colour instead of violet colour.*
- *Proper care should be taken while heating the samples in test tube. Keep the mouth of the test tube away from yourself and your friends.*
- *Proper care should be taken while using acids like HCl and HNO_3, as they may harm your skin.*
- *Always run a suitable control by taking water in a test tube instead of protein sample.*

Viva-Voce

Q.1 Why does the skin turn yellow when it inadvertently comes in contact with HNO_3? NCERT

Ans The skin turns yellow when it inadvertently comes in contact with HNO_3 because the aromatic amino acid present in our skin protein forms nitro-complex in a reaction with nitric acid, which gives yellow colour to the area of contact. This reaction is called xanthoproteic reaction.

Q.2 Why are only few drops of $CuSO_4$ solution added during Biuret test? NCERT

Ans Only few drops of $CuSO_4$ solution should be added during Biuret test because excess $CuSO_4$ will produce blue colour instead of violet colour.

Q.3 What are the building blocks of proteins?

Ans Amino acids are the building blocks of proteins, which are held together by peptide bonds.

Q.4 What are the major sources of protein?

Ans The major sources of protein are milk, cheese, albumin of egg, pulses and nuts.

Q.5 Give the general formula of an amino acid.

Ans The general formula of an amino acid is

$$NH_2 - \overset{\displaystyle H}{\underset{\displaystyle R}{\overset{|}{\underset{|}{C}}}} - COOH$$

(where, *R* varies from one amino acid to another).

Q.6 What is the role of a peptide bond?

Ans Peptide bond links amino acid together to form proteins. They joins the amino and carboxyl groups of successive amino acids.

Q.7 How much energy is released by degradation of 1 g of protein?

Ans 4 kcal of energy is released by degradation of 1 g of protein.

Q.8 What are prosthetic groups or cofactors?

Ans Some proteins have a non-peptide group attached to their structures, such external groups are called as prosthetic groups or co-factors.

Experiment 7.c

AIM

To test the presence of fats in suitable plant and animal materials.

Theory/Principle

Fats can be defined as 'esters of fatty acids and glycerol'. These are insoluble in water but soluble in organic and non-polar solvents like chloroform and benzene.

Fats are a rich source of energy that yield 9 kcal of energy per gram of fat and are stored in body in the adipose tissues. These tissues provide warmth and necessary padding in areas like thighs. Some of the sources of fats are butter, ghee, meat, milk, fish, groundnut oil, coconut oil, etc. There are three types of fat (lipids) on the basis of their chemical structure, i.e. simple lipids, compound lipids and derived lipids. Cholesterol is a type of lipid in our body, excess of which can cause heart ailment. Specific red colour with Sudan III gives the confirmatory test for fats.

Requirements

Test tubes, test tube stand, test tube holder, droppers, Sudan III, ethyl alcohol, water, chloroform, ether, benzene, oil, ghee or butter and groundnuts.

Procedure

1. Crush some groundnuts after soaking in water and filter their extract in a test tube.
2. Use this filterate or other sources of fat like oil, ghee or butter, etc. for performing following different tests given in the observation table to check its presence.

Observation and Result

Tests	Observations	Results
	(i) Sudan III test	
(a) Take 2 mL of oil or butter or groundnuts extract in a test tube add 2 mL of water and a pinch of Sudan III. (b) Gently shake the tube. (c) The lipid layer will show change in colour while layer of water will remain uncoloured.	Red colour appear in the lipid layer.	It indicates and confirms the presence of fats.
	(ii) Solubility test	
(a) Take 5 different test tubes and place small pieces of butter/mustard oil/ghee in each test tube. (b) Add 2 mL of water in test tube *A*, 2 mL of ether in test tube *B*, 2 mL of chloroform in test tube *C*, 2 mL of benzene in test tube *D* and 2 mL of ethyl alcohol in test tube *E*.		

Tests	Observations	Results
(c) Shake thoroughly.	Oil, ghee or butter is broken into small droplets in water which float at the surface indicating that fat is insoluble in water. But in ether chloroform, benzene and ethyl alcohol no such droplets are formed as the oil, ghee or butter dissolves in these organic solvents.	It shows the presence of fats as they are insoluble in water.
	(iii) **Emulsion test**	
(a) Take 2 mL of sample + 2 mL water in a test tube.		
(b) Gently shake the tube.	Two layers are observed, i.e. layer of oil over water.	It shows the presence of fats.
	(iv) **Translucence test**	
Crush peanuts or butter piece and rub it on a piece of white paper.	The paper becomes translucent.	It shows the presence of fats.

PRECAUTIONS

- *Small quantities of sample extracts and chemicals should be used to avoid wastage.*
- *The test tubes should be washed thoroughly before and after use.*
- *The organic solvents should be used under the guidance of teachers.*
- *Proper care must be taken while using Sudan III because it may stain the clothes.*
- *Use different droppers for different reagents.*

Viva-Voce

Q.1 What are the simplest forms of fat? NCERT

Ans The simplest forms of fat are fatty acids and glycerol.

Q.2 Will fat dissolved in an organic solvent give a positive result with Sudan III? NCERT

Ans Sudan III will not give a positive result with organic solvent because the fat gets dissolved in it. But if fat is mixed with water, Sudan III will stain the fat molecules with red colour and will give positive result.

Q.3 Which test for fats can be done without the use of chemicals?

Ans When fat or oil is rubbed on white paper, it makes the paper translucent. This translucence test for fats is done without using any chemical.

Q.4 Which chemical gives the confirmatory test for fat?

Ans Sudan III gives the specific red colour with fats, and is also used as a confirmatory test for them.

Q.5 Name two solvents that can dissolve fat in them.

Ans Non-polar solvents like chloroform and benzene can dissolve fat in them.

Q.6 Name the fat (lipid) that can cause heart ailment.

Ans Excess of cholesterol in our body causes heart ailment.

Q.7 Give a difference between oils and fats.

Ans Oils are mainly unsaturated fatty acids which are liquid at room temperature, whereas fats are mostly saturated fatty acids and are solid at room temperature.

Q.8 Can oils be changed into fats? How?

Ans Oils can be changed into fats by the process of hydrogenation, which converts unsaturated fatty acids into saturated fatty acids.

Q.9 What amount of energy is released by the degradation of 1g of fat?

Ans Energy of 9 kcal is released by the degradation of 1g of fat.

Q.10 Give the types of fats (lipids) on the basis of their chemical structure.

Ans On the basis of their chemical structure, fats (lipids) are classified as follows:

(i) Simple lipids

(ii) Compound lipids

(iii) Derived lipids

Experiment 8

AIM

Separation of plant pigments through paper chromatography.

Theory/Principle

Chloroplast contains **photosynthetic pigments** such as chlorophyll-*a* and *b*, carotenes and xanthophylls. These pigments absorb solar radiation at different wavelengths of the visible spectrum for photosynthesis. They differ in their chemical structures and hence, their physiochemical properties, such as molecular weight, solubility in the solvent, etc. are also different.

Paper chromatography is a popular technique widely used for separating various chlorophyll pigments from a mixture. It is based on the principle of partition chromatography, which involves two phases:

(i) **Stationary phase** Chromatographic paper made up of cellulose fibre holds water between its fibres. The hydrated paper acts as stationary phase.

(ii) **Mobile phase** Organic solvent acts as mobile phase, which moves by capillary action of paper.

In chromatography, pigments move to different distances, depending on their solubility in the solvent system, on a cellulose paper (Whatmann No. 1 chromatography paper). The solvent system components vary in density and thus move at different rates due to wick action through the chromatography paper. Lighter components move faster than the heavier components. Differential solubility of pigments in the solvent system and the differential rates of mobility of solvent system components is used for separation of pigments.

Mono-dimensional Chromatography

It is of two types:

(i) **Descending paper chromatography** Development of chromatogram is done by allowing the solvent to travel down the paper.

(ii) **Ascending paper chromatography** Solvent travels in upward direction of the chromatographic paper.

Both of the above techniques are used for separation of organic and inorganic substances. Separation of photosynthetic pigments by paper chromatography is also an application of **mono-dimensional ascending chromatography**.

Two-dimensional Chromatography

Square or rectangular paper is used. The sample is applied to one of the corners and chromatogram is developed at right angle to the direction of first run.

Note *R_f value or retention factor or relative front value is defined as the ratio of distance moved by the solute (pigment) to the distance moved by the solvent on the chromatographic paper.*

$$R_f \text{ value} = \frac{\text{Distance moved by the solute (pigment)}}{\text{Distance moved by the solvent}}$$

Requirements

Fresh green spinach leaves (mucilage-free), blotting sheet, chromatographic paper/ Whatmann no. 1 chromatography paper, mortar and pestle, a wide mouth test tube or chromatography chamber, 100 mL and 10 mL measuring cylinders, 50 mL beaker, black, capillary tube, petroleum ether, acetone, scissors, pins, sand, test tube stand, funnel, rubber cork, pencil and muslin cloth.

Procedure

1. Take 10-15 fresh spinach leaves (mucilage-free) and remove their petiole and mid rib.
2. Cut the leaves into small pieces and grind them in mortar and pestle with few mL of acetone and a pinch of sand, until the leaf extract becomes dark green coloured.
3. Now, filter this extract through muslin cloth and collect the filtrate in a 50 mL beaker or a test tube.
4. Make a solution of petroleum ether and acetone in the ratio of 9 : 1 and pour 3-5 mL of this, solution into the wide mouth test tube or chromatography chamber. Close the chamber or wide mouth test tube by placing a split cork tightly over the mouth of the test tube. Keep the tube in standing position in a test tube stand.
5. Cut a strip of Whatmann no.1 chromatography paper according to the size of the test tube.
6. Make one end of this chromatographic paper into a triangular shape with a pointed end using scissors.[Fig. 8.1(a)]
7. Apply the leaf extract on the loading spot (a point marked in the centre of the chromatographic paper strip at a distance of about 2 cm from the notch) with a very fine capillary tube or tip of a pin or toothpick. Allow it to dry and repeat the procedure for about 4-5 applications. Make sure that the diameter of the loaded spot is not more than 3-5 mm.

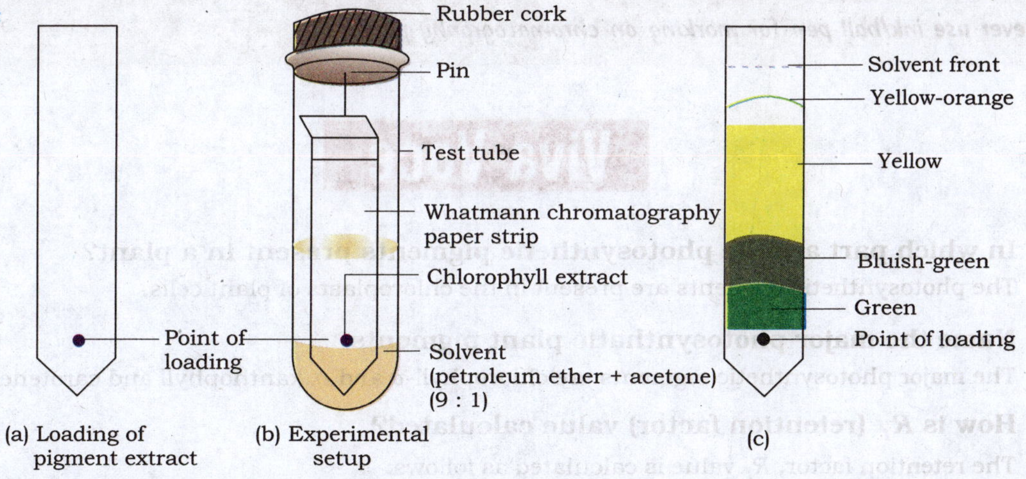

Fig. 8.1 Demonstration of paper chromatography to show separation of plant pigments

8. Suspend the loaded chromatography paper vertically in the wide mouth test tube with the help of a drawing pin fixed on the cork. The paper should not touch the wall of the tube and make sure that the loaded spot is clearly above the solvent. [Fig. 8.1(b)]
9. Leave the apparatus undisturbed till the solvent rises to about three-fourth of the strip.
10. Take out the strip and cover the chromatogram with black paper to prevent photo-oxidation.
11. With the help of pencil, mark the bands. [Fig. 8.1(c)]

Observation

Sequentially from the bottom, the four colours visible are : green, bluish-green, yellow and orange. Identify the pigments on the basis of colours as given in the table below.

Pigments	Colours of the band
Chlorophyll-*b*	Green
Chlorophyll-*a*	Bluish-green
Xanthophyll	Yellow
Carotene	Yellow-orange

Result

The different type of photosynthetic pigments can be identified with the help of colour of their bands as given in the table above.

PRECAUTIONS

- *Loading of extract must be done at the same point each time.*
- *Let the paper dry after each loading.*
- *The solvent should not touch the loading spot.*
- *The leaf used should be fresh and green.*
- *Only lamina of the leaf should be used.*
- *Paper should be dried in air, not in the sunlight.*
- *Mark the solvent front and bands immediately after taking the paper out from the tube.*
- *Never use ink/ball pen for marking on chromatography paper.*

Viva-Voce

Q.1 In which part are the photosynthetic pigments present in a plant?

Ans The photosynthetic pigments are present in the chloroplasts of plant cells.

Q.2 Name the major photosynthatic plant pigments.

Ans The major photosynthetic pigments are chlorophyll-*a* and *b*, xanthophyll and carotene.

Q.3 How is R_f (retention factor) value calculated?

Ans The retention factor, R_f value is calculated as follows:

$$R_f \text{ value} = \frac{\text{Distance travelled by the solute (pigment)}}{\text{Distance travelled by the solvent}}$$

Q.4 Why the chromatographic paper should not be dried in sunlight?

Ans The chromatographic paper should not be dried in sunlight because the pigments may get oxidised in sunlight and may lose colour, making it difficult to identify them.

Q.5 What is chromatography?

Ans Chromatography is a technique used to separate and analyze components in a mixture by passing it through a medium where different components move at different rates.

Q.6 What is the colour of the following pigments?

(i) Chlorophyll-*a*   (ii) Chlorophyll-*b*

(iii) Xanthophyll

Ans The colour of the given pigments are as follows:

(i) Chlorophyll-*a* — Bluish-green

(ii) Chlorophyll-*b* — Green

(iii) Xanthophyll — Yellow

Q.7 Among the two solvent system in chromatography, which moves farthest and why? NCERT

Ans Mobile phase moves farthest in two solvent systems in chromatography because it percolates over the stationary phase carrying components along with the direction of flow. Components dissolved in the mobile phase also move with the flow.

Q.8 Give a reason as to why acetone is used in paper chromatography?

Ans Acetone is an organic solvent, which dissolves the pigments so that they can be easily separated through chromatography technique. Therefore, acetone has an important role in paper chromatography.

Q.9 Which photosynthetic pigment moves farthest on a paper chromatogram and why? NCERT

Ans Carotene moves farthest because it is light and has highest R_f value among other photosynthetic pigments.

Q.10 Leaves in general appear green although they possess yellow and orange pigments. Comment. NCERT

Ans Leaves in general appear green although they possess other pigments like carotene and xanthophyll because chlorophyll-b and chlorophyll-*a* is present in larger amount than any other pigment in leaves. Combination of different pigments make different shades of green.

Q.11 Why do we add sand while preparing the pigment extract? NCERT

Ans While preparing the pigment extract we add sand because it facilitates the fine crushing of leaves and accurate separation of pigments.

Q.12 How can you identify different compounds by paper chromatography?

Ans The different compounds separated by paper chromatography can be identified by calculating their R_f values and matching the same with the standard R_f values of the compounds.

Q.13 Why organic solvents are used in chromatography experiment?

Ans Plant pigments are soluble in organic solvent and not in water hence, they are used in chromatography experiment.

Experiment 9

AIM

To study the rate of respiration in flower buds or leaf tissues and germinating seeds.

Theory/Principle

Respiration is a vital process in all the living organisms that generates energy through breakdown of food materials in the presence/absence of O_2.

Types of Respiration

Process of respiration is of two types:

(i) **Anaerobic respiration** (in absence of O_2)

$$\text{Pyruvate} \xrightarrow{\text{Yeast}} \underset{\text{Ethyl alcohol}}{C_2H_5OH} + CO_2 + \text{Energy}$$

or,

$$\text{Pyruvate} \xrightarrow{\textit{Lactobacillus}} \underset{\text{Lactic acid}}{C_3H_6O_3} + \text{Energy}$$

(ii) **Aerobic respiration** (in presence of O_2)

$$\text{Glucose} \xrightarrow{\text{Glycolysis}} \text{Pyruvic acid} \xrightarrow{\text{Krebs' cycle}} CO_2 + H_2O + \text{Energy}$$

The energy released during respiration is used for all the life processes. Rate of respiration depends on various internal and external factors like age, physiological status and type of cell, availability of light, temperature and oxygen. There is net gain of 36 ATP (in eukaryotes) and 38 ATP (in prokaryotes) from 1 glucose molecule by aerobic respiration.

Respiratory Quotient /Respiratory Ratio

It can be defined as the ratio of the volume of CO_2 evolved to the volume of oxygen consumed in respiration over a period of time.

$$RQ = \frac{\text{Volume of } CO_2 \text{ evolved}}{\text{Volume of } O_2 \text{ consumed}}$$

(a) For carbohydrates, RQ = 1.

$$C_6H_{12}O_6 + 6O_2 \longrightarrow 6CO_2 + 6H_2O + \text{energy; } RQ = \frac{6\ CO_2}{6\ O_2} = 1$$

(b) For fats, RQ < 1.

$$2(C_{51}H_{98}O_6) + 145O_2 \longrightarrow 102CO_2 + 98H_2O + \text{energy; } RQ = \frac{102\ CO_2}{145\ O_2} = 0.7$$

(c) For organic acids, RQ>1, because they are rich in oxygen.

$$C_4H_6O_5 + 3O_2 \longrightarrow 4CO_2 + 3H_2O + \text{energy; } RQ = \frac{4\ CO_2}{3\ O_2} = 1.3$$

(d) For proteins, RQ is variable (ranges from 0.7-0.9, i.e. *RQ* < 1) depending upon the oxygen content of substrates.

Requirements

Germinating seeds, flower buds and leaf tissue, conical flask, hollow glass tube bent twice at right angle, rubber cork with a hole, beaker containing water, potassium hydroxide (KOH) solution, small test tube, string, pencil, practical notebook, etc.

Procedure

1. Take some germinating seeds, flowering buds and leaf tissues in conical flasks A, B and C, respectively.
2. Hang a small test tube, containing KOH, in the conical flasks with the help of a string as shown in fig 9.1.
3. Pass a hollow glass tube (bent twice at right angle) through the hole of the cork, in such a way that one end of the tube is in the beaker containing water and the other end is in the conical flask.
4. Make the apparatus air tight.
5. Note the initial level of water as *'a'* in the bent tube.
6. Keep the apparatus undisturbed for few hours.
7. Note the final position of water as *'b'* in the bent tube and record the data in the observation table.

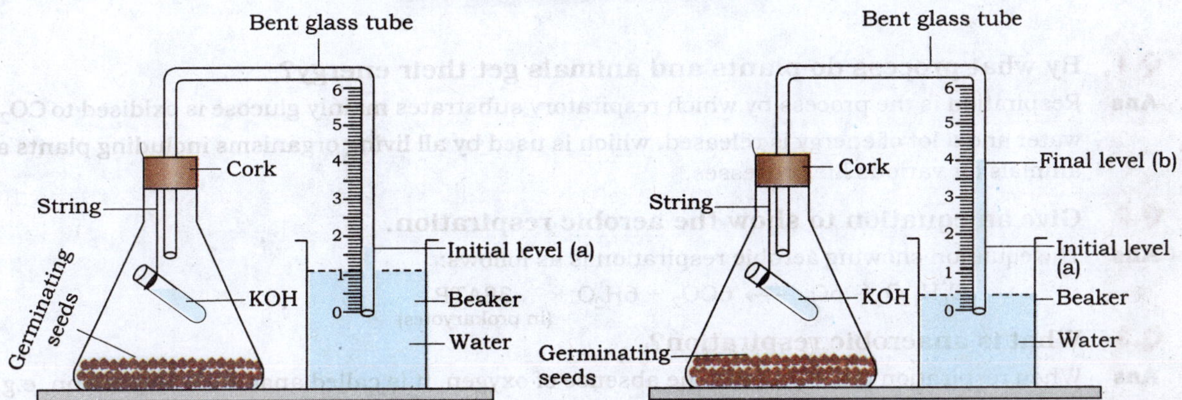

Fig. 9.1 Study of rate of respiration

Observation

The volume of water will rise in the capillary tube and it will be equivalent to the amount of CO_2 produced by the germinating seeds, flower buds and leaf tissues during aerobic respiration. The CO_2 thus evolved is absorbed by KOH in the test tube and some partial vacuum is created in the conical flask. To fill in this space, water enters through delivery tube. The observations can be noted in the observation table as follows:

S.No.	Initial level of water (*a*)	Final level of water (*b*)	Rise in the level of water (b – a = h)
A.			
B.			
C.			

Result

In the germinating seeds, flower buds and leaf tissue, the energy source or substrate for respirations are different and the rise of water levels shows difference. It is because of various types of substrates utilized at differential rates, that there is variation in respiration.

PRECAUTIONS

- *The apparatus should be airtight.*
- *Fresh KOH should be used for the experiment.*
- *The initial and final level of water should be noted carefully.*
- *Only germinating seeds can respire aerobically, therefore, the seeds with broken seed coat should be used instead of the recently soaked seeds.*

Viva-Voce

Q.1 By what process do plants and animals get their energy?

Ans Respiration is the process by which respiratory substrates mainly glucose is oxidised to CO_2 and water and a lot of energy is released, which is used by all living organisms including plants and animals for various life processes.

Q.2 Give an equation to show the aerobic respiration.

Ans The equation showing aerobic respiration is as follows:

$$C_6H_{12}O_6 + 6O_2 \longrightarrow 6CO_2 + 6H_2O + \underset{\text{(in prokaryotes)}}{38ATP}$$

Q.3 What is anaerobic respiration?

Ans When respiration takes place in the absence of oxygen, it is called anaerobic respiration, e.g. fermentation in yeast.

$$C_6H_{12}O_6 \longrightarrow 2C_2H_5OH + 2CO_2 + 2ATP$$

Q.4 What is the role of KOH used in the experiment? NCERT

Ans KOH absorbs CO_2 that is released by the respiring seeds, thus creating partial vacuum which eventually leads to rise in level of water in the glass tube.

Q.5 Why fermentation or anaerobic respiration yields less energy than aerobic respiration?

Ans In fermentation or anaerobic respiration, the carbohydrate is incompletely oxidised to produce alcohol and CO_2 while, the complete oxidation in aerobic respiration yields more amount of energy. Therefore, less energy is produced in anaerobic respiration than aerobic respiration.

Q.6 What is Respiratory Quotient (RQ)?

Ans The ratio between the volume of CO_2 evolved and the volume of O_2 consumed is called respiratory quotient.

Q.7 What are the other materials, apart from germination seeds that can be used to study the rate of respiration in plants?

Ans Flowering buds or leaf tissues can also be used in place of germinating seeds in the experiment for aerobic respiration because these plant tissues also respire actively and aerobically.

Q.8 Do plants breathe?

Ans Yes, plants breathe. They need O_2 for respiration and release CO_2. Exchange of gases takes place through stomata and lenticels in plants.

Q.9 Why do we use only germinating seeds in this experiment?

Ans We use germinating seeds in this experiment because the germinating seeds are more active than non-germinating seeds and they can also respire aerobically.

Q.10 What will happen if the setup is not air tight? NCERT

Ans If the setup is not air tight, the germinating seeds will absorb O_2 from the air entering through the loose setup and no rise in the water level will be observed. This will give fake results or errors in the results of the experiment.

Q.11 Why does the air bubble move in the pipette towards the boiling tube? NCERT

Ans The air bubble move towards the boiling tube due to the change in gas volume resulting from the respiration of the germinating seeds.

Q.12 What is catabolic process?

Ans A catabolic process involves the breakdown of complex molecules into simpler ones. This degradation releases energy, which is used by cells for various metabolic activities and maintenance.

Q.13 Why is the rate of respiration not measured by the energy released?

Ans The rate of respiration is not measured by the energy released because the energy is immediately transformed into various other forms, making it difficult to measure directly.

Experiment 10

AIM

To detect the presence of urea in urine.

Theory/Principle

Urea is mainly excreted out of the body into urine through kidneys. An adult man normally passes out 1-1.5 L of urine per day. Its specific gravity is more than that of plasma (i.e. 1.020-1.03).

The characteristics of urine are give below.

Composition Urine contains 95% water, 2% urea, 0.03% uric acid, traces of creatinine, chloride, potassium, etc.

Colour Pale yellow due to the pigment **urochrome** which is produced by the breakdown of haemoglobin.

pH Ranges from 4.5-8.0; average pH 6.0. Urine is normally acidic, but when kept in open atmosphere, it splits and ammonia is released which makes the stored urine alkaline.

Odour Unpleasent; if allowed to stand for some time, it imparts strong smell like that of ammonia.

Nitrogen present in amino acids is removed as urea. Normally, a healthy adult excretes about 15 g of nitrogen per day; 95% of this is excreted as urea in urine. The amino groups of amino acids are ultimately removed as ammonia (NH_3). This NH_3 is highly toxic and is ultimately converted into urea. Urea is formed in the liver from ammonia and carbon dioxide (CO_2). Its excretion in urine is dependent on amount of protein ingested.

At optimum pH and temperature urease enzyme decomposes urea into ammonia and carbon dioxide which form ammonium carbonate (an alkaline substance), which changes slightly acidic solution to alkaline solution. When phenol red is used as indicator in this reaction mixture, the colour of solution changes from yellow to pink.

Uremia

It is the presence of an excessive amount of urea in the blood. It is due to its decreased excretion by kidneys.

Requirements

Urine sample, test tubes, test tube stand, test tube holder, spirit lamp, water, sodium hypobromite, phenol red, dilute sodium hydroxide, 2% acetic acid, urease tablet, 1% $CuSO_4$ solution and 2% Na_2CO_3 solution.

Procedure

1. Sodium Hypobromite Test

(i) Take 2 mL of urine sample in a test tube.

(ii) Add 3 to 5 drops of sodium hypobromite solution in it.

(iii) Record your observations.

2. Urease Test

(i) Take 2 mL of urine in one test tube and 2 mL of water in other test tube.

(ii) Add a drop of phenol red indicator to each tube.

(iii) Add 2% Na_2CO_3 solution drop by drop till the pink colour appears in both the test tubes and the solution becomes alkaline in nature.

(iv) Now, add 2% acetic acid to the test tubes drop by drop till the pink colour disappears, turning it into an acidic solution.

(v) Add half of a urease tablet, in place of urease tablet, soyabean powder or aqueous extract of arhar (*Cajanus cajan*) can also be used as a source of urease to the sample and rotate the tube between the palms or warm the tubes to about 60°C. Repeat this step with the other test tube as well.

(iv) Record your observations.

Note *This test is a specific test for urea because the enzyme urease shows its specificity for the substrate urea. The optimum pH (just acidic) and temperature (60°C) must be maintained for the activity of the enzyme urease. Urea is formed in the liver from ammonia and carbon dioxide. Ammonia is the product of deamination of amino acids. Therefore, urea excretion in urine is dependent on the amount of protein ingested.*

3. Biuret Test

(i) Take 2 mL of urine sample in a test tube and heat it on low flame, till it is completely evaporated leaving behind the residue in the test tube.

(ii) Cool the test tube and add 3 mL of water. Shake it.

(iii) Add 1 mL of dilute NaOH and 1 or 2 drops of 1% $CuSO_4$ solution to the test tube. Avoid using excess drops of $CuSO_4$ as it will give false positive result.

(iv) Record your observations.

Observation

(i) **Sodium Hypobromite Test** Brisk effervescence of nitrogen appears in the test tube, which indicates the presence of urea in the sample.

$$\underset{\text{Urea}}{(NH_2)_2CO} + \underset{\text{Sodium hypobromite}}{NaOBr} \longrightarrow CO_2 + N_2 + NaBr + H_2O$$

$$CO_2 \xrightarrow{+NaOH} NaHCO_3$$

(ii) **Urease Test** The solution which contains urine turns pink, thus indicating the presence of urea in the sample.

$$\underset{\substack{\text{Urea}\\\text{(neutral)}}}{(NH_2)_2CO} \xrightarrow[Na_2CO_3]{\text{Urease}} \underset{\substack{\text{Ammonium carbonate}\\\text{(alkaline)}}}{(NH_4)_2CO_3} \xrightarrow{\text{Heating}} 2NH_3 + H_2CO_3$$

$$2NH_3 \xrightarrow{+H_2O} NH_4OH$$

(iii) **Biuret Test** The pink colour develops indicating the presence of urea. If excess amount of $CuSO_4$ is added, it will form $Cu(OH)_2$ with NaOH forming a blue colour, which can be mistaken as a positive Biuret test.

Result

The above tests show that the given sample of urine contains urea.

PRECAUTIONS

- *The test tubes must be cleaned and dried thoroughly before use.*
- *Use standard reagents.*
- *Heating must be done carefully and by using test tube holder.*
- *Overheating should be avoided to prevent denaturation of enzyme.*
- *Required amount of reagents should be used to prevent false positive results.*
- *The test tubes must be washed after use.*
- *Fresh sample of urine should be used because if the urine is kept exposed to the atmosphere, it split and ammonia is released.*

Q.1 Give the composition of urine.

Ans The composition of urine can be given as

(i) Water – 95-96%

(ii) Urea – 2%

(iii) Dissolved substances – 2% (contains sugar, albumin, ketone bodies, bile salts, etc.)

Q.2 Give the reaction for urease test.

Ans The reaction for urease test can be shown as follows:

$$\underset{\substack{\text{Urea}\\\text{(neutral)}}}{(NH_2)_2CO} \xrightarrow[Na_2CO_3]{\text{Urease}} \underset{\substack{\text{Ammonium carbonate}\\\text{(alkaline)}}}{(NH_4)_2CO_3} \xrightarrow{\text{Heating}} 2NH_3 + H_2CO_3$$

$$2NH_3 \xrightarrow{+H_2O} NH_4OH$$

Q.3 What is the normal volume of urine excreted by an adult?

Ans Normal volume of urine excreted by an adult is 1-1.5 litres/day.

Q.4 What is the colour of urine and name the pigment responsible for this characteristic colour? NCERT

Ans The urine is pale yellow or amber coloured due to the presence of urochrome.

Q.5 In which organ of our body, highly toxic ammonia is converted into urea? NCERT

Ans Ammonia is converted into urea in the liver.

Q.6 Name the disorder that shows the presence of excess urea in the urine. NCERT

Ans Uremia is the disorder, which shows the presence of excess urea in the urine.

Q.7 What is micturition?

Ans The process of discharge of urine from the urinary bladder through the urethra is called micturition.

Q.8 What is the other name of hypobromite ion?

Ans Hypobromite ions are also known as alkaline bromine water (BrO^-).

Q.9 Which bond is responsible for the colour production in biuret test?

Ans The peptide bond is responsible for the colour production in biuret test.

Q.10 Which other organ of our body excretes urea in small amount? NCERT

Ans A small amount of urea can also be excreted through the skin (*via* sweat).

Q.11 What do you call those animals that eliminate nitrogen mainly in the form of urea? NCERT

Ans The animals that eliminate nitrogen in the form of urea are called ureotelic.

Experiment 11

AIM

To detect the presence of sugar in urine.

Theory/Principle

Urine is the major excretory product of kidney in mammals. Normal urine does not contain glucose. The presence of glucose in urine is called **glycosuria**. There are three main tests, i.e. **Benedict's test, Fehling's test** and **Seliwanoff's test**, which are used for detection of reducing sugars like glucose, fructose, etc. in urine.

$CuSO_4$ present in Benedict's solution or Fehling's solution is reduced on boiling by the reducing substances (glucose, fructose etc.) to form the coloured precipitate of cuprous oxide. The light green, green, yellow and brick red precipitates of cuprous oxides depend on the concentration of reducing substances present in urine.

Glucose reduces the blue cupric sulphate of Benedict's reagent or Fehling's reagent to a coloured insoluble precipitate.

$$\underset{\substack{\text{Glucose}\\\text{(reducing sugar)}}}{CH_2OH(CHOH)_4CHO} + \underset{\substack{\text{Cupric sulphate}\\\text{(blue solution)}}}{2Cu^{++}SO_4^-} + 2H_2O \xrightarrow{\text{heating}} \underset{\substack{\text{Gluconic acid}\\\text{(oxidised sugar)}}}{CH_2OH(CHOH)_4COOH} + \underset{\substack{\text{Cuprous oxide}\\\text{(red precipitate)}}}{Cu_2O} + 4H^+ + SO_4^-$$

Requirements

Test tubes, beakers, test tube stand, test tube holder, spirit lamp, pipette, urine sample, Benedict's reagent, Fehling's solution A, Fehling's solution B and Seliwanoff's reagent.

Procedure

Preparation of Reagents

Prepare Benedict's and Fehling's reagent as prepared in experiment 7(a).

Note *It is not necessary that we perform Benedict's and Fehling's test to test the presence of glucose only. These can also be used to test presence of other reducing sugars in urine such as lactose (in pregnant and lactating mothers), fructose (in fructosuria), galactose (in galactosuria), homogentistic acid (in alkaptonuria), glucuronates and mucin.*

Seliwanoff's Reagent

1. Dissolve 50 mg of resorcinol in 33 mL of concentrated HCl.
2. Dilute the above solution with distilled water to make up final volume of 100 mL.

Note *In absence of appropriate samples having abnormal urine components like glucose or albumin, they can be added in normal urine sample.*

After preparation of reagents, perform the following tests.

1. Benedict's Test

(i) Take 0.5 mL of freshly passed urine sample in a test tube and add 5 mL of Benedict's reagent into it.

(ii) Boil the solution for 2 minutes holding the test tube firmly with a test tube holder in the inclined position and keep shaking the tube continuously as the contents of the test tube have a tendency to spurt out.

(iii) Note down the colours of the precipitate.

2. Fehling's Test

(i) Take equal volumes (2 mL) of Fehling's solutions A and B in a test tube and mix them well.

(ii) Add the solution prepared in step (i) dropwise to 1 mL of urine sample taken in another test tube.

(iii) Heat the solution after each drop is added.

(iv) Observe the colour of the precipitate.

3. Seliwanoff's Test

(i) Take 3 mL Seliwanoff's reagent in a test tube and add 1 mL of urine sample to it.

(ii) Boil the solution for 2 minutes in water bath.

(iii) Observe if there is any colour change in test tube.

(iv) If no colour appears in 2 minutes, continue boiling for 5 minutes.

Note *The qualitative Benedict's test is not very specific test for glucose, since other reducing sugars also give positive test, such as fructose, galactose, lactose, maltose, pentose. Other urinary constituents, drugs and contaminants in the urine may give false positive results. For detecting whether glucose or fructose is present in the urine, Seliwanoff test should be performed. This test is to be performed when urine sample gives positive test for Benedict's or Fehling's test.*

Observations

1. **Benedict's Test** The appearance of green, yellow, light green and brick-red coloured precipitate, indicate the presence of reducing substances in urine. The various coloured precipitates depends on the concentration of reducing sugar in the urine sample which gives a rough estimate of the concentration as given below.

	Colour of precipitate	% of reducing sugar present
1.	Light green	0.1-0.5 (traces of glucose)
2.	Green	0.5-1.0 (moderate amount of glucose)
3.	Yellow	1.0-2.0 (moderate amount of glucose)
4.	Brick-red	above 2 (large amount of glucose)

2. **Fehling's Test** A yellow or orange or brick-red coloured precipitate is formed, which indicates the presence of reducing sugars in urine.

3. **Seliwanoff's Test** Presence of red to orange colour after step (ii) gives positive test for fructose, while appearance of faint orange or no colour after step (iv) gives the positive test for glucose.

Result

The given sample of urine contains reducing sugar such as glucose, fructose, etc.

However, it is important to note that the test that are done in this experiment are sensitive to 50-80 mg glucose /100 mL urine. Less than this amount in the urine will not be detected by these tests.

PRECAUTIONS

- *The test tube must be washed before and after use.*
- *The chemicals should be poured or used in a proper amount to avoid the false positive results.*
- *Proper care must be taken while heating the test tube.*
- *Standard reagents and chemicals must be used.*
- *Do not mix the droppers used for pouring solutions or reagents.*
- *One must use gloves, while working with urine sample to keep themselves protected from infections.*

Viva-Voce

Q.1 What is the end product of Benedict's and Fehling's tests?

Ans The end product of Benedict's and Fehling's tests is a coloured insoluble precipitate.

Q.2 What is the basic principle of Benedict's and Fehling's test?

Ans The basic principle of Benedict's and Fehling's solution is that glucose or any other reducing agent reduces the blue cupric sulphate of Benedict's and Fehling's reagents to a coloured insoluble precipitate.

Q.3 Name any two reducing sugars.

Ans Maltose and fructose, are reducing sugars.

Q.4 What is the significance of appearance of different colours, while performing Benedict's test? NCERT

Ans The appearance of different colours, while performing Benedict's test indicates or gives the idea about the quantity of sugar present in the solution, e.g. light green precipitate indicates the presence of glucose in traces, while red precipitate indicates the presence of higher concentration of glucose in urine.

Q.5 What is the significance of performing Seliwanoff's test? NCERT

Ans Seliwanoff's test is used for detecting the presence of glucose and fructose in urine. It is performed when urine sample gives positive test for Benedict's or Fehling's test.

Q.6 What is a reducing sugar?

Ans A sugar which has free aldehyde or ketone group is called reducing sugar. In other words, we can say that the sugar that is capable of being oxidised and causes the reduction of other substances without being hydrolysed first is known as a reducing sugar.

Q.7 Give a difference between diabetes mellitus and diabetes insipidus.

Ans Diabetes mellitus is caused when sugar level increases in blood and appears in urine, due to the deficiency of insulin hormone. **Diabetes insipidus** is caused when water level increases in urine and most of the water is excreted out in urine due to the deficiency of Anti-diuretic Hormone (ADH).

Q.8 Name any two non-reducing sugars.

Ans Sucrose and trehalose are the non-reducing sugars.

Q.9 Which test is used to differentiate between aldehydes and ketones?

Ans Fehling's test is used to differentiate between aldehydes and ketones.

Q.10 Name the disorder in which glucose level is high in urine. NCERT

Ans Diabetes mellitus is the disorder in which glucose level is high in urine.

Experiment 12

AIM

To detect the presence of albumin in urine.

Theory/Principle

Albumin is a protein in plasma which is important for the maintenance of fluid balance within the vascular system. Proteins are usually reabsorbed from the kidney by blood and not passed out in urine after filtration process.

In normal urine, a trace of protein which is less than 250 mg (in 24 hours urine) is found. But, under pathological conditions like albuminuria, albumin is found in urine above normal level. This amount is so negligible that it escapes detection by any of the simple test.

Analysis of Albumin

Nitric acid causes the precipitation of albumin. When heated or treated with sulphosalicylic acid, albumin undergoes coagulation, which is measured by the degree of turbidity.

Requirements

Test tubes, test tube stand, test tube holder, graduated pipette (5 mL capacity), spirit lamp, urine sample, concentrated nitric acid, acetic acid, Robert's solution, sulphosalicylic acid (or solution containing 13% salicylic acid and 20% sulphuric acid).

Procedure

1. Sulphosalicylic Acid Test

(i) Take 3 mL of urine sample in a test tube.

(ii) Add few drops of sulphosalicylic acid to it.

(iii) Heat the tube gently.

(iv) Note down the observed changes.

2. Nitric Acid Ring Test

(i) Take 5 mL of concentrated nitric acid in a test tube.

Note *In place of nitric acid, Robert's solution (mixture of* $MgSO_4$ *solution and conc.* HNO_3*) can be used.*

(ii) Add the urine sample with a dropper or graduated pipette keeping the tube inclined, so that the urine flows down slowly along the side of the test tube to form a separate layer.

(iii) Observe any changes and record in your notebook.

3. Heat Coagulation Test

(i) Take 6-8 mL of urine in a test tube.

(ii) Incline the test tube at an angle and on a low flame, heat the tube in a way so that only upper one-third of test tube gets heated.

(iii) The heated portion develops turbidity.

(iv) Add 1% acetic acid drop by drop in the test tube and boil its contents or simply add a drop of 33% acetic acid. Look out for any change in turbidity.

Observations

1. **Sulphosalicylic Acid Test** Appearance of cloudy or whitish turbid solution or precipitate (coagulation) in the solution shows the presence of albumin. The turbidity increases on gentle heating.
2. **Nitric Acid Ring Test** A white ring is formed at the junction of two liquids (Robert's solution or nitric acid and urine solution) which confirms the presence of albumin in the sample of urine.
3. **Heat Coagulation Test** Persistence of turbidity after step (iv) confirms presence of albumin in urine.

Note *Disappearance of turbidity confirms the presence of phosphates.*

Result

The above tests confirm the presence of albumin in urine.

PRECAUTIONS

- *Wash the test tubes thoroughly before and after use.*
- *Heat the contents gently, do not boil unless required.*
- *Use standard reagents and do not waste excess of reagents or chemicals.*

Viva-Voce

Q.1 Which reagents will demonstrate the presence of protein in urine? NCERT

Ans Sulphosalicylic acid and Robert's reagent are used to detect the presence of protein in urine sample.

Q.2 Name the condition in which albumin is significantly detected in urine.

Ans The presence of albumin in urine is significantly detected in albuminuria.

Q.3 Why is the test tube put in inclined position while adding urine sample?

Ans The test tube is inclined while adding the urine sample with a dropper, so that it flows down slowly along the side of the test tube to form a separate layer.

Q.4 What is the cause of albuminuria?

Ans Albuminuria refers to the condition of high concentration of albumin being passed out in the urine sample of an individual. It may result from inflammation of glomeruli in kidneys or a condition called nephritis. High blood pressure may also cause this diseased condition.

Q.5 Explain the following conditions:

(i) Uremia **(ii) Hematuria**

(iii) Glycosuria

Ans (i) **Uremia** It refers to the condition when excess amount of urea is detected in the blood.

(ii) **Hematuria** It refers to the condition when blood cells are detected in urine.

(iii) **Glycosuria** It is the presence of high concentration of glucose in urine.

Q.6 Give appropriate terms for the animals which secrete the following nitrogenous wastes.

(i) Urea as nitrogenous waste.

(ii) Ammonia as nitrogenous waste.

(iii) Uric acid as nitrogenous waste.

Ans (i) Animals that excrete urea – Ureotelic

(ii) Animals that excrete ammonia – Ammonotelic

(iii) Animals that excrete uric acid – Uricotelic

Q.7 Name the three processes by which urine is formed in human body.

Ans Urine is formed by the following three processes:

(i) Ultrafiltration or glomerular filtration

(ii) Selective reabsorption

(iii) Tubular secretion.

Experiment 13

AIM

To detect the presence of bile salts in urine.

Theory/Principle

In human body, old and damaged RBCs are removed from the circulation mostly in the spleen, and to some extent, in the liver by macrophages. Haemoglobin of the RBCs is broken down in the cytoplasm of macrophages. When iron is removed from heme component of haemoglobin, the iron-free portion of heme is converted to biliverdin, a green pigment and then into bilirubin, a yellow orange pigment. Bilirubin enters the blood and is transported to the liver from spleen. Bilirubin is then secreted by liver cells into bile, which passes into the small intestine and later into the large intestine. Bilirubin is detected in urine in certain pathological conditions only.

Urine Analysis for Bile Salts

Various tests can be performed for detection of bile salts in urine sample, but among all these, Fouchet's test is considered as a confirmatory test. In this test, the colourless bilirubin is oxidised by the ferric ion of ferric chloride (present in Fouchet reagent) to green biliverdin. This can be shown as follows:

$$\underset{\text{(Colourless)}}{\text{Bilirubin}} + Fe^{3+} \longrightarrow \underset{\text{(Green)}}{\text{Biliverdin}} + Fe^{2+}$$

Requirements

Test tubes, 10 mL measuring cylinders, funnel, dropping pipette or drop bottle, test tube stand, test tube holder, cotton, filter paper, distilled water, urine sample, Lugol's iodine solution, barium chloride solution (10%), Fouchet reagent, trichloroacetic acid, ferric chloride and concentrated nitric acid.

Preparations of Reagents

(i) Lugol's iodine solution : Dissolve 1 g of iodine crystals and 2 g of potassium iodide in 100 mL of distilled water.

(ii) Fouchet reagent : Dissolve 25 mL of trichloroacetic acid (TCA) in 75 mL of distilled water. Now add 1 g of ferric chloride to this solution and mix.

(iii) 10% Barium chloride solution : Dissolve 10 g of $BaCl_2$ in 90 mL of distilled water and make up the solution to 100 mL with water.

Procedure

1. Lugol's Iodine Test

(i) Take 4 mL of urine sample in a test tube.

(ii) Add 4 drops of Lugol's Iodine solution in it with the help of dropping pipette.

(iii) Shake the tube well.

(iv) Record your observations.

2. Gmelin's Test

(i) Take 5 mL of conc. HNO_3 in a test tube.

(ii) Add an equal volume of urine sample to it slowly along the sides of the test tube.

(iii) Record your observations.

Note *Bile pigments present in urine sample react with conc. nitric acid to form a coloured ring at the junction between urine and acid layer.*

3. Fouchet's Test

(i) Take 5 mL of urine sample.

(ii) Add 2-5 mL of $BaCl_2$ in the test tube and shake it well to mix the two solutions.

(iii) A precipitate is formed. Filter the mixture with the help of filter paper.

(iv) Add 2 drops of Fouchet reagent to the precipitate present on filter paper.

(v) Record your observations.

Observations

(i) **Lugol's Iodine Test** Light to dark green colour indicates the presence of bile pigments, while faint yellow to brown colour indicates the absence of bile pigments.

(ii) **Gmelin's Test** The presence of bile pigments in the given urine sample is indicated by the formation of a green, blue, yellow or red ring at the junction of the two solutions.

(iii) **Fouchet's Test** The precipitate turns green which shows the presence of bile pigments.

Result

The above tests show the presence of bile salts in the urine sample.

PRECAUTIONS

- *Urine sample taken must be fresh.*
- *The reagents must be prepared fresh.*
- *Wastage of chemicals and reagents should be avoided.*
- *The test tubes must be washed before and after use.*
- *Don't mix droppers used for different chemicals.*

Viva-Voce

Q.1 Give the names of the pigments found in bile. NCERT

Ans Bilirubin and biliverdin are the two bile pigments.

Q.2 What are the colours of biliverdin and bilirubin?

Ans Biliverdin is green in colour, while bilirubin is a yellow-orange pigment.

Q.3 Which pigment provides colouration to the bile? NCERT

Ans Bilirubin.

Q.4 What are the different tests to detect the presence of bile pigments in urine? NCERT

Ans Gmelin's test, Fouchet's test and Lugol's iodine test.

Q.5 Which organ of the body produces bile pigments? NCERT

Ans Liver is responsible for producing bile pigment.

Q.6 How are bile pigments produced? NCERT

Ans Bile pigments are formed by the breakdown of haemoglobin. Iron-free portion of heme is converted into biliverdin and then into bilirubin.

Q.7 What are the functions of bile pigments? NCERT

Ans Bile pigments help in digestion and absorption of fats.

Q.8 Give a very primary symptom of jaundice.

Ans The primary symptom of jaundice is yellowing of eyes and skin.

Q.9 Write the other name of urochrome.

Ans Urobilin is the other name of urochrome.

Q.10 How is the urochrome formed?

Ans Urochrome is formed by breakdown of bilirubin.

Q.11 Why siblings or parents are preferred for kidney transplantation?

Ans To avoid rejection of transplanted kidney due to the difference in tissues at chemical and genetic levels, siblings or parents are usually preferred as organ donors as they have similar tissues due to the similar genetic constitution.

Q.12 Mention the name of the diseases in which bile pigments occurs in urine. NCERT

Ans Some of the diseases during which bile pigments are excreted include jaundice, hepatitis and cirrhosis.

SECTION-B

Experiment 1

AIM

To study the parts of a compound microscope.

Theory/Principle

Microscope is an extensively used instrument that enlarges the image of the object seen through it, using combination of various lenses.

A **compound microscope** is a complex assemblage or combination of different lenses that enable highly magnified image formation of the microscopic living organisms and help in studying the intricate details of cells and tissues. Compound microscope uses natural light to magnify and resolve the image of the object. A monocular mono-objective compound microscope is normally used in biological laboratory.

The principle of a microscope is based on magnification and resolution to observe fine details of small objects.

i. **Magnification**

The ratio of enlarged image to that formed on retina of an unaided normal eye is termed as magnification of the microscope. The strength of magnification of a microscope is generally indicated as 5X, 10X or 40X.

Magnification of compound mircoscope = Magnifying power of objective lens × Magnifying power of eye piece of ocular lens

e.g. a 5X eye piece and a 40X objective will magnify the image $5 \times 40 = 200$ times.

Generally, in a compound microscope eye piece lens are 10X or 15X and objective lens are 10X as well as 40X.

ii. **Resolving Power**

Resolution of a microscope is its ability to ditinguish between two closely spaced points as separate entities. The formula for obtaining the resolving power of microscope is $R = \dfrac{\lambda}{2NA}$

where, λ = wavelength of light source, NA = numerical aperture.

Since, numerical aperture is negligible, it can be ignored.

$\therefore$ Resolving power $(R) = \lambda / 2$

λ of visible light = 4000-7000 Å.

If we take the average as 6000 Å, the resolving power $= \dfrac{6000}{2} = 3000$ Å.

Therefore, the resolving power of a light compound microscope = 0.30 μ or 3000 Å or 300 nm.

Requirements

A compound microscope, any permanent or temperory slide, silk cloth, lens cleaning fluid and lens cleaning paper.

Procedure

1. Place the microscope on the working table.
2. Remove dust by wiping the microscope with the help of silk cloth.
3. Clean the lenses with the help of lens cleaning fluid and lens cleaning paper.
4. Identify the various parts of the microscope and draw a well labelled diagram of microscope by labelling its various parts.
5. Take a permanent slide preparation or temporary slide prepared by you and keep it on the stage, fix with clips after focusing and view.
6. Learn to use the microscope by adjusting the focus, by moving the coarse adjustment and fine adjustment knobs.

Observations

Compound microscope has following two types of parts:

Mechanical Parts

Base or foot	A horse shoe-shaped metallic structure that supports the microscope.
Pillar	A small vertical projection of the base.
Arm	It is the vertical and curved part of microscope which connects the body tube to the base of the microscope and is used for handling the instrument. It can be tilted to different angles at the inclination joint.
Inclination joint	The arm is attached to the pillar at this joint.
Stage	It is a flat/round/square/ rectangular platform which is attached to the arm. Slide or object to be magnified is kept on it.
Stage clips	These are two metal clips that hold the slide firmly in place. These are attached to the stage. The material to be observed is adjusted by moving the slide and then fixing it at the desired position with the help of clips.
Diaphragm	It is attached to the base of stage and regulates or adjusts the amount of light entering into the microscope, i.e. it regulates the aperture size.
Condenser	It is a system of two or more lenses to receive parallel light rays and to converge these on to the object through the iris and hole present in the stage. Some microscopes don't have this part.
Body tube	It is a tubular hollow part which is attached to the upper part of the arm. It connects the eye piece to the objective lenses and can be moved up and down with the help of screws.
Nose piece	It is a circular, metallic and rotating structure attached below the body tube. Three different objective lenses can be fitted into it. The viewer can spin the nose piece to select the different objective lenses.
Coarse adjustment screw	A big sized screw which helps in moving the objective lens up or down for general focusing of object or specimen. It is used for low magnification focusing.
Fine adjustment screw	A small sized screw used for fine tuning or focusing of the object to increase the details of the specimen. It is used for high magnification focusing.

Optical Parts

Mirror It is attached to the lower end of the arm and has plano-concave surfaces which are used to reflect the converging light rays from an external source up through the diaphgram and condenser in order to get brightly illuminated image of object.

Objective lens This lens is attached to the nose piece and is the most important part of a compound microscope. It is a lens system made up of many lenses in a definite pattern. It is of three types:

(i) **Low power objective lens** with magnifying power 10X.

(ii) **High power objective lens** with magnifying power 40X. It is also called as high dry objective lens because it is used with only air as the imaging medium between specimen and objective.

(iii) **Oil immersion objective** lens with magnifying power of 100X treated as third objective lens in some microscope. It uses mineral oil as imaging medium.

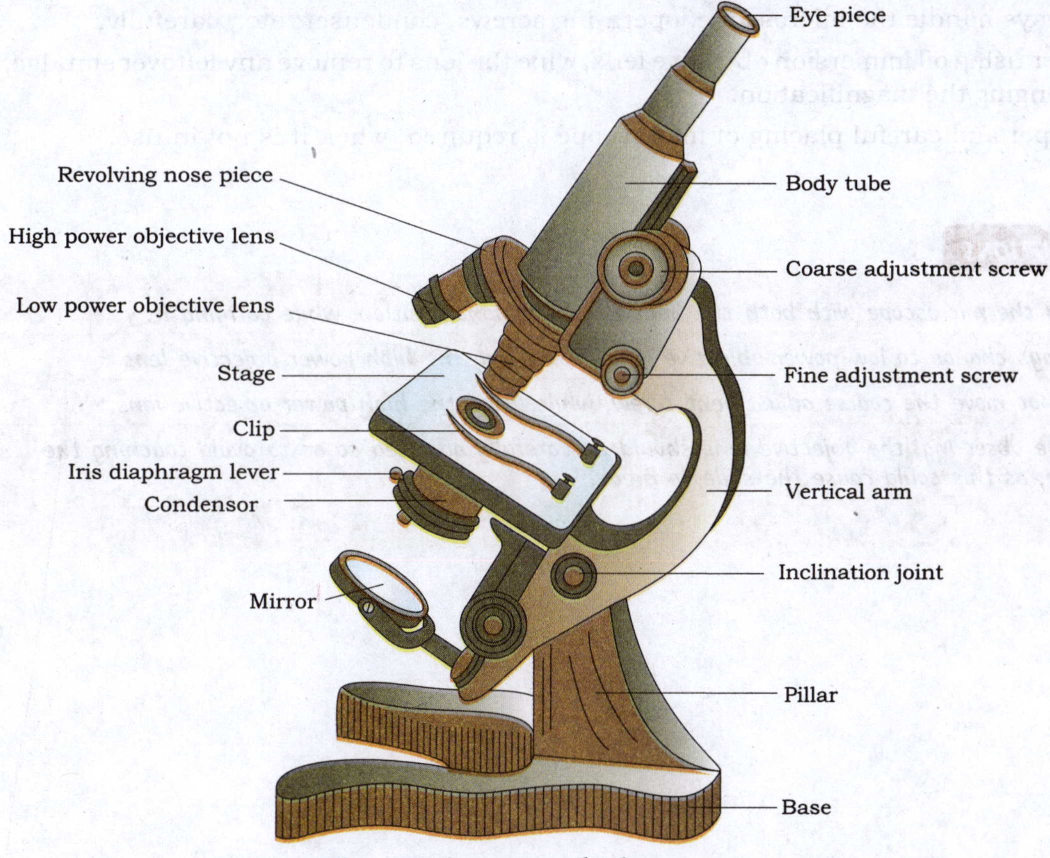

Fig. 1.1 A compound microscope

Eye piece lens or ocular lens This lens is fitted at the top of the body tube through which the magnified image of the object canbe seen. It has the magnification of 5X, 10X or 15X.

Working of Microscope

1. The mirror is adjusted in diffused source of light so that sufficient light enters into the microscope.
2. The light entering into the microscope should be regulated by the help of diaphragm and adjustment screws.

3. Keep a clean prepared slide on the centre of the stage such that it lies just under the objective lens and is completely illuminated by diaphragm.
4. Locate the object and focus it under low power objective by using coarse adjustment screw. For obtaining the higher magnification turn the nose piece to next higher power objective and use fine adjustment screw to focus.
5. The higher power objective should be used only when object is properly mounted under cover-slip.

Handling of Microscope

1. The lens and metal parts should be cleaned with the help of tissue paper or silk cloth before and after use.
2. It should be covered when not in use.
3. Objective lens should not be removed ordinarily from the nose piece.
4. The slides should be focused in low power first and then changed to high power.
5. Always handle the microscope, operating screws, condenser, etc., carefully.
6. After using oil immersion objective lens, wipe the lens to remove any leftover smudge, before changing the magnification.
7. Proper and careful placing of microscope is required, when it is not in use.

PRECAUTIONS

- *Hold the microscope with both the hands in an upright position, while carrying it.*
- *Always change to low power objective lens after using the high power objective lens.*
- *Do not move the coarse adjustment screw, while using the high power objective lens.*
- *While observing, the objective lens should be carefully adjusted so as to avoid touching the slide, as this could cause the slide to break.*

Viva-Voce

Q.1 Which of the following parts provides support and supports the weight of a microscope? NCERT

(a) Arm (b) Stage
(c) Body tube (d) Foot

Ans (d) Basal foot or base provides stable support and supports the weight of a microscope.

Q.2 To which part of a microscope is the objectives fitted? NCERT

(a) Nose piece (b) Diaphragm
(c) Stage (d) Arm

Ans (a) The objective lenses are fitted to the nose piece which is a circular, rotating, metallic structure below the body tube.

Q.3 What do you mean by magnification power of a microscope?

Ans The ability of the microscope to enlarge the object under its focus is termed as magnification power.

Q.4 Magnification power of a microscope is calculated by NCERT

(a) magnifying power of eye piece × magnifying power of mirror.

(b) magnifying power of eye piece × magnifying power of objective.

(c) magnifying power of objective × magnifying power of plane mirror.

Ans (b) Magnification power of a microscope is calculated by magnifying power of eye piece × magnifying power of objective.

Q.5 What is the resolving power of a microscope?

Ans The ability of the microscope to distinguish between two closely spaced points as two separate entities is known as resolving power.

Q.6 Give the formula to calculate the resolving power.

Ans Resolving power $(R) = \frac{\lambda}{2NA}$

where, λ = Wavelength of light source

NA = Numerical aperture

Since, NA is negligible therefore,

$$R = \frac{\lambda}{2}$$

Q.7 What is the resolving power of a light microscope?

Ans The resolving power of a light microscope is 0.30 μ or 300 nm.

Q.8 What is the resolving power of human eye?

Ans Resolving power of human eye is 100 μ.

Q.9 What would happen if direct sun rays are focused by the mirror into the body tube? NCERT

Ans If the direct sun rays are focused by the mirror into the tube body, it will harm our eyes as well as distort the view of the specimen. Therefore, diffused light used for focussing the object.

Q.10 What measures can be taken if natural light is not sufficient?

Ans An artificial source of light can be used.

Q.11 Give a difference between light microscope and electron microscope.

Ans The light microscope uses sunlight as a source of illumination while, beam of electrons in vacuum is used as source of illumination in an electron microscope.

Q.12 What is the difference between a dissecting and a compound microscope? NCERT

Ans The dissecting microscope has lower magnification and is used to magnify small animals, objects or to perform dissection of small animal or to see large section, while compound microscope has high magnification power as well as resolving power and is used to see the minute details of cells and tissues.

Q.13 When should the concave surface and plane surface of the mirror be used in the microscope?

Ans Concave mirrors are used to concentrate light onto the specimens, which is useful when the light is dim or when enhanced illumination is needed. Plane mirrors are used to direct light within the optical path onto the eye piece, without focusing it and are not specifically chosen based on light brightness.

Q.14 What is the magnification of a dissecting microscope?

Ans The magnification of a dissecting microscope may be 10X to 40X.

Q.15 Give the formula to calculate the numerical aperture.

Ans Numerical aperture can be calculated as

$$NA = \eta \sin \theta$$

where, η = Refractive index of medium

θ = half angle of the maximum cone of light that can enter the lens.

Q.16 What is the difference in resolving power of a compound microscope and that of a dissecting microscope?

Ans A compound microscope has a higher resolving power and is used for detailed microscopic analysis, while a dissecting microscope has a lower resolving power and is used for viewing large specimens with lower magnification.

Q.17 What is the magnification achieved when a 15X eye piece and a 40X objective are used together? NCERT

Ans The magnification achieved when a 15X eye piece and 40X objective are used together will be $15 \times 40 = 600$ times.

Experiment 2

AIM

Study of the specimens/slides/models and identification with reasons: Bacteria, *Oscillatoria*, *Spirogyra*, *Rhizopus*, Mushroom, Yeast, Liverwort, Moss, Fern, Pine, Monocotyledonous and Dicotyledonous plant (one each) and Lichen.

Theory/Principle

Morphology is the study of the characteristic features of an organism including external and internal features. Morphological studies help in identification and classification of organisms. As large number of organisms are present around us and it becomes very difficult to study them individually. Hence, they are classified into different groups based on their characteristics. In 1969, RH Whittaker proposed a five kingdom classification to simplify the study of wide variety of organisms in a very systemic manner. Some important characteristic features of five major kingdoms can be tabulated as follows:

Main Characteristics	Monera	Protista	Fungi	Plantae	Animalia
Body organisation	Unicellular prokaryotes	Unicellular eukaryotes	Multicellular eukaryotes, cell wall made up of chitin.	Multicellular eukaryotes, cell wall is made up of cellulose.	Multicellular eukaryotes, cell wall is absent.
Mode of nutrition	Autotrophic	Autotrophic and heterotrophic	Heterotrophic, (saprophytic and parasitic)	Autotrophic	Heterotrophic
Asexual reproduction	Fission	Binary and multiple fission	Spores	Vegetative propagation and spores.	Budding, fragmentation, parthenogenesis. etc.
Sexual reproduction	Conjugation	Syngamy	Syngamy	Syngamy with alteration of generation	Syngamy
Important members	Archaebacteria, eubacteria and cyanobacteria	Protozoans and slime moulds	Bread mould, yeast and mushrooms	Algae, bryophyte, pteridophyte, gymnosperm and angiosperm.	Sponges, cnidarians, echinoderms, chordates, etc.

The term 'Plantae' is more commonly used for all eukaryotic and chlorophyll containing organisms (autotrophs), except for few plants, like insectivorous plants, which are heterotrophs. Classification of important plant group summarised as follows

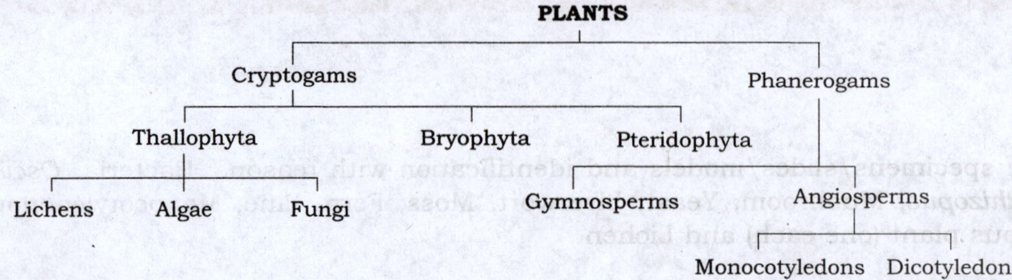

Requirements

Prepared slides or preserved specimens or models of the given species, pencil, record file, hand lens and laboratory guide.

Procedure

1. Observe the permanent slides under a microscope and note down the characters. Microorganisms like bacteria, algae, fungi can be studied with the help of microscope only.
2. Large sized specimens or models can be observed directly with unaided eye or with the help of a hand lens.
3. Draw the well labelled diagrams of different specimens in your practical book.
4. Write the classification and comments about the specimen in your practical book.

Observations

Bacteria

Classification

Kingdom – Monera
Class – Eubacteria

Identification Characteristics

Bacteria are identified on the basis of their colony characteristics, shapes and Gram staining.

General Characteristics

1. Bacteria are prokaryotic, unicellular organism which can be seen by microscope only.
2. These are of different shapes, i.e. coccus (spherical), bacillus (rod-shaped), spirillum (spiral-shaped), vibrio (comma-shaped) and filamentous.
3. They possess rigid cell wall and do not bear true nucleus and membrane bound organelles like mitochondria, Golgi bodies, etc.
4. They possess mesosomes and plasmid (extrachromosomal material).
5. Bacteria have double stranded circular DNA as their genetic material in the nucleoid region.
6. They reproduce by binary fission. Some of them form endospores during unfavourable conditions.

7. Based on their Gram staining ability, bacteria are classified into Gram-positive bacteria and Gram-negative bacteria.

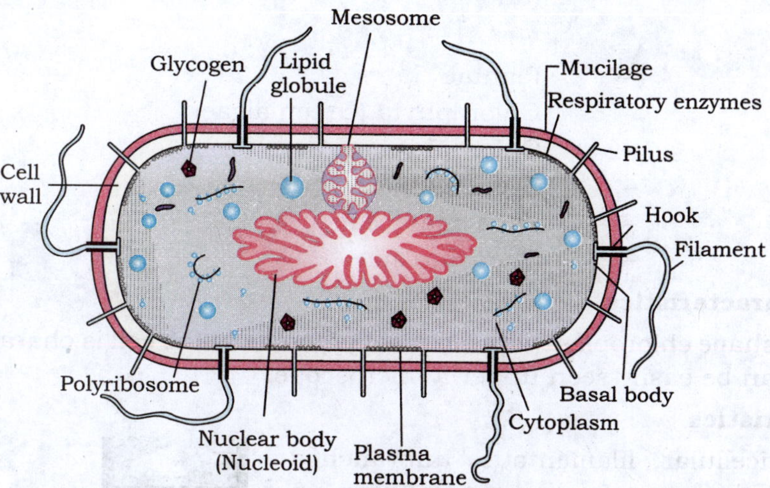

Fig. 2.1 An ultrastructure of bacterial cell

Oscillatoria

Classification

Kingdom	–	Monera
Division	–	Cyanophyta
Class	–	Cyanophyceae
Order	–	Oscillatoriales
Family	–	Oscillatoriaceae
Genus	–	*Oscillatoria* sp.

Identification Characteristics

1. Prokaryotic cell structure, presence of hormogonia is characteristic feature of *Oscillatoria.*
2. Thallus filamentous unbranched and multicellular. The cells are arranged one above the other like a pack of cards.

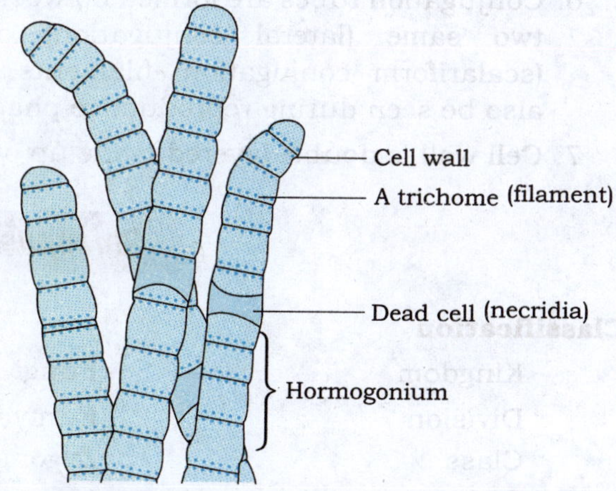

Fig. 2.2 An *Oscillatoria* filament (blue-green alga)

General Characteristics

1. It is a blue-green algae, which is found in freshwater bodies, stagnant water, ponds, pools, etc.
2. Each cell has a definite cell wall.
3. Some cells of the filament may be dead and appear as blank spaces in the filament. These are called dead cells.
4. Group of living cells lying between dead cell or necridia called **hormogonia**, are responsible for reproduction.
5. Fresh specimen of the filaments show oscillatory movement and hence named as *Oscillatoria.*

Spirogyra

Classification

Kingdom	–	Plantae
Division	–	Chlorophyta (Green algae)
Class	–	Chlorophyceae
Order	–	Zygnematales
Family	–	Zygnemataceae
Genus	–	*Spirogyra* sp.

Identification Characteristics

Long spiral ribbon shape chloroplast with several pyrenoids in the cell is characteristic feature of *Spirogyra*, which can be easily seen under a microscope.

General Characteristics

1. It is a multicellular, filamentous, unbranched green algae, which is covered by mucilagenous sheath.
2. It occurs in stagnant freshwater bodies like ditches, ponds, lakes, etc. It is commonly called as **water silk** or **pond scum** because of its silky slippery and green coloured thread-like filaments.
3. Each filament consists of long, cylindrical cells that are placed one above the other in a single row.
4. The cytoplasm lies in the periphery of the cell, enclosing a single large vacuole.
5. It reproduces asexually by **fragmentation** and sexually by **conjugation**.
6. Conjugation tubes are formed between the cells of two same (lateral conjugation) or different (scalariform conjugation) filaments. These can also be seen during reproductive phase.

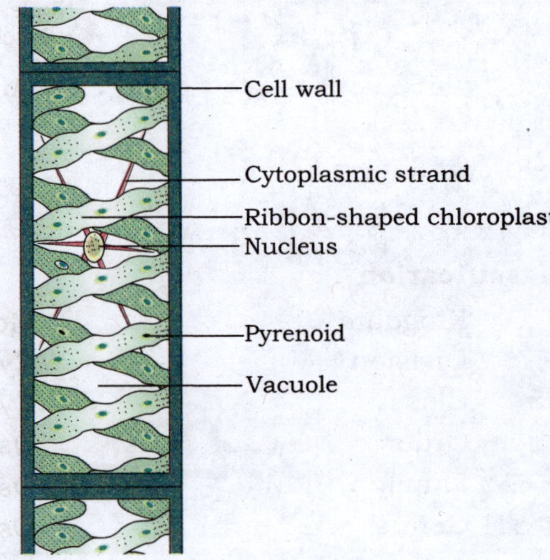

Fig. 2.3 Structure of a cell of *Spirogyra*

7. Cell wall is double layered made up of cellulose and pectin.

Rhizopus (Bread Mould)

Classification

Kingdom	–	Fungi
Division	–	Eumycota
Class	–	Zygomycetes
Order	–	Mucorales
Family	–	Mucoraceae
Genus	–	*Rhizopus*
Species	–	*stolonifer*

Identification Characteristics

The presence of tubular, coenocytic hyphae (hyphae without septal wall) is the characteristic feature of *Rhizopus*.

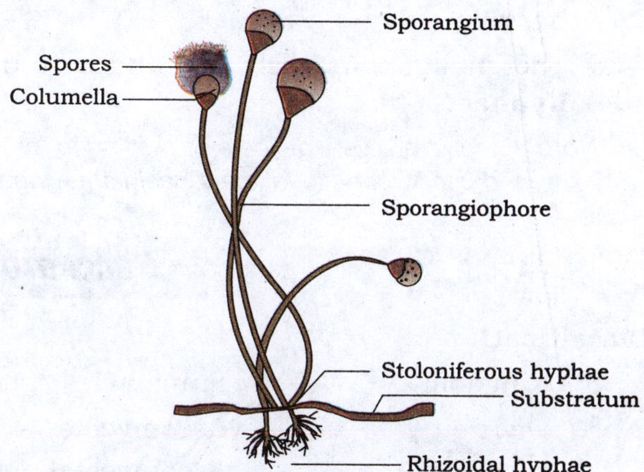

Fig. 2.4 *Rhizopus stolonifer*

General Characteristics

1. *Rhizopus* is also called as bread mould. They grow on stale bread, decaying vegetables and fruits. They are saprophytic in their mode of nutrition.
2. It occurs in the form of interwoven mass of very fine thread-like structures known as **hyphae**. The hyphae together constitute **mycelium** or thallus of the plant body.
3. Some hyphae are horizontal and grow parallel on the surface on the substratum. These are called **stoloniferous hyphae**.
4. Some hyphae grow down into the substratum, and are called **rhizoidal hyphae**.
5. Some hyphae grows vertically upwards and are called **sporangiopores**. A single sporangiopore bears a globular sporangium, containing dome-shaped **columella**. The cavity between the columella and the sporangial wall is filled with numerous black spores.

Agaricus (Mushroom)

Classification

Kingdom	–	Fungi
Division	–	Eumycota
Class	–	Basidiomycetes
Order	–	Agaricales
Family	–	Agaricaceae
Genus	–	*Agaricus*
Species	–	*campestris*

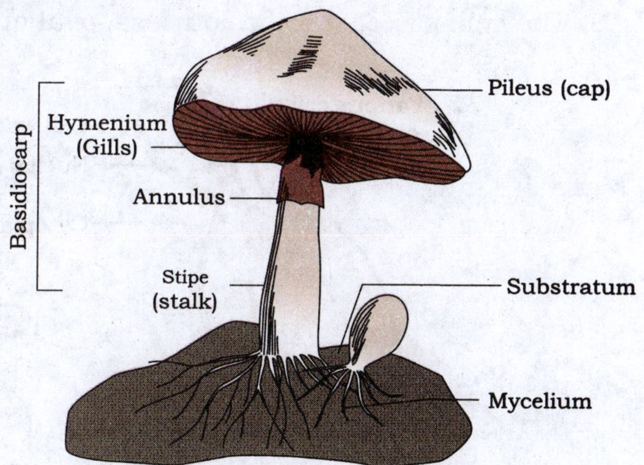

Fig. 2.5 *Agaricus* (mushroom)

Identification Characteristics

1. It has characteristic mushroom shape with a stalk-like stipe and a cap-like pileus.
2. The underside of pileus bears gills that produces naked spores.

General Characteristics

1. *Agaricus* is a saprophytic fungus that grows in humus rich soils, pile of straw and rotting wooden logs with thick layer of semi-decomposed organic matter.
2. Common edible mushroom is the fruiting body or basidiocarp of *Agaricus*.
3. A basidiocarp consists of an stalk or erect **stipe** composed of vertically arranged hyphae and an umbrella like **pileus** attached ventrally at the centre to the stalk.
4. A collar like ring known as **annulus** is present on the stalk, at the base of the stipe and is the remnant of the covering of young basidiocarp.

5. These gills bear club-shaped **basidia** on either sides and **basidiospores** are placed on the basidia.
6. The thallus possesses an underground, highly interwoven mass of thick colourless **hyphae**.

Note *Fungus are very delicate so they need to be handled carefully while observing. Avoid inhaling of spores and use forceps to take out basidia having black spores.*

Saccharomyces (Yeast)

Classification

Kingdom	–	Fungi
Division	–	Ascomycota
Class	–	Ascomycetes
Order	–	Saccharomycetales
Family	–	Saccharomycetaceae
Genus	–	*Saccharomyces*
Species	–	*cerevisiae*

Identification Characteristics

It has an eukaryotic unicellular structure which is typically oval or spherical in shape.

General Characteristics

1. It is an saprophytic fungus growing on fruit surfaces, nectar, cane juices, etc.
2. It is a unicellular fungus having single nucleus in each cell.
3. The cells of yeast are colourless, oval or spherical in shape with one large vacuole.

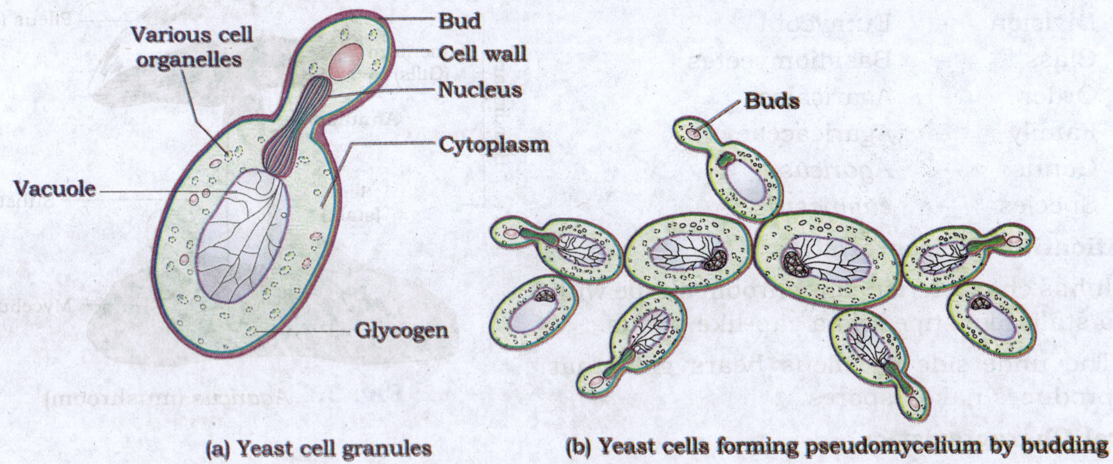

(a) Yeast cell granules

(b) Yeast cells forming pseudomycelium by budding

Fig. 2.6 Yeast

4. Each cell has a distinct cell wall, cytoplasm and contains a single nucleus. It also contains mitochondria and glycogen granules.
5. Reserve food is present in the cytoplasm in the form of volutin granules and glycogen droplets.

Lichen (A Symbiotic Association)

Identification Characteristics

Lichens are characterised by their thallus like structure, which can be lobed, flat or cylindrical and display a range of colours.

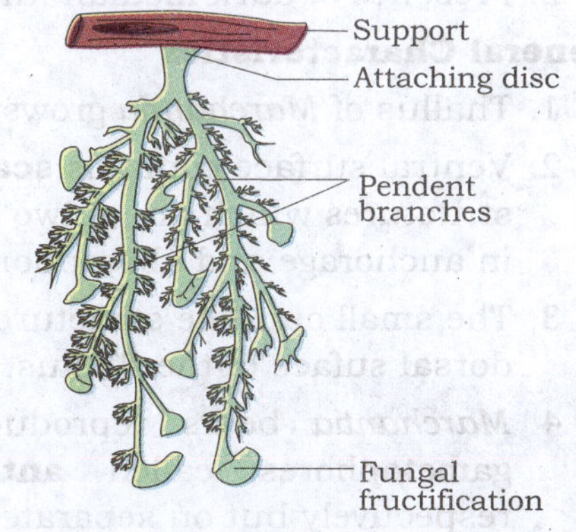

Fig. 2.7 Lichen (symbiotic relation)

General Characteristics

1. These are the composite organisms representing a symbiotic association between a fungus and an alga.
2. Alga constitutes **phycobiont** and carries out photosynthesis, whereas fungus constitutes **mycobiont** and absorbs water and minerals for the alga.
3. Lichens may grow on land, rocks, tree trunks and walls of houses and exposed soil surfaces.
4. On the basis of their general growth, form and nature of attachment to the substratum, lichen thallus is divided into three main categories.
   (i) **Crustose** These lichen form a thin, flat and inconspicuous layer that closely adheres to the surfaces such as stone, rock or tree bark.
   (ii) **Foliose** These lichens have a leafy appearance with flat, lobed thalli that spread horizontally. They are attached to the substrates by rhizoid like structure.
   (iii) **Fruticose** These lichens have a shruby form with cylindrical, flat or ribbon like thalli that are often branched and pendulous. They are anchored to their substrates by disc like structure at their bases.

Crustose

Foliose

Fruticose

Fig. 2.8 Types of lichens

Marchantia (Liverwort)

Classification

Kingdom	–	Plantae
Division	–	Bryophyta
Class	–	Hepaticopsida
Order	–	Marchantiales
Family	–	Marchantiaceae
Genus	–	*Marchantia* sp.

Identification Characteristics

1. The thallus is dorsiventrally flat which is dichotomously branched or lobed.
2. Presence of dark median furrow called midrib on dorsal side that extends into each lobe.

General Characteristics

1. Thallus of *Marchantia* grows flat on the surface of the soil substratum.
2. Ventral surface contains **scales** and **rhizoids**. The rhizoids are colourless, unicellular structures which are of two types (i) **smooth walled** (ii) **tuberculate**. The rhizoids help in anchorage and absorption of water through their capillary action.
3. The small cup-like structure called **gemma cups** are present on the median groove on dorsal suface of the thallus. Gemma cups bear **gemmae** for vegetative propagation.
4. *Marchantia* bears reproductive organs, i.e. **antheridia** and **archegonia** on erect gametophores called **antheridiophores** (male) and **archegoniophores** (female) respectively but on separate thalli.
5. The antheridiophores has a flat, more or less convex head or receptacle bearing antheridia. The archegoniophores are umbrella shaped structure, with outwardly projected ribs. Between the ribs, archegonia are present.
6. Liverworts grow on moist, shady and humid places of hills.

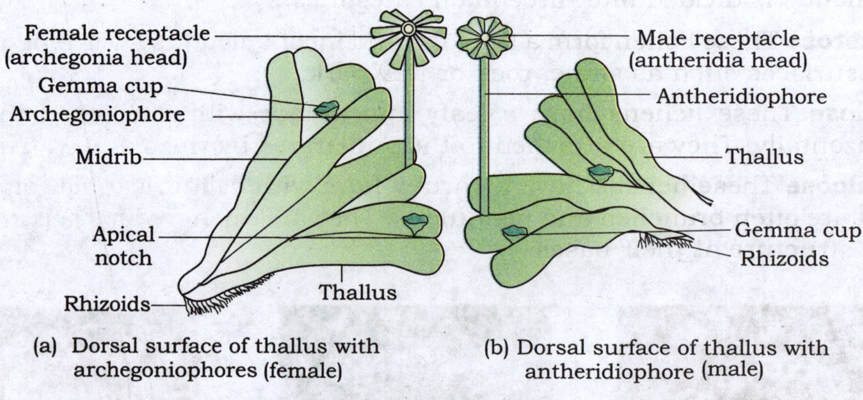

Fig. 2.9 Marchantia (Liverwort)

Funaria (Moss)

Classification

Kingdom	–	Plantae
Division	–	Bryophyta
Class	–	Musci/ Bryopsida
Order	–	Funariales
Family	–	Funariaceae
Genus	–	*Funaria*
Species	–	*hygrometrica*

Identification Characteristics

1. Thallus is plant like body with root-like rhizoids, with seta and capsule.
2. Leaves are green and arranged spirally.

General Characteristics

1. It is found on tree trunks or moist and damp places, on walls of houses and crevices of rocks.
2. Rhizoids are long, colourless, septate and interwined, multicellular and branched structures that serve as roots, i.e. they fix the plant to the soil and absorb water and minerals.
3. The main axis may be branched or unbranched that bears flat, green, spirally arranged leaves.
4. Leaves are sessile with a distinct midrib.
5. Reproductive organs are borne on separate branches of the same thallus.
6. The male branch is called **antheridiophore** as it bears **antheridia** which are club-shaped, while the female branch is called **archegoniophore** as it bear **archegonia** which are flask shaped at its tip.
7. After fertilisation, a sporophyte is formed on female shoot which consists of a long stalk known as **seta,** a **foot** which is embedded into tissues of the gametophyte and a **capsule** that contains spores which play an important role in reproduction of the gametophyte.
8. The spores germinate into **filamentous protonema**, which forms the adult leafy gametophyte.

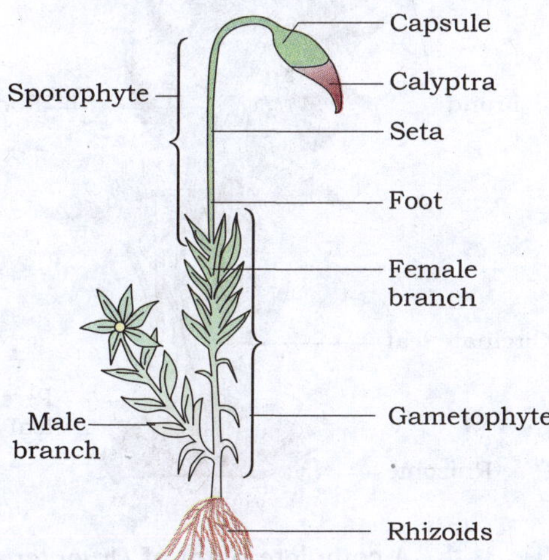

Fig. 2.10 *Funaria* (moss) : A bryophyte

Dryopteris (Male Fern)

Classification

Kingdom	–	Plantae
Division	–	Pteridophyta
Class	–	Filicineae
Order	–	Polypodiales
Family	–	Dryopteridaceae
Genus	–	*Dryopteris*
Species	–	*filix-mas*

Identification Characteristics

1. The plant shows the presence of pinnately compound leaves (fronds).
2. Presence of midrib called 'rachis' is seen.
3. Presence of sac-like 'sori' on ventral surface is evident.

General Characteristics

1. These are perennial land plants, mostly found in moist and shady places.
2. Plant body is sporophyte which is differentiated into root, stem (underground rhizome) and pinnately compound leaves called fronds.
3. The rhizome are short, thick and are covered with scaly leaves, remnants of leaf bases and cluster of adventitious roots. It is covered by brown, hairy structure called **ramenta**.
4. Stem is underground growing horizontally bearing roots on its lower surface and is also called as **root stock.**
5. Young leaves are coiled-like a spring and are called **circinate** leaves. Petiole is long, cylindrical and covered with hairs (ramenta) when young.
6. Leaves are long and pinnately compound with leaflets having wavy margin, sub sessile arranged on either side of midrib called **rachis,** which is the extended part of the petiole. leaves look like a branch or aerial shoot and are thus named as **fronds.**

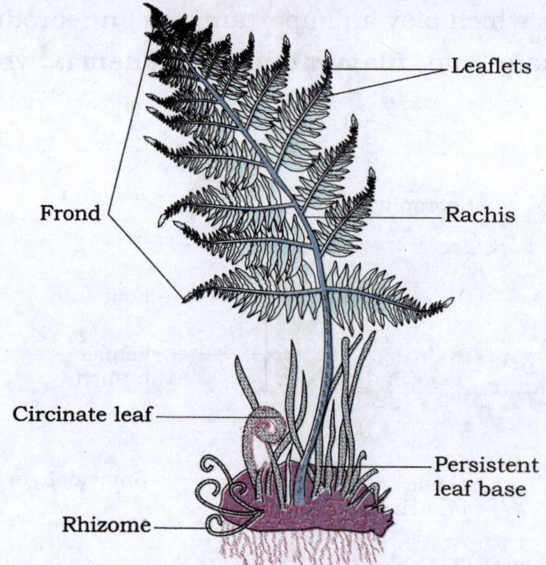

Fig. 2.11 A complete plant of *Dryopteris* (fern)

Pinus (Pine) : Gymnosperm

Classification

Kingdom	–	Plantae
Division	–	Gymnospermae
Class	–	Pinopsida
Order	–	Pinales
Family	–	Pinaceae
Genus	–	*Pinus*
Species	–	*roxburghii*

Identification Characteristics

1. *Pinus* is a pyramid or cone-shaped tall tree.
2. Well-differentiated body with roots, stems and leaves are present.
3. The presence of needle-like and scale-like leaves is characteristic of these plants.
4. Big male and female cones are unique to this class of Plantae.

General Characteristics

1. *Pinus* is a evergreen tree that grows in temperate and sub-tropical regions on the slope of hills.
2. Roots have tap root system and often associated with mycorrhizae.
3. Stem is hard, woody, cylindrical, rough and is covered with bark and bears two types of branches (dimorphic), i.e.
   (a) **Long shoots** bear scaly leaves and grow indefinitely or show unlimited growth.
   (b) **Dwarf shoots** bear needle-like leaves and scaly leaves. Dwarf shoots are borne on long shoots and show limited growth.
   Both types of branches bear large number of brown membranous scaly leaves.

Fig. 2.12 Pinus (gymnosperm) showing long and dwarf shoots and cones

4. Leaves are of two types
   (a) **Needle or acicular leaves** Foliage leaves are needle-like and are present on the apex dwarf shoots. These are long, acicular and green in colour. Dwarf shoot with needle leaves is called **spur** shoot.
   (b) **Scale leaves** These are thin, membranous, non-photosynthetic and protective in function. These are present on long shoots and base of dwarf shoot.
5. *Pinus* is monoecious that bears, both of its reproductive parts, male and female cones, on different branches of the same plant.
6. Male cones occur in clusters on long branches.
7. Male cone is small and green in colour. A number of **microsporophylls** (membranous) are arranged spirally around its axis. Each microsporophyll bears two microsporangia which bear winged microspores or **pollen grains**.
8. Female cones are large, 10-30 cm in length consisting of megasporophylls. Megasporophylls are compact when young but spread apart when mature. Each megasporophyll has bract scale and ovuliferous scale which bear 2 ovules on ventral side.

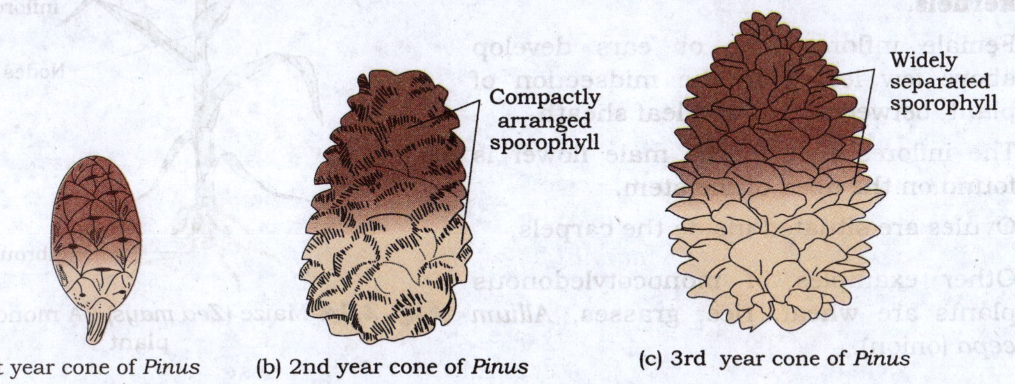

(a) 1st year cone of *Pinus* (b) 2nd year cone of *Pinus* (c) 3rd year cone of *Pinus*

Fig. 2.13 Cones of *Pinus*

9. Female cones are of three types
   (i) **First year cone** Small, greenish red with small sporophylls for pollination to occur.
   (ii) **Second year cone** Large with woody sporophylls that are compactly arranged for seed development to take place.
   (iii) **Third year cone** Large and woody cone with sporophylls that are widely separated from each other for dispersal of seeds.

Maize (Monocotyledonous)

Classification

Kingdom	–	Plantae
Division	–	Angiospermae
Class	–	Monocotyledonae
Order	–	Poales
Family	–	Poaceae
Genus	–	*Zea*
Species	–	*mays*

Identification Characteristics

1. Leaves show parallel venation which is unique feature of monocots.
2. Seeds have one cotyledon.
3. The plant body is differentiated into roots, stem and leaves.
4. Fibrous root system is present.
5. Flowers appear in clusters. Each flower is trimerous, i.e. it's every whorl is in multiple of 3.

General Characteristics

1. It is an annual, herbaceous plant.
2. **Roots** are fibrous or adventitious.
3. **Stem** is unbranched with distinct nodes and internodes.
4. **Leaves** are grown from each nodes and are simple or compound.
5. The leafy stalk produces ears that contain the grains or seeds. These are called as **kernels**.
6. Female inflorescence or ears develop above few leaves in the midsection of plant, between stem and leaf sheath.
7. The inflorescence of the male flower is found on the apex of the stem.
8. Ovules are situated inside the carpels.
9. Other examples of monocotyledonous plants are wheat, rice, grasses, *Allium cepa* (onion).

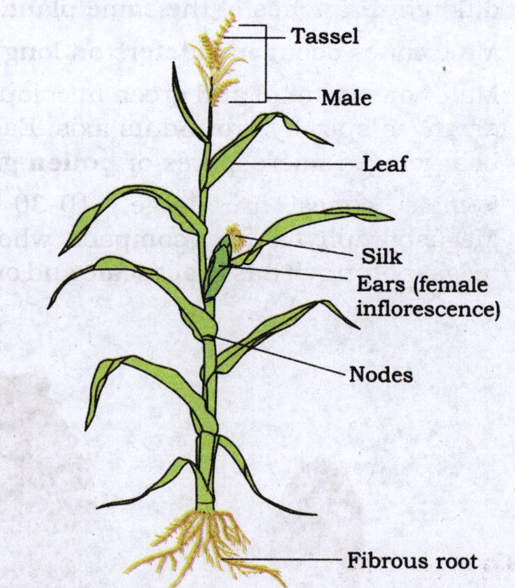

Fig. 2.14 Maize (*Zea mays*) : A monocotyledonous plant

Brassica (Dicotyledonous)

Classification

Kingdom	–	Plantae
Division	–	Angiospermae
Class	–	Dicotyledonae
Order	–	Brassicales
Family	–	Brassicaceae
Genus	–	*Brassica*
Species	–	*campestris*

Identification Characteristics

1. Plant body is differentiated into roots, leaves and stem.
2. Leaves have reticulate venation which is the characteristic of dicot plants.
3. Stem is branched, bears leaves, fruits, flowers and seeds.
4. Seed have two cotyledons.

General Characteristics

1. It is a cultivated biennial herb.
2. **Root** The plant has tap root system with branches on lateral side.
3. **Stem** The plant has soft green stem with distinct nodes and internodes.
4. **Leaves** The plant bears simple, alternate leaves with lobed margin.
5. **Flowers** are tetramerous, yellow coloured and are meant for sexual reproduction. Each flower is bisexual and with cruciform corolla.
6. The fruits is an elongated capsule-like with a false septum (replum) called **siliqua**.
7. Seeds are enclosed within the fruit that contains an embryo with two cotyledons. They are small rounded and yellow or black-coloured.
8. Other examples of dicotyledons plants are pea, gram, *Hibiscus*, lady finger, etc.

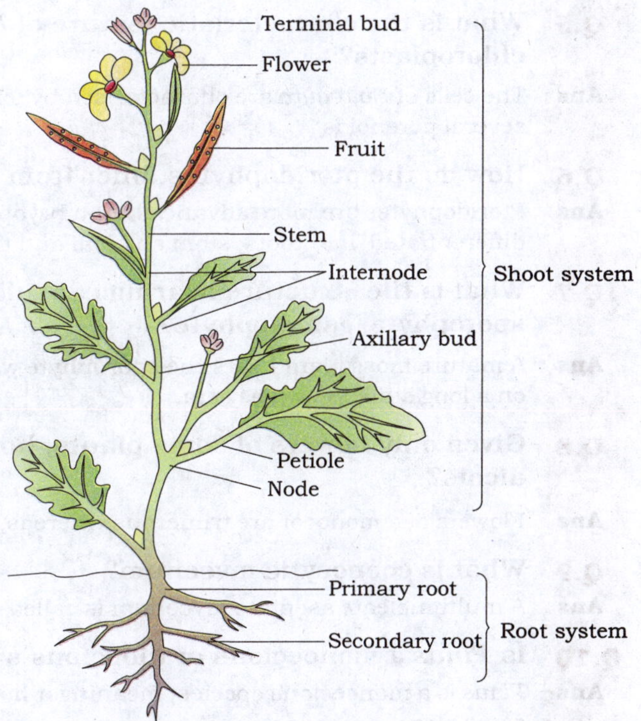

Fig. 2.15 Mustard plant (*Brassica campestris*): A dicotyledonous plant

PRECAUTIONS

- *Handle the specimens in separate specimen bottles carefully.*
- *Do not rush towards the specimen to observe it.*
- *Be careful while using microscope to observe slides.*

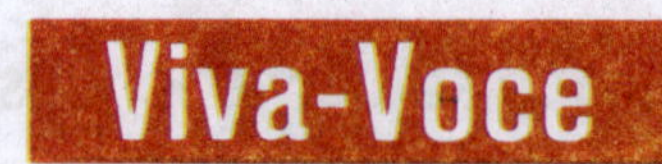

Viva-Voce

Q.1 Who gave two and five kingdom classification system?

Ans Linnaeus gave two kingdom classification system and RH Whittaker (1969) developed the five kingdom classification system.

Q.2 An unlabelled slide shows filamentous structures with linearly arranged cells and blank spaces occurring intermittently. Name the specimen. NCERT

Ans *Oscillatoria* is the specimen shown on the slide.

Q.3 Mention the characteristic features on the basis of which organisms are classified into kingdom– Monera.

Ans Monerans are unicellular prokaryotes that have an autotrophic mode of nutrition. They reproduce asexually by amitosis and show sexual reproduction also. Some of the examples include archaebacteria, eubacteria and cyanobacteria.

Q.4 Bryophytes are called the amphibians of plant kingdom. Explain why?

Ans Bryophytes are called the amphibians of plant kingdom because they occur in damp, moist places and water is very essential for the transfer of gametes.

Q.5 What is the characteristic feature of *Spirogyra* with reference to their chloroplasts?

Ans The cells of *Spirogyra* are characterised by long, spiral and ribbon-shaped chloroplasts with several pyrenoids.

Q.6 How do the pteridophytes differ from bryophytes?

Ans Pteridophytes are more advanced than bryophytes because they have independent sporophyte differentiated into roots, stem and leaf and these also possess vascular tissues.

Q.7 What is the structure bearing capsules in a moss called as a sporophyte/gametophyte? NCERT

Ans A mature moss plant bears the sporophyte which consists of a prominent conical capsule raised on a long stalk known as seta.

Q.8 Given only flowers of some plants, how would you clasify them as monocots and dicots? NCERT

Ans Flowers of a monocot are trimerous whereas, flowers in a dicot are tetramerous or pentamerous.

Q.9 What is coenocytic mycelium?

Ans A multinucleate aseptate mycelium is called coenocytic mycelium.

Q.10 Is *Pinus* a monoecious or dioecious species?

Ans *Pinus* is a monoecious species, meaning it has both male and female reproductive organs on the same plant.

Q.11 List some important features of dicot plant.

Ans Dicot plants have two cotyledons, reticulate leaf venation, floral organs in multiple of four or five, and a tap-root system.

Q.12 List some important features of monocot plants.

Ans Monocot plants have one cotyledon, parallel leaf venation, floral organs typically in multiple of three, and a fibrous root system.

Q.13 Give reason why the two kingdom classification system was rejected?

Ans The two kingdom classification system was rejected because it had following drawbacks:

(i) Prokaryotes and eukaryotes were placed together.

(ii) Unicellular and multicellular organisms were not separated.

(iii) Fungi, having their own physiological, biochemical and structural organisation were kept in Plantae.

Q.14 Give characteristic features of gymnosperms.

Ans The characteristic features of gymnosperms are as follows:

(i) They possess naked ovules /without ovary.

(ii) Vascular tissues are less developed.

(iii) Have sporophytic life.

Q.15 How are Thallophyta different from plants?

Ans Thallophyta are the plants that have thallus-like body that are not differentiated into roots, stem and leaves. These are non-vascular plants, having no embryo.

Q.16 Yeast is unicellular but it is placed under fungi. Why is it so?

Ans Yeast possess chitinous cell wall, glycogen as food reserve and produce ascospores for reproduction like other fungi, therefore these are placed under fungi even when they are unicellular.

Q.17 What type of leaves are found in fern? NCERT

Ans Leaves of a fern are long, upto 1-1.5m length , compound with leaflets arranged on either side of midrib called rachis. Each compound leaf arises from a bud and is rolled from apex, downwards like a spring. The young leaf has circinate venation.

Q.18 What is alternation of generation?

Ans When two phases of life cycle, i.e. gametophytic and sporophytic generation alters with each other and are interdependent of each other, it is called alternation of generation.

Q.19 What are the similarities and differences observed in gymnosperms and angiosperms? NCERT

Ans Gymnosperms and angiosperms both have vascular tissues, produce seeds, and possess roots, stems and leaves, but gymnosperms have exposed seeds on cones and rely mainly on wind pollination, while angiosperms have seeds enclosed in fruits and are pollinated by wind, animals and insects.

Q.20 What type of symbiotic relationship is found in lichens?

Ans Lichens exhibit a mutualistic and symbiotic relationship between fungi and algae or cyanobacteria. In this relationship, the fungus provides protection, while the algae or cyanobacteria perform photosynthesis to produce nutrients.

Q.21 Name some of the important prokaryotes.

Ans Cyanobacteria, Archarbacteria, Mycoplasma and Eubacteria.

Q.22 Which organisms are wall-less prokaryotes?

Ans Mycoplasma.

Q.23 What is prothallus?

Ans It is the gametophyte stage in life cycle of ferns and other pteridophytes. It is a small, typically heart shaped and photosynthetic structure that produces the reproductive organ necessary for sexual reproduction.

Experiment 3

AIM

To study the characters of virtual specimens/slides/models and identifying features of *Amoeba, Hydra,* Liverfluke, *Ascaris*, Leech, Earthworm, Prawn, Silkworm, Honeybee, Snail, Starfish, Shark, Rohu, Frog, Lizard, Pigeon and Rabbit.

Theory/Principle

Diversity among animal kingdom is enormous. A systematic study of such a huge number of animals would not have been possible without a proper classification system. The animal kingdom comprises of unicellular protozoans and multicellular animals or metazoans. These animals have been classified on the basis of their morphological similarities and dissimilarities as well as on their phylogenetic relationships.

The broad classification of kingdom–Animalia is as follows:

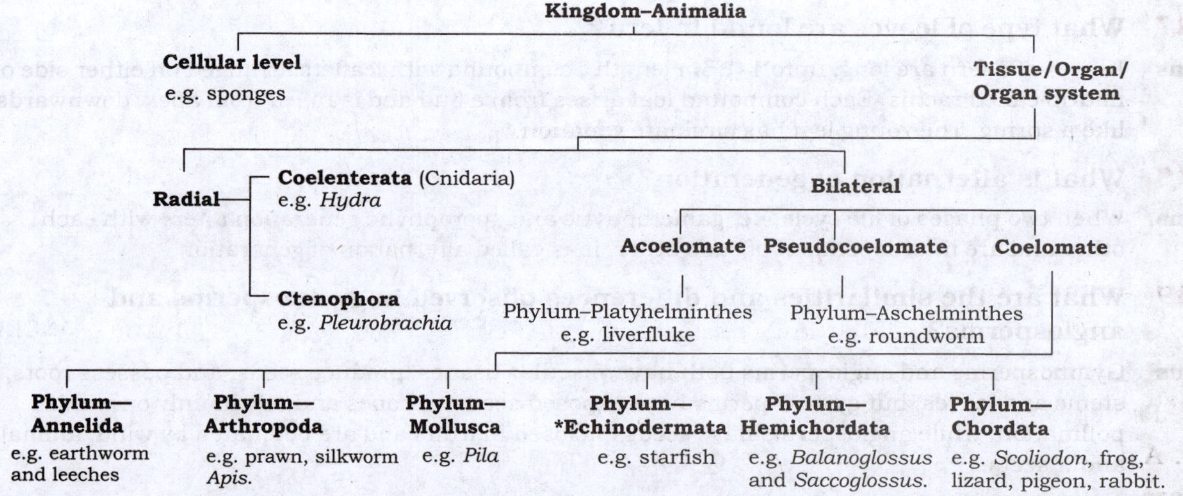

* Echinodermata exhibits radial and bilateral symmetry depending on the stage of life cycle.

Phylum-Chordata is further divided into following sub-phylums

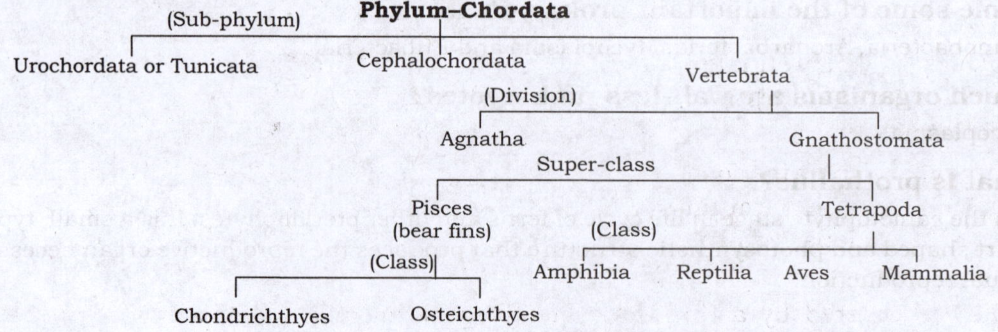

Fasciola hepatica (Liverfluke)

Classification

Kingdom	–	Animalia
Phylum	–	Platyhelminthes
Class	–	Trematoda
Order	–	Digenea
Genus	–	*Fasciola*
Species	–	*hepatica*

Identification Characteristics

1. Triangular, flat, leaf-like body.
2. Presence of ventral and oral sucker.
3. Anterior part is broader with a conical end.

General Characteristics

1. *Fasciola* is an endoparasite found in the bile duct of vertebrates like cow, sheep, goat, man, etc. It causes a serious liver disease called **liver rot.**
2. The entire body of *Fasciola* is covered by cuticle with spinules.
3. Body possesses two suckers. Oral sucker is located at the anterior end and on the ventral surface of the body, another sucker is present which is called **acetabulum.** It helps it to attach to the host.
4. Liver fluke is bisexual (**hermaphrodite**) and the ventral surface of the body contains a single genital opening called **gonopore** (near acetabulum).
5. The posterior end of the body bears an excretory pore.

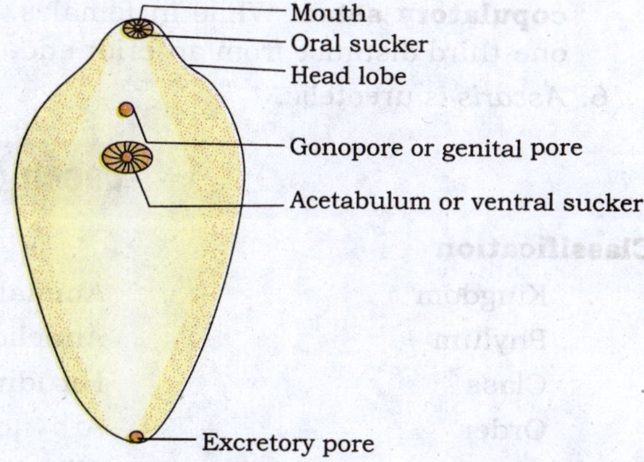

Fig. 3.3 *Fasciola hepatica* (liverfluke)

6. It has **digenetic** (double host) life cycle. The secondary host of liver fluke is snail.

Ascaris

Classification

Kingdom	–	Animalia
Phylum	–	Nemathelminthes or Aschelminthes
Class	–	Chromadorea
Order	–	Ascaridida
Genus	–	*Ascaris*
Species	–	*lumbricoides*

Identification Characteristics

1. Cylindrical body that is tapering at both ends, posterior end of male is ventrally curved.
2. Presence of triradiate mouth.
3. Presence of penial setae in males and genital aperture in females.
4. It has 20-40 cm long, cylindrical (5-6 mm diameter) body with no segments present on its surface.

5. A dorsal, a ventral and two lateral lines extend all along the entire length of the body of the organism.

General Characteristics

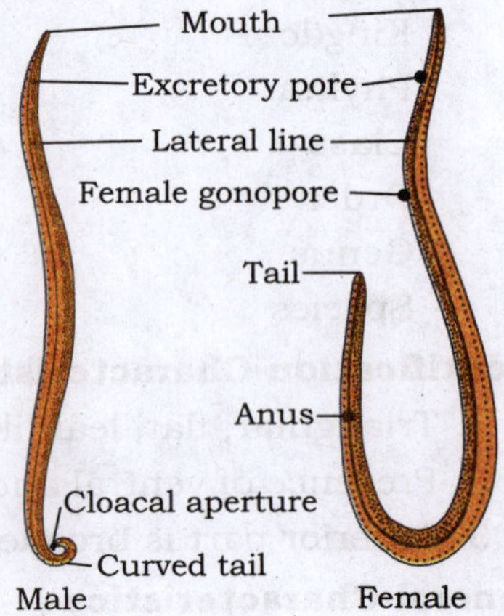

Fig. 3.4 *Ascaris lumbricoides*

1. *Ascaris lumbricoides* is a common intestinal parasite of man, particularly in small children, pigs, cattle, monkey, etc. The infection occurs through contaminated food and water. This organism is commonly called as **roundworm**.
2. The anterior or the front end of the body has a terminal **triradiate mouth** surrounded by three lips, one present mid-dorsally and the rest two lips are situated ventro-laterally. A little behind anterior end, there is a small **excretory pore** which lies in ventral position.
3. The animal shows **sexual dimorphism**, i.e. separate male and female individuals are found.
4. Males are smaller in size than females and in females, the genital pore and anus open separately.
5. Posterior end of male is curved having cloacal aperture with two needle-like **penial** or **copulatory setae**. While in females, genital aperture is present mid-ventrally at about one-third distance from anterior end.
6. *Ascaris* is ureotelic.

Leech (*Hirudinaria*)

Classification

Kingdom	–	Animalia
Phylum	–	Annelida
Class	–	Hirudinea
Order	–	Arhynchobdellida
Genus	–	*Hirudinaria*
Species	–	*granulosa*

Identification Characteristics

1. Presence of annuli and 33 true segments.
2. Presence of small anterior and large posterior sucker.
3. Dorsal surface is convex and dark green in colour while ventral surface is flat and yellow-brown in colour.

General Characteristics

1. It is found in freshwater ponds, lakes and swamps. It is also an **ectoparasite**, that sucks the blood of cattles, frogs and even humans.
2. It feeds on blood, thus also called as **sanguivorous animal**.
3. Size of the organism varies from 6 to 10 cm in length. However, leaches may contract or elongate their body much beyond the limits mentioned.
4. The mouth is present in the centre of anterior sucker while ventral sucker is also present at posterior end. Anus is dorsal in position, at the junction of the last metamere and the posterior sucker.

5. Body surface remains moist due to the secretion of mucus from the body wall.

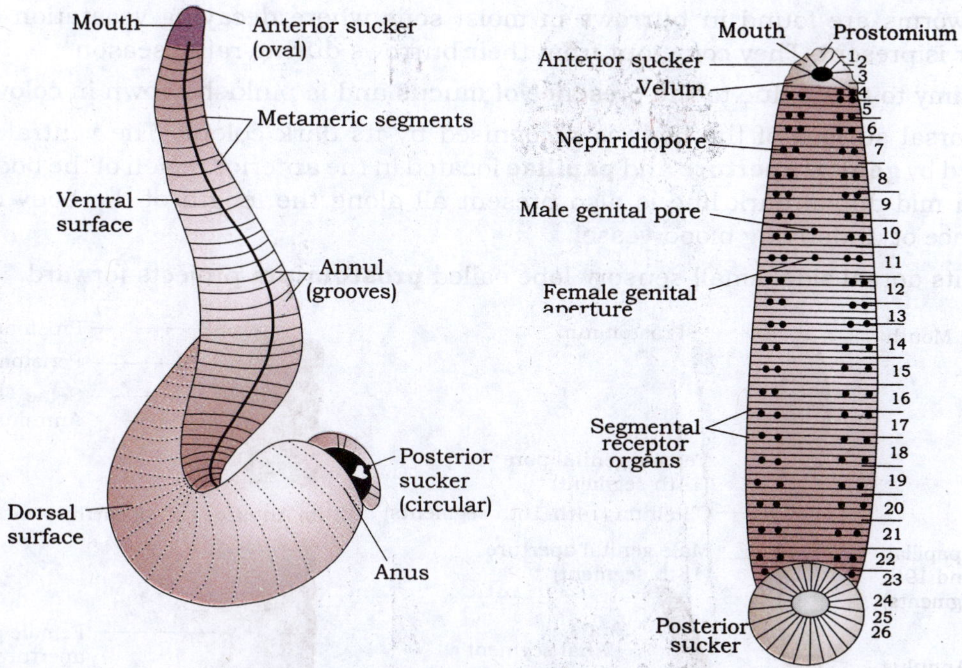

Fig. 3.5 *Hirudinaria granulosa* (leech)

6. There are 17 pairs of ventro-laterally arranged **nephridiopores** in the metameres starting from 6th to 22nd.
7. Male and female genital apertures are located on the ventral surface in the middle of the 10th and 11th metameres.
8. Segments 9, 10, 11 develop into a temporary **clitellum** during breeding season.
9. Leech is a **hermaphrodite** but shows cross fertilisation.

Pheretima (Earthworm)

Classification

Kingdom	–	Animalia
Phylum	–	Annelida
Class	–	Oligochaeta
Order	–	Opisthopora
Genus	–	*Pheretima*
Species	–	*posthuma*

Identification Characteristics

1. It has an elongated (about 150 mm in length), narrow, bilaterally symmetrical, cylindrical (3 to 5 mm in diameter) and segmented body with 100-120 segments.
2. Presence of prostomium and peristomium.
3. On the ventral surface, 4 pairs of openings of **spermathecae** are situated ventro-laterally in the grooves between 5/6, 6/7, 7/8 and 8/9 segments.
4. In the adult earthworm, the skin or body wall around the segments 14th and 16th is comparatively thick and it is called **clitellum**.

General Characteristics

1. Earthworms are found in burrows in moist soils where decaying vegetation or organic matter is present. They come out from their burrows during rainy season.
2. It is slimy to touch due to the presence of mucus and is pinkish brown in colour.
3. The dorsal surface of the body is recognised by its dark colour. The ventral surface is marked by **genital aperture** and **papillae** located in the anterior region of the body. Besides this, a mid-dorsal dark line is also present all along the length of the body due to the presence of underlying blood vessel.
4. From its dorsal side, small sensory lobe called **prostomium** projects forward.

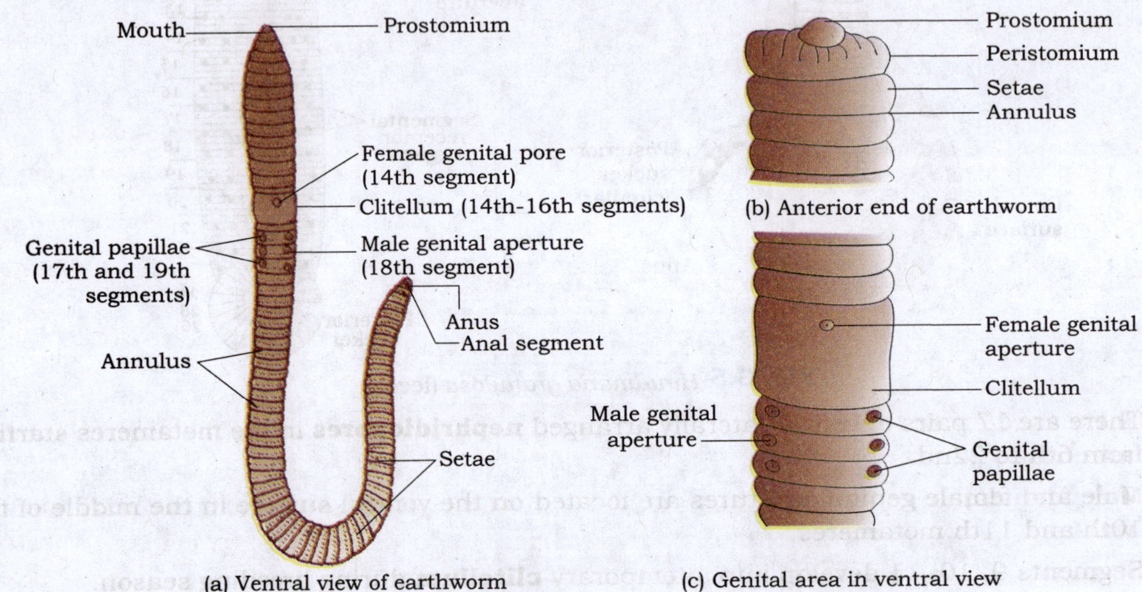

Fig. 3.6 *Pheretima posthuma* (earthworm)

5. A single female genital aperture is found mid-ventrally in 14th segment which is covered by clitellum and releases **ova**.
6. Two male genital appertures are present on the ventro-lateral surface in the 18th segment that release **sperms**.
7. The **genital or copulatory papillae** are present ventrolaterally on the 17th and 19th segments just above and below the male genital apertures.
8. **Anus** is present in the last body segment that excretes undigested waste.
9. It is hermaphrodite having both the sex organs, i.e. testis and ovary in the same body but shows **cross fertilisation.**

Palaemon serratus (Prawn)

Classification

Kingdom	–	Animalia
Phylum	–	Arthropoda
Class	–	Crustacea
Order	–	Decapoda
Genus	–	*Palaemon*
Species	–	*serratus*

Identification Characteristics

1. Head and thorax is fused to form cephalothorax.
2. Cephalothorax is identified by presence of carapace and rostrum.
3. Cephalothorax is identified by presence of 13 pairs of appendages.
4. Pair of compound eye at the anterior end of cephalothorax.

General Characteristics

1. It is found in fresh water resources as in rivers, ponds, lakes, swamps, etc.
2. The size of this animal is variable (20-30 cm). It is usually orange-red in colour, which is also variable. Body of prawn is elongated or curved, a bit compressed and bilaterally symmetrical. It is divided into cephalothorax and abdomen.
3. In the cephalothoracic region, there are 13 pairs of jointed appendages of which **antennules**, **antenna**, **chelate legs**, and **non-chelate legs** are the prominent ones.
4. The cephalothorax has eight pairs of segmented legs out of which five pairs are used for walking.
5. Abdomen consist of 6 segments out of which the first five segments having a pair of **pleopods** each. These help in swimming and the sixth segment having **uropods**.
6. There is a conical **telson** at the end of the abdominal segment.

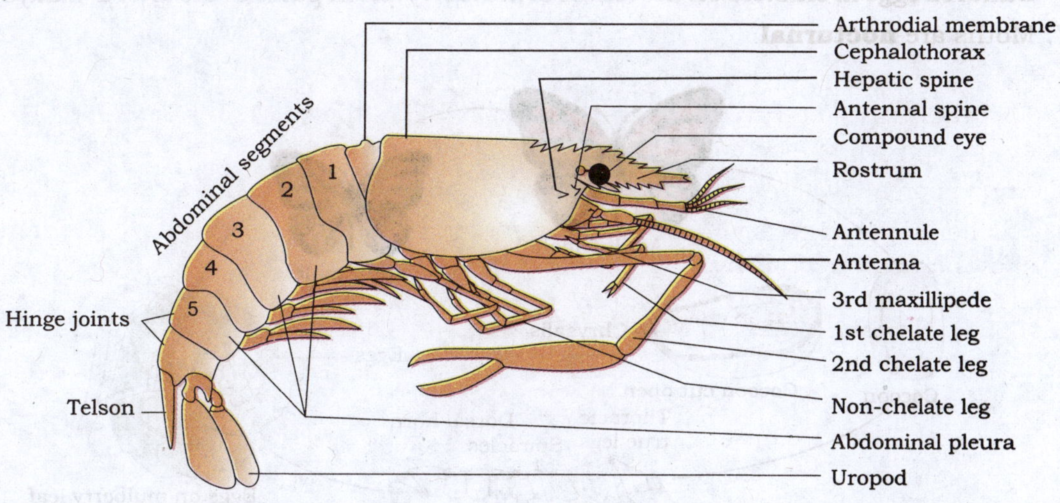

Fig. 3.7 *Palaemon* (prawn)

Bombyx mori (Silkworm)

Classification

Kingdom	–	Animalia
Phylum	–	Arthropoda
Class	–	Insecta
Order	–	Lepidoptera
Genus	–	*Bombyx*
Species	–	*mori*

Identification Characteristics

1. Body is divisible into head, abdomen and thorax.
2. Presence of 2 pairs of wings and 3 pairs of joint appendages.
3. In sitting posture, the wings remain outstretched (like the wings of aeroplane).
4. Body and wings are covered by minute scales.

General Characteristics

1. Silkworm is a creamy white, 2-3 cm long organism found on mulberry plant. These are reared for producing silk and this process is called **sericulture**.
2. Head is comparatively small and bears a pair of compound eyes and a pair of short and thick **antennae.**
3. The abdomen is short, thick and segmented. Abdominal segments are continuous with thoracic segments.
4. Silkworms are **unisexual.**
5. The life cycle of moth shows four stages, i.e. Egg → Larva → Pupa → Adult (moth).
6. The moth is a non-feeding stage. Male moth mates with female which lays three to five hundred eggs in clusters on the leaves of mulberry. Both parents die after 2-3 days of mating.
7. Moths are **nocturnal**.

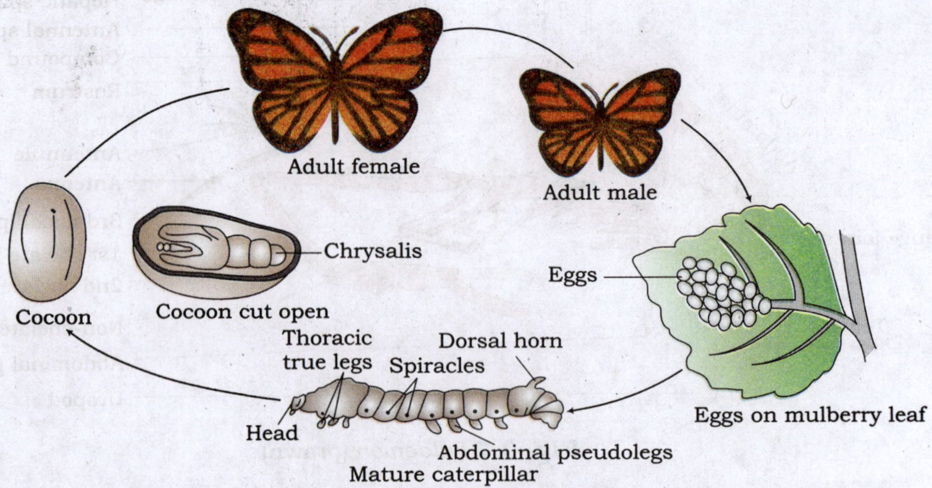

Fig. 3.8 Different life stages of silkworm (*Bombyx mori*)

Apis indica (Honeybee)

Classification

Kingdom	–	Animalia
Phylum	–	Arthropoda
Class	–	Insecta
Order	–	Hymenoptera
Genus	–	*Apis*
Species	–	*indica*

Identification Characteristics

1. Body is divisible into head, abdomen and thorax.
2. Presence of ocelli and compound eyes.
3. Presence of **polymorphism**.
4. Presence of poisonus sting in last abdominal segment.

General Characteristics

1. Honeybee is a social insect that lives in a colony. It is found in warmer environments and shows great **division of labour**. They collect nectar from flowers.
2. The body is covered with thick, tough and non-living chitinous cuticle, which forms the exoskeleton.
3. Head is wide and triangular that bears a pair of antennae and a pair of **compound eyes**. The ventral side bears specialised mouthparts.
4. Thorax is divided into three segments, i.e. **anterior prothorax, middle mesothorax** and **posterior metathorax**.
5. Thorax bears three pairs of legs (one in each segment ventrally in thoracic region) and two pairs of membranous wings are present dorsally in metathorax and metathorax region.
6. Abdomen is a narrow region having poisonous **sting** and present behind the metathorax.
7. Honeybee produces honey, beewax and royal jelly.
8. The colony or beehive consists of **queen** (fertile female), **drones** (fertile males) and **workers** (sterile females). All these organisms can be identified by their own specific features.

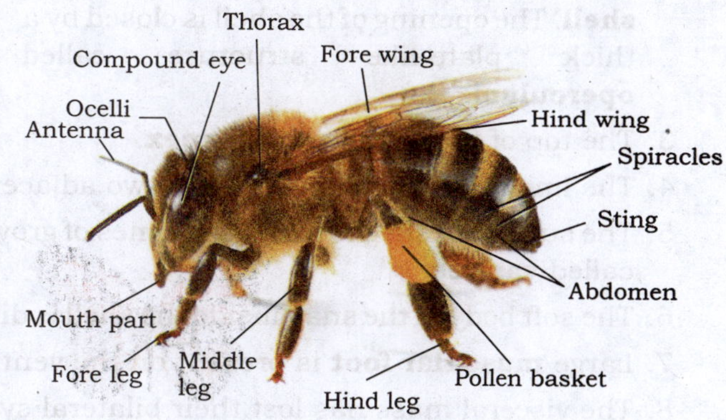

Fig. 3.9 *Apis indica* (honeybee)

(a) **Queen** is largest in size (15-20 mm). Every colony has single queen bee. Abdomen is long and tapering. Wings, eyes and legs are small. Abdominal segment lacks wax gland.

(b) **Drones** are larger than workers, but smaller than queen. Wax gland is absent and eyes are very large.

(c) **Workers** are smallest in size. Abdominal segments bear wax glands, which are present ventrally on the four posterior abdominal segments. Pollen collecting baskets are present on thoracic legs.

Pila globosa (Apple snail)

Classification

Kingdom	–	Animalia
Phylum	–	Mollusca
Class	–	Gastropoda
Order	–	Architaenioglossa
Genus	–	*Pila*
Species	–	*globosa*

Identification Characteristics

1. Calcareous shell is globose and spiral.
2. The presence of peristome.
3. The presence of ctenidia.

General Characteristics

1. *Pila* or apple snail is most commonly found in shallow freshwater sources such as streams, ponds, ditches, lakes, rice fields, etc. It is an aquatic animal, but can live without water for some time. It is most common molluscs seen during the rainy season.
2. *Pila* is sluggish organism with soft, slimy and unsegmented body enclosed within a hard, one-piece spirally coiled **calcareous shell**. The opening of the shell is closed by a thick plate-like structure called **operculum**.

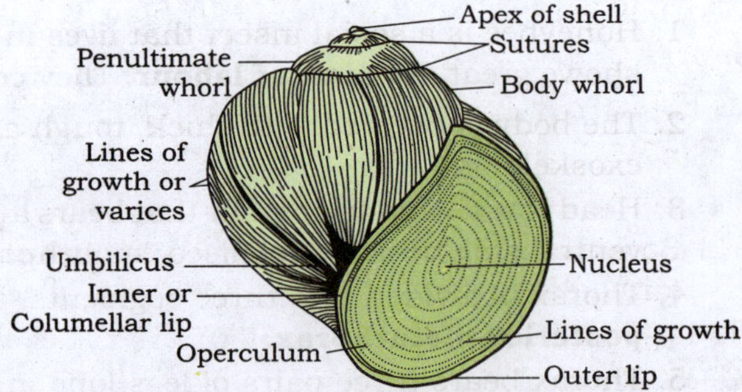

Fig. 3.10 *Pila globosa* (apple snail)

3. The top of the shell is called **apex**.
4. The line that is present between two adjacent whorls is called **suture**.
5. The surface of shell is marked by lines of growth, some of which are dark well-marked ridges called **varices**.
6. The soft body of the snail inside the shell is differentiated into **head**, **foot** and **visceral mass**.
7. Large **muscular foot** is present on the ventral side which helps it in creeping.
8. The visceral mass has lost their bilateral symmetry due to coiling or **torsion.**
9. **Mantle** covers the viscera.
10. Respiration in *Pila* occurs through gill called **ctenidium** in water and by **pulmonary sac** when it is on land.
11. Separate sexes are present with slight sexual dimorphism.

Asterias rubens (Starfish)

Classification

Kingdom	–	Animalia
Phylum	–	Echinodermata
Class	–	Asteroidea
Order	–	Forcipulatia
Genus	–	*Asterias*
Species	–	*rubens*

Identification Characteristics

1. Star-shaped body structure.
2. Presence of five ambulacral grooves on the ventral surface.
3. Tube feet are present in ambulacral groove.
4. Presence of distinct madreporite on the aboral surface.
5. Spines present all over the body.

General Characteristics

1. Starfish is an unique marine animal which is found crawling on rocky sea bottom in shallow water.
2. The whole body is covered by numerous small-sized blunt protuberances called **ossicles.**
3. Body is distinguished into **oral surface** (which is directed downward) and **aboral surface** (directed upward).
4. The oral surface bears a mouth in the central disc.
5. Two rows of tubular projections called **tube feet** or **podia** help in locomotion, food capture and respiration.
6. **Aboral surface** bears large number of short and movable spines. **Anus** is present in the centre of the disc on the aboral side of body.
7. Starfish possesses power of regeneration and shows autotomy.

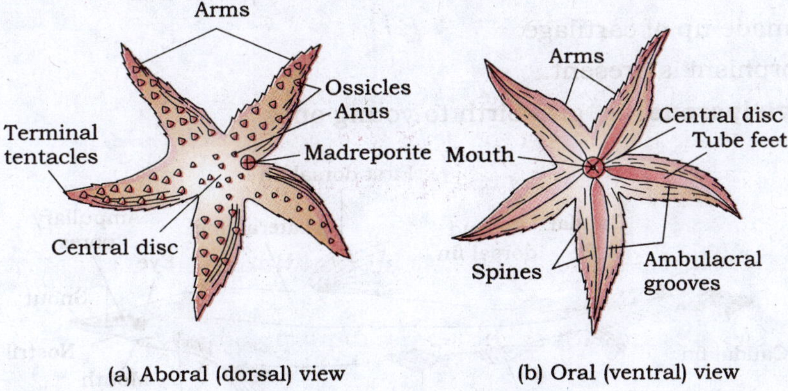

Fig. 3.11 *Asterias* (starfish)

Scoliodon (Shark or Dog Fish)

Classification

Kingdom	–	Animalia
Phylum	–	Chordata
Sub-phylum	–	Vertebrata
Super-class	–	Pisces
Class	–	Chondrichthyes
Order	–	Carcharhiniformes
Genus	–	*Scoliodon*
Species	–	*dumerili*

Identification Characteristics

1. Streamlined body covered with placoid scales.
2. Presence of two types of fins, i.e. median unpaired fins and lateral paired fins.
3. Elongated tail with heterocercal caudal fins present.
4. Male shark have claspers.
5. A pair of lateral eyes and five pairs of gill-slits (clefts) are present on the lateral side between mouth and pectoral fins, which are not covered.

General Characteristics

1. *Scoliodon* is commonly known as shark or dog fish and is found in the coastal waters of India. It is a **cartilagenous fish**.
2. Body of dog fish is elongated, spindle-shaped or streamlined, dorsoventrally flattened at anterior and laterally compressed at posterior and with a long pointed **snout**.
3. The body of *Scoliodon* is differentiated into **head**, **trunk** and **tail**.
4. A crescentic mouth and nasal aperture are present in ventral position on the head behind tip. Mouth has sharp and backwardly pointed teeth on both upper and lower jaws that help it to catch the prey.
5. **Cloacal aperture** is situated ventrally between two pelvic fins.
6. Skeleton is made up of cartilage.
7. Sexual dimorphism is present.
8. Sharks are **viviparous**, i.e. give birth to young ones.

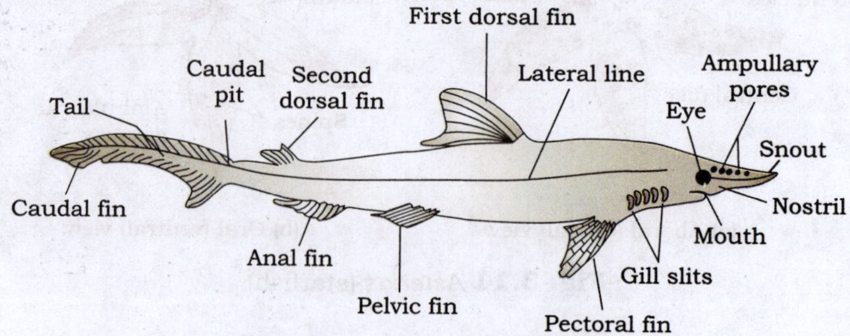

Fig. 3.12 *Scoliodon* (dog fish)

Labeo rohita (Rohu)

Classification

Kingdom	–	Animalia
Phylum	–	Chordata
Sub-phylum	–	Vertebrata
Super-class	–	Pisces
Class	–	Osteichthyes
Order	–	Cypriniformes
Genus	–	*Labeo*
Species	–	*rohita*

Identification Characteristics

1. Streamlined body covered with cycloid scales.
2. Gills are covered by operculum.
3. Presence of thick and fringed lower lips.
4. Caudal fin is homocercal (symmetrical).
5. The margin of the lower lip is fimbriated.

General Characteristics

1. Rohu or the Indian carp, is found in clear and sluggish rivers, streams, ponds, etc. These are called **freshwater dwellers** and are widely used as food in our country.
2. The body is laterally compressed and streamlined. It is grey or black on the dorsal side and silvery on the ventral surface. Its size can be 1 m in length.
3. The region extending between the depressed and obtuse **snout** and the posterior end of the operculum forms the **head** part of rohu.
4. A pair of nostrils and lateral eyes are present on its head. Eyes are without eyelids.
5. Fins are present for locomotion. Three median unpaired (**dorsal**, **anal** and **caudal**) fins and two paired fins (**pectoral** and **pelvic**) are present.
6. Sexes are separate and males are without **claspers**, which are present in some other types of fishes.
7. Females are oviparous, i.e. they lay eggs.

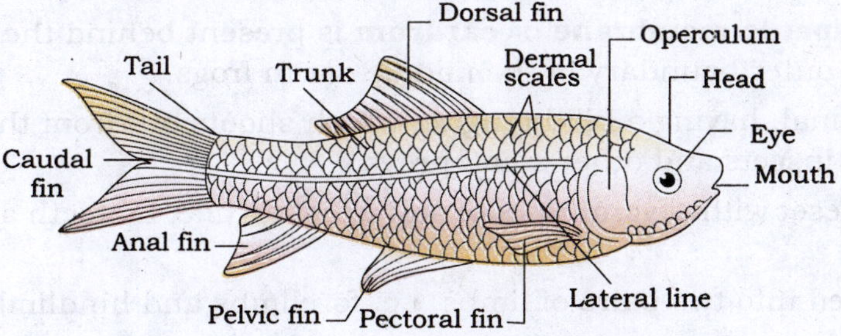

Fig. 3.13 *Labeo rohita* (Rohu : A bony fish)

Rana tigrina (Frog)

Classification

Kingdom	–	Animalia
Phylum	–	Chordata
Class	–	Amphibia
Order	–	Anura
Genus	–	*Rana*
Species	–	*tigrina*

Identification Characteristics

1. Bilaterally symmetrical body with head and trunk.
2. Skin is naked and slimy.
3. Feet are webbed and in males possess nuptial pads.
4. Forelimbs are smaller than hind limbs.

General Characteristics

1. Frogs are commonly found during rainy season in or near ponds, pools, lakes, rivers and other humid places.
2. The skin is moist, lacks scales and is covered by mucus.
3. The skin is usually olive green in colour with dark spots and a medium streak that represents **mid-dorsal line**. It can change its colour according to its environment.
4. On the ventral side, skin colour is creamish with white spots.
5. Head is small, triangular in shape and immovably fixed with trunk. Two nostrils are present on either side of the head.

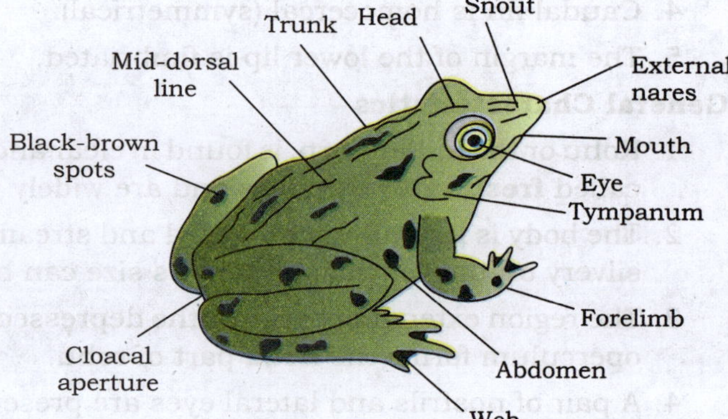

Fig. 3.14 *Rana tigrina* (Indian frog)

6. Two large bulging eyes are present on head with thick pigmented upper eyelids while lower eyelids are rudimentary. A **nictitating membrane** is present that covers the eye and constitutes **third eyelid**.
7. A circular **tympanic membrane** or **eardrum** is present behind the eyes. It is transparent and forms the outer boundary of the middle ear in frogs.
8. Mouth is terminal, having a bifid tongue, which shoots out from the mouth with a rolling effect to catch insects and other small preys.
9. Upper jaw is beset with several rows of spiny teeth while, no teeth are present in the lower jaw.
10. Trunk is divided into two pairs of limbs, i.e. forelimbs and hindlimbs.
11. Forelimbs have four and hind limbs have 5 clawless digits.
12. Hindlimbs are webbed for swimming and leaping. An inter-digital, web-like membrane is present in the hind limbs, which is used for swimming.
13. At the posterior side of the body, **cloacal aperture** is present, which is an opening for excreting out fecal matter.

14. Frog shows sexual dimorphism during breeding season. Male frogs are smaller in size and possess **vocal sacs** for sound production and **nuptial pad** or **copulatory pad** on the base of the first digit of fore limb, which aids them in **amplexus**. Female frog is bigger in size and does not have vocal sac or nuptial pad.

Calotes versicolor (Garden lizard)

Classification

Kingdom	–	Animalia
Phylum	–	Chordata
Class	–	Reptilia
Order	–	Squamata
Genus	–	*Calotes*
Species	–	*versicolor*

Identification Characteristics

1. Body is covered with rough epidermal scales.
2. Presence of triangular head and tympanum.
3. Presence of two pairs of pentadactyl limbs and clawed digits.
4. The body is differentiated into head, neck, trunk and elongated tail.

General Characteristics

1. Lizard is most commonly found in open fields, hedges on trees and gardens. It is commonly known as 'girgit'.
2. Eyes are dorso-lateral in position.
3. Limbs (forelimbs and hindlimbs) are provided with tiny microscopic structures called setae. These are adapted for running and sticking on the wall.
4. Neck is short. It is an **insectivorous** animal.
5. The tail of lizard shows **autotomy**, i.e. it is ringed and fragile and can be easily broken and regenerated again. The skin provides the animal with protective colouration in its environment.

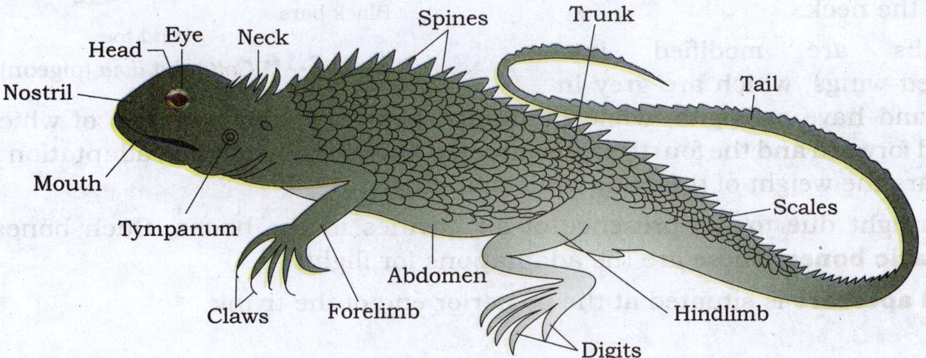

Fig. 3.15 *Calotes versicolor*

Columba livia (Pigeon)

Classification

Kingdom	–	Animalia
Phylum	–	Chordata
Class	–	Aves
Order	–	Columbiformes
Genus	–	*Columba*
Species	–	*livia*

Identification Characteristics

1. Body is covered with feathers and is streamlined.
2. Forelimbs modified into wings.
3. Mouth is modified into a beak.
4. Hindlimbs have talons.
5. Eyes have nictitating membrane.
6. Small and rounded head.

General Characteristics

1. It is very common bird, which makes its nests in scantily inhabited houses, godowns, railway stations and old buildings. It feeds on grains, fruits and insects.
2. The head contains large eyes and nostrils and a short and stout beak that has no teeth. Opening of ears is present which is covered with feathers.
3. Cylindrical neck is very flexible to facilitate mobility of the head. A narrow fluorescent bound occurs around the neck.

Fig. 3.16 *Columba livia* (pigeon)

4. Forelimbs are modified into feathered wings, which are grey in colour and have no digits, while hindlimbs bear four clawed digits of which three are directed forward and the fourth one is directed backward. This is an adaptation for perching and bears the weight of the body while standing.
5. Body is light due to the presence of air cavities in the bones. Such bones are called **pneumatic bones**. These are the adaptations for flight.
6. **Cloacal aperture** is situated at the posterior end of the trunk.

Oryctolagus cuniculus (Rabbit)

Classification

Kingdom	–	Animalia
Phylum	–	Chordata
Class	–	Mammalia
Order	–	Lagomorpha
Genus	–	*Oryctolagus*
Species	–	*cuniculus*

Identification Characteristics

1. Body covered with fur and have bushy tail.
2. Presence of pair of eyes and pinnae.
3. Short limbs used for leaping and burrowing.
4. Head is pear-shaped with a blunt snout.
5. The upper lip bears sensitive hair called as **vibrissae** or **whiskers** and has a cleft in the middle which is called as **rabbit cleft** and through which the incisor teeth get exposed.

General Characteristics

1. It is a medium sized, viviparous animal found in the fields, gardens, etc. It makes burrows in the field and feeds on vegetation or green plants.
2. The body is divisible into head, neck, trunk and small tail.
3. Head and trunk are joined together by a short neck, which allows the head to move in various directions.
4. Sexes are separate showing **sexual dimorphism.** Females have slit-like *vulva*, four to five pairs of mammary glands with nipples along thorax and abdomen, while males have a pair of testes in a pair of scrotal sacs and a small, cylindrical and muscular penis.

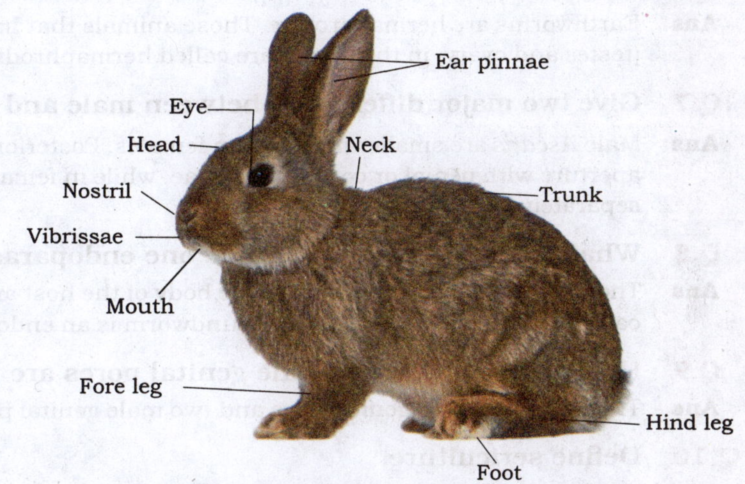

Fig. 3.17 *Oryctolagus cuniculus* (rabbit)

PRECAUTIONS

- *Handle the specimens in specimen bottles and on slides with great care.*
- *Draw the figure as seen in the specimen bottle.*
- *Be careful while using microscopes and slide specimens.*
- *Do not rush towards the specimen to observe it.*

Viva-Voce

Q.1 What is hypostome?

Ans The free distal end in *Hydra* has a small conical projection called hypostome.

Q.2 What are nematoblasts meant for?

Ans The tentacles in *Hydra* bear large number of stinging cells or nematoblasts that are meant for defence and offence against their predator and their prey respectively.

Q.3 Which disease is caused by *Fasciola*?

Ans *Fasciola* or liverfluke causes disease called liver rot (fasciolosis).

Q.4 What do you mean by the term 'metazoans'?

Ans The multicellular organisms are called metazoans.

Q.5 How do these organisms multiply?

(i) *Amoeba*

(ii) *Hydra*

Ans *Amoeba* multiplies by binary fission and *Hydra* by budding.

Q.6 State whether earthworms are hermaphrodite or not.

Ans Earthworms are hermaphrodite. Those animals that have both the sex organs or gonads (testes and ovary) in their body are called hermaphrodite, e.g. leech and earthworms.

Q.7 Give two major differences between male and female *Ascaris*. NCERT

Ans Male *Ascaris* are smaller in size than females. Posterior end of male is curved having cloacal aperture with penial or copulatory setae, while in females the genital pore and anus open separately.

Q.8 What are endoparasites? Name one endoparasite.

Ans Those organisms that live inside the body of the host and derive their nutrition from them are called endoparasites. *Ascaris* or roundworm is an endoparasite.

Q.9 How many male and female genital pores are present in an earthworm?

Ans There is one female genital pore and two male genital pores in an earthworm.

Q.10 Define sericulture.

Ans Rearing of silkworm for getting raw silk is called sericulture.

Q.11 What is cephalothorax?

Ans When head and thorax are fused together, it is called cephalothorax.

Q.12 What are the important differences between workers, queen and drones in honeybee? NCERT

Ans Workers are the smallest in size and are unfertile female. Drones are males which are larger than workers, but smaller than queen. Queen is the only fertile female. Each colony has a single queen bee.

Q.13 How does an *Amoeba* move? Which mode of nutrition is shown by *Amoeba*?

Ans Amoeba moves by special organs called pseudopodia. It shows holozoic mode of nutrition.

Q.14 Which animal possess ambulacral grooves?

Ans Starfish (a member of Echinodermata) possesses ambulacral grooves.

Q.15 Match the characters given in Column A with the name of animals given in Column B. NCERT

	Column A		Column B
(a)	Hypostome	(i)	*Amoeba*
(b)	Cephalothorax	(ii)	*Hydra*
(c)	Ambulacral groove	(iii)	Earthworm
(d)	Pseudopodia	(iv)	Prawn
		(v)	Starfish

Ans (a)- (ii), (b)-(iv), (c)-(v), (d)-(i)

Q.16 What are the fundamental features on which the animal kingdom is based?

Ans The fundamental features on which the animal kingdom is based are:

(i) Level of organisation.
(ii) Symmetry.
(iii) Body cavity or coelom.

Q.17 What are the characteristic features of phylum-Chordata?

Ans The characteristic features of phylum-Chordata are

(i) Presence of notochord.
(ii) Gill slits in embryonic stage.
(iii) Triploblastic and coelomate body.
(iv) Closed blood vascular system.

Q.18 Give the characteristic features of phylum–Arthropoda.

Ans The characteristic features of phylum– Arthropoda are

(i) Segmented body with joint appendages.
(ii) Body is covered by chitinous exoskeleton.
(iii) Body segments not separated by septa.

Q.19 List the characteristics of super class–Pisces.

Ans Super-class–Pisces consists of water dwelling animals that have the following characteristics:

(i) Paired appendages in the form of pectoral and pelvic fins.
(ii) Have exoskeleton dermal scales.
(iii) Respiration occurs by gills.
(iv) Two-chambered heart.

Q.20 Why do some animals like earthworm, leech and frog have moist skins?

Ans Skin of some animals like earthworm, leech and frog are moist because it helps in the cuticular respiration.

Q.21 Define the term 'triploblastic'.

Ans Animals that have been developed from three germinal layers, i.e. ectoderm, mesoderm and endoderm are said to be triploblastic.

Q.22 Why are the earthworms also called as farmer's friends?

Ans The earthworm ploughs the soil by making burrows in it. This makes the soil porous which makes water easily available to the plant and helps its roots to breathe properly for healthy growth. Therefore, earthworms are called farmer's friends.

Q.23 **Give the name of some coelenterates besides *Hydra*.**

Ans Jelly fish, sea anemone, sea pen are some coelenterates.

Q.24 **What is bilateral symmetry? Name two organisms that are bilaterally symmetrical.**

Ans Symmetry where the animal body can be divided into two equal halves through one plane passing through the centre is called bilateral symmetry. Frog and toad show bilateral symmetry.

Q.25 **Give the definition of clitellum and state its function.**

Ans Clitellum is the circular band of glandular tissue in 14th-16th segments in earthworm. It helps in the formation of cocoons.

Q.26 **What is meant by sexual dimorphism?**

Ans When the two sexes, i.e. male and females of an organism can be easily differentiated from their external features, they are called sexually dimorphic, e.g. *Ascaris*.

Q.27 **What is the use of honey and beeswax?**

Ans Honey is the food with high nutritive value and is used in cough and cold as medicines. Whereas, beeswax is used in making cosmetics and polishes.

Q.28 **What features contribute to the success of reptiles on land?**

Ans The features that contribute to the success of reptiles on the land are as follows

1. Keratinised scales on their bodies prevent water loss.
2. Internal fertilisation.
3. A shell around the egg to prevent dessiccation.

Q.29 **What are pneumatic bones and where are they found?**

Ans Pneumatic bones are bones that contain air cavities to reduce weight of the body. These bones are present in birds, making them light and aiding them in flight.

Experiment 4

AIM

To study the mitosis in onion root tip cells and animal (grasshopper) cells from permanent slides.

Theory/Principle

Somatic growth in plants and animals takes place by the increase in the number of cells. A cell divides mitotically to form two daughter cells wherein, the number of chromosomes remains the same (i.e. unchanged) as in the mother cell.

Cell cycle is the sequence of stages that a cell passes between two consecutive cell divisions. It consists of four stages, i.e. G_1, S, G_2 and M.

Cell division phase has two parts, i.e. karyokinesis (division of nucleus) and cytokinesis division of cytoplasm).

In plants, such divisions occurs rapidly in meristematic tissues of root and shoot apex, where the stages of mitosis can be easily observed. In animals, mitotically dividing cells can be easily viewed in the bone marrow tissue of a vertebrates, epithelial cells of gills in fishes and in the tail of growing tadpole larvae of frog.

Mitosis is generally similar in plant and animal cells, animal cells use centrioles for spindle formation and cytokinesis occurs through a cleavage furrow. In contrast, plant cells lack centrioles and undergo cytokinesis by forming a cell plate.

Requirements

Permanent slides of mitosis in onion root tip cells and animal cells (grasshopper), compound microscope.

Procedure

1. Place the permanent slide on the stage of a compound microscope.
2. First, observe the slide under lower magnification (10X objective) to locate the dividing cells.
3. Now, observe the dividing cells under higher magnification (40X objective) to examine different stages of mitosis.
4. Observe all the slides in the same way.

Observations/Results

Under lower magnification, rectangular cells with pink nucleus are seen scattered. Under higher magnification, different stages become distinct. Those cells which are not in the phases of cell division are considered to be in the interphase. Different stages of cell cycle are described as follows.

Interphase

1. It is a non-dividing phase of the cell cycle between two successive cell divisions.
2. The cells are mostly rectangular, oval or even circular in shape.
3. Nuclear envelope is distinct and the nucleus is homogenous, situated at centre and looks granular.

4. Chromatin fibres appear in the form of an interconnected network within the nucleus.
5. One or few nucleoli are also observed inside the nucleus.

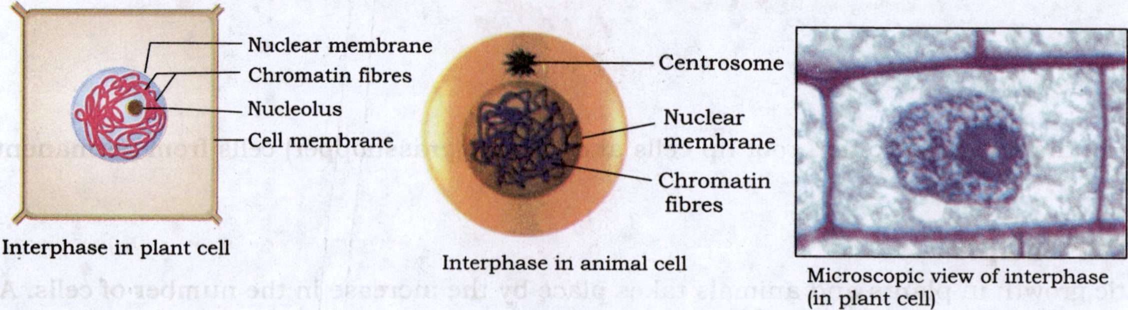

Fig. 4.1 Interphase

Stages of Mitosis

I. Prophase

1. Nucleus is enlarged and occupies most of the cell volume. Intact nuclear outline is seen.
2. Chromatin (seen as homogenous material in the nucleus at interphase) gets condensed and appears as long thread-like structures called **chromosomes**.
3. In late prophase stage the nuclear membrane starts disappearing. Nucleoli may or may not be visible.
4. If the cell is in early stage of prophase, then the chromatin fibres are very thin. However, in the cells observed at late prophase stage, comparatively thicker chromatin fibres would be visible with no nuclear membrane.

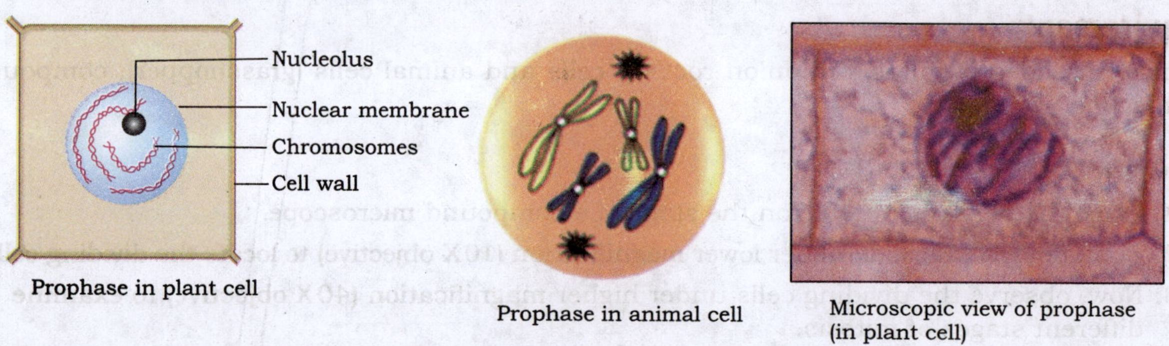

Fig. 4.2 Prophase

II. Metaphase

1. Chromosomes become shorter and thicker and hence become distinct and clearly visible under the compound microscope.
2. Nuclear membrane completely disappears.
3. Chromosomes align at the cell's equatorial plane, known as **metaphase plate**.
4. Each chromosomes consists of two sister chromatids joined at the centromere, which can be seen by changing the resolution of microscope.
5. The spindle apparatus is fully formed and extends from the poles to the **kinetochores** or **centromere**.

6. Nucleoli is not visible.

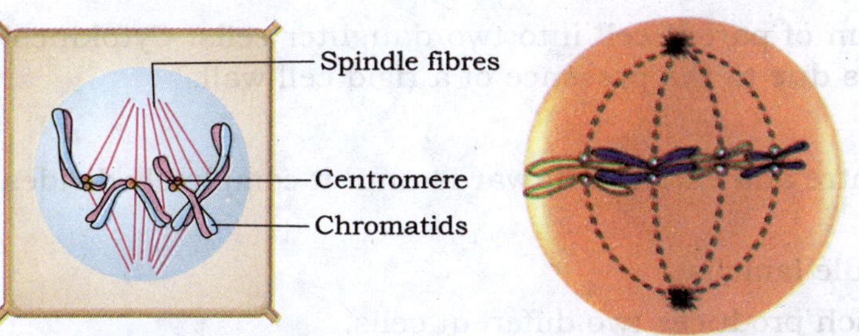

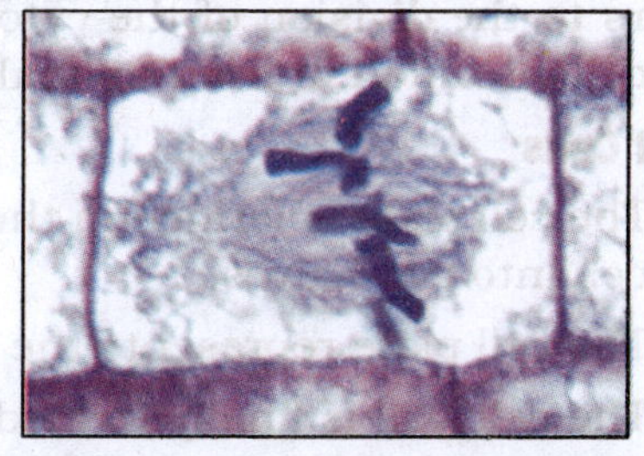

Metaphase in plant cell   Metaphase in animal cells   Microscopic view of metaphase in plant cell

Fig. 4.3 Metaphase

iii. Anaphase

1. The two sister chromatids of each chromosome separate from the centromere and move towards the opposite poles.
2. Each chromatid now represents a separate chromosome having its own centromere.
3. The daughter chromosomes (separated chromatids) appear in V, J and I shapes, depending upon the position of centromere on the chromosomes.
4. Anaphase is designated as early, mid and late, depending on the position of moving chromosomes with respect to the opposite poles.

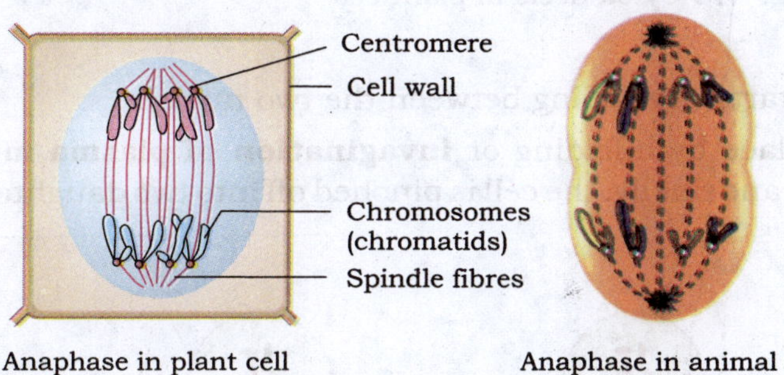

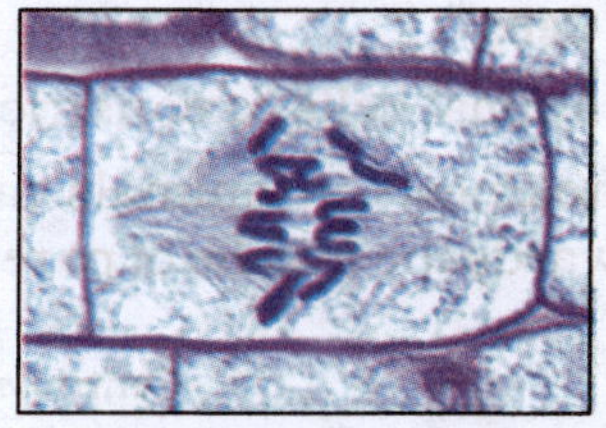

Anaphase in plant cell   Anaphase in animal cell   Microscopic view of anaphase in plant cell

Fig 4.4 Anaphase

iv. Telophase

1. Chromosomes reach the opposite poles, lose their individuality and look like a mass of chromatin again.
2. Nuclear membrane reappears to form the nuclei of two future daughter cells.
3. Nucleolus gets reconstituted.
4. Two daughter nuclei formed at the two poles of a cell, are similar to the parent nucleus both quantitatively and qualitatively.

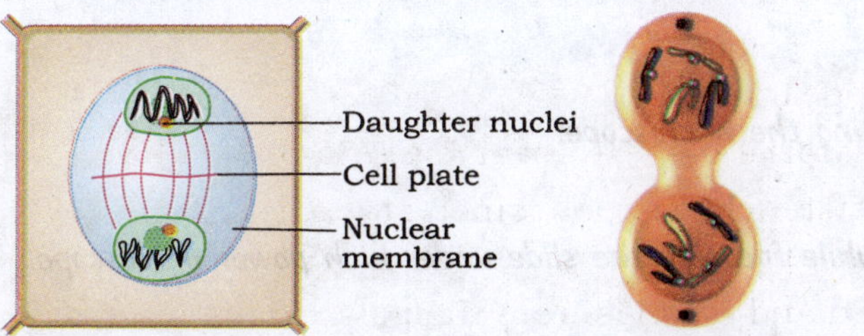

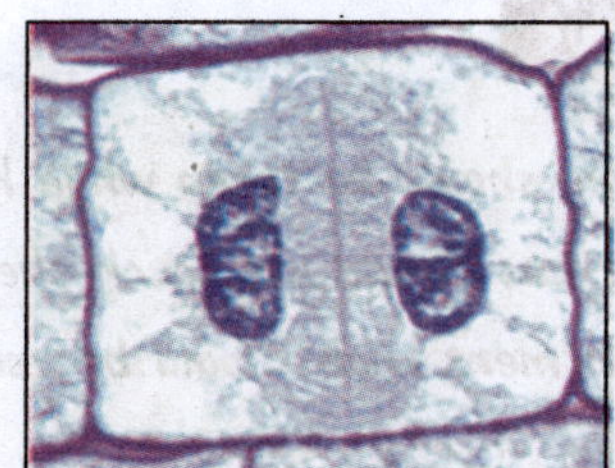

Telophase in plant cell   Telophase in animal cell   Microscopic view of telophase in plant cell

Fig. 4.5 Telophase

Cytokinesis

It refers to the division of the cytoplasm of parent cell into two daughter cells. Cytokinesis in plant cells is different from animal cells due to the presence of a rigid cell wall.

In Plant Cells

1. The cell plate is formed in the centre and extends outwards until it completely divides the cell into two halves.
2. The cell plate represents the middle lamella.
3. The cell wall is finally formed which produces two different cells.
4. As a result of mitosis, two daughter cells are formed which are qualitatively and quantitatively similar to the parent cell.

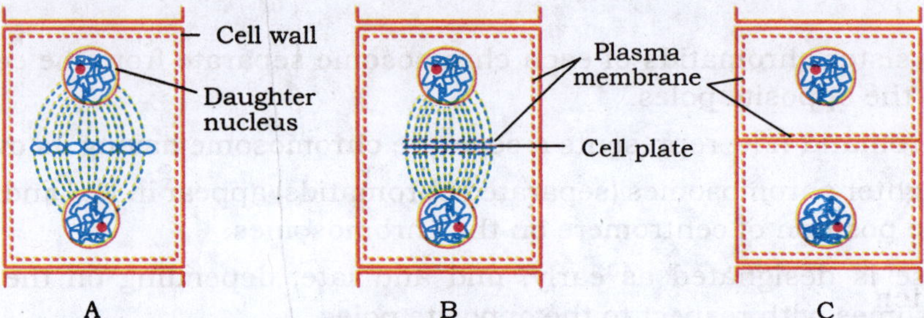

Fig. 4.6 Cytokinesis in plant cell

In Animal Cells

1. In animal cells, a constriction starts developing between the two nuclei.
2. Cytokinesis in animals takes place by infolding or **invagination of plasma membrane** towards the middle of parent cell and finally, the cell is pinched off into two daughter cells.

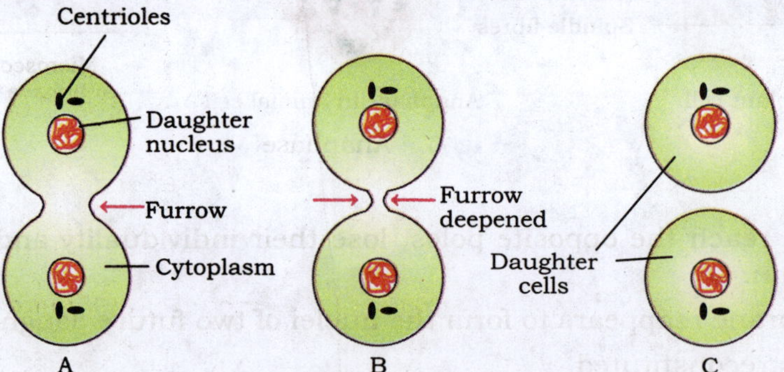

Fig. 4.7 Cytokinesis in animal cell

PRECAUTIONS

- *Proper care should be taken while handling the microscope.*
- *Objective lens should not touch the slide.*
- *Fine adjustment knob should be used, while focusing the slide under high power mircoscope.*

Viva-Voce

Q.1 Which type of cell division is seen in somatic cells?

Ans Somatic cells show mitotic cell division.

Q.2 Can we study the process of mitosis in leaf cells?

Ans No, the process of mitosis can not be studied in leaf cells because the cells of leaf do not divide.

Q.3 To study the process of mitosis why do we use onion root tip or grasshopper larva cells?

Ans Onion root tips and grasshopper larvae contain mitotically active cells which are in dividing stage. Therefore, process of mitosis is better studied in these cells.

Q.4 Mitosis is referred as equational division. Explain why?

Ans Mitosis is called equational division because the two daughter cells produced as a result of mitosis have equal number of chromosomes, which are qualitatively and quantitatively similar to the parent cell.

Q.5 At which stage of cell division do the chromatids start moving towards opposite poles?

Ans At anaphase stage, the chromatids start moving towards opposite poles.

Q.6 What is daughter chromosome?

Ans At anaphase, each chromatid behaves as an independent chromosome and is known as daughter chromosome.

Q.7 What is the difference between karyokinesis and cytokinesis?

Ans Karyokinesis is the division of nucleus into two daughter nuclei, while cytokinesis is the division of cytoplasm along with cell organelles into two daughter cells.

Q.8 What is the difference between cytokinesis in plant cell and cytokinesis in animal cell?

Ans Cytokinesis in plant cell involves outward extension of cell plate from the centre thereby dividing a cell into two cells, while in animal cell, cytokinesis occurs by infolding or invagination of plasma membrane that grows inward. This separates the parent cells into two daughter cells.

Q.9 At which stage of cell division, chromosomes can be best seen?

Ans Chromosomes can be best seen at metaphase stage of cell division.

Q.10 Which cellular elements participate in anaphase movement? NCERT

Ans Spindle fibres are cellular elements that participate in anaphase movement. The shortening of spindle fibres causes the movement of chromatids towards the respective poles.

Q.11 Name the stain which is used to study the chromosomes.

Ans Acetocarmine is used to study the chromosomes because it stains them in deep red colour while the cytoplasm remains unstained.

Q.12 Where do the spindle fibres originate from?

Ans Spindle fibres originate from centriole in animals and from cytoplasm in plants.

Q.13 Who was the first to observe the process of mitosis in plant cell?

Ans Strasburger was the first to observe the mitotic cell division in plant cell (1875).

Q.14 What would happen if mitosis NCERT

(i) does not take place at all?

(ii) takes place at a rate faster than the normal rate?

Ans (i) Mitosis is the process by which cell divides. If mitosis does not occur then no new cells will be formed. No growth and development will happen and life will cease to exist.

(ii) If mitosis occurs at a rate faster than normal, there will be accumulation of cells. There will be no control over growth and number of cells produced. Excessive cell production will lead to tumour or cancer.

Q.15 Why is chromatin network seen during the prophase stage of mitosis? NCERT

Ans The chromatin network is seen during prophase because it condenses and coils to form distinct chromosomes. This visible chromatin network helps to facilitate the accurate segregation of genetic material during cell division.

Q.16 What would happen if cytokinesis does not take place after karyokinesis? NCERT

Ans If cytokinesis does not follow karyokinesis, the cells will become multinucleated, potentially leading to disrupted function and diseases like cancer.

Q.17 What would happen if the chromosomes fail to move during anaphase? NCERT

Ans If chromosomes fail to move during anaphase, proper segregation won't occur, leading to cells with abnormal chromosomal numbers. This can result in cell malfunction, diseases or cell death.

Q.18 What is the significance of mitosis?

Ans Mitosis is vital for growth, repair and asexual reproduction as it produces two genetically identical daughter cells. It also maintains genetic stability and ensures the continuity of cell function.

Q.19 What triggers a cell to undergo mitotic division?

Ans A high nucleocytoplasmic ratio, triggers a cells to undergo mitotic division. As the cell grows, the cytoplasm content increases, and thus the volume of cytoplasm is more than the nucleus. This disturbs the ratio in terms of volume between nucleus and cytoplasm. The nucleus is unable to control the activities of large cytoplasm. Hence, the cell undergoes mitosis and form two daughter cells to restore the nucleo-cytoplasmic ratio.

Experiment 5

AIM

To study and identify different types of inflorescence (cymose and racemose).

Theory/Principle

Inflorescence plays an important role in the taxonomical studies and identification of plants. The arrangement of flowers on the shoot of a plant is called **inflorescence**. It is the reproductive shoots composed of a number of shoots of limited growth (dwarf shoots) termed flowers. Peduncle and pedicel are the main parts of the flower which help in determining the infloresence. The peduncle is the main stalk supporting an inflorescence, while the pedicel is the smaller stalk supporting an individual flower or fruit within the inflorescence.

Types of Inflorescence

On the basis of position in the shoot system, inflorescence is of the following types

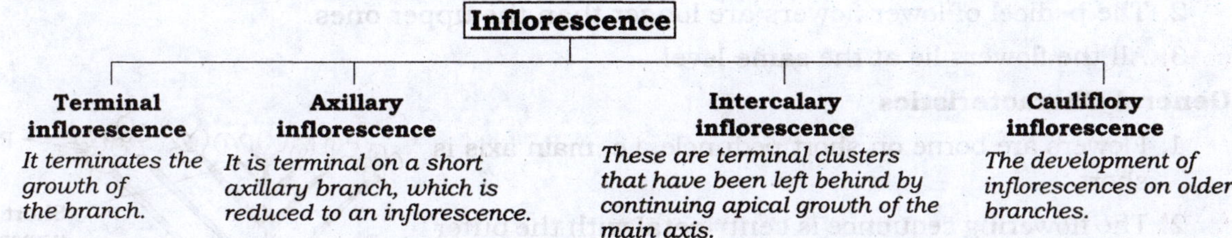

On the basis of sequence of development of flowers on the peduncle, the inflorescence is of the following types.

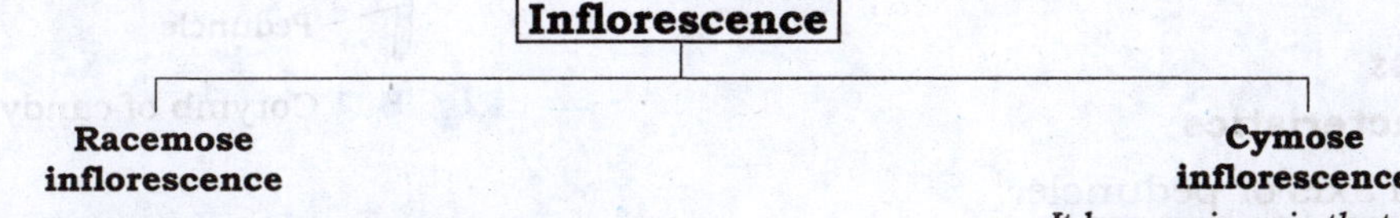

Requirements

Practical record book, pencil, eraser, hand lens, fresh or preserved inflorescences of locally available plants, beaker and water.

Procedure

1. Collect the inflorescences of locally available plants. Keep them in a beaker with water.
2. Observe the collected inflorescence.
3. Identify the type of inflorescence and comment on it.
4. Draw a well labelled diagram of each inflorescence showing the arrangement of flowers on the peduncle and any other features of special interest.

Observations

Racemose Inflorescence

I. Raceme : Mustard

Identification Characteristic

The inflorescence shows the indefinite growth of peduncle and terminal bud does not form the flower.

General Characteristics

1. Main axis or peduncle is elongated and unbranched that bears numbers of flowers laterally.
2. Flowers are stalked (or pedicillate) and show acropetal succession, i.e. older flowers at the base and younger flowers towards tip.
3. Larkspur, radish and *Crotalaria* also show raceme inflorescence.

Fig. 5.1 Raceme of mustard

II. Corymb : Candytuft

Identification Characteristics

1. The peduncle is unbranched and bears pedicellate flowers in an acropetal manner.
2. The pedicel of lower flowers are longer than the upper ones.
3. All the flowers lie at the same level.

General Characteristics

1. Flowers are borne on short peduncle, i.e. main axis is short.
2. The flowering sequence is centripetal with the outer or lower flowers opening first.
3. *Cassia auriculata* and *Gynanadropsis* are the other examples of corymb inflorescence.

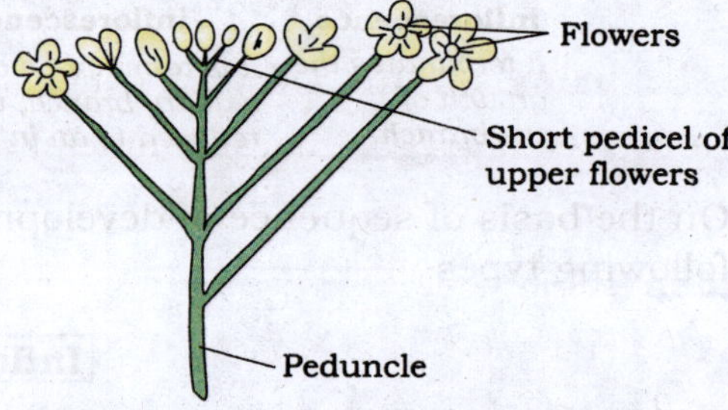

Fig. 5.2 Corymb of candytuft

III. Spike : *Achyranthes*

Identification Characteristics

1. It has elongated axis or peduncle.
2. Flowers are sessile and bisexual.

General Characteristics

1. Peduncle is unbranched and grows indefinitely.
2. Flowers are arranged in acropetal succession, i.e. older flowers at lower sides and young flowers at top.
3. *Callistemon* (bottle brush), *Amaranthus* (chaulai) are the other examples of spike inflorescence.

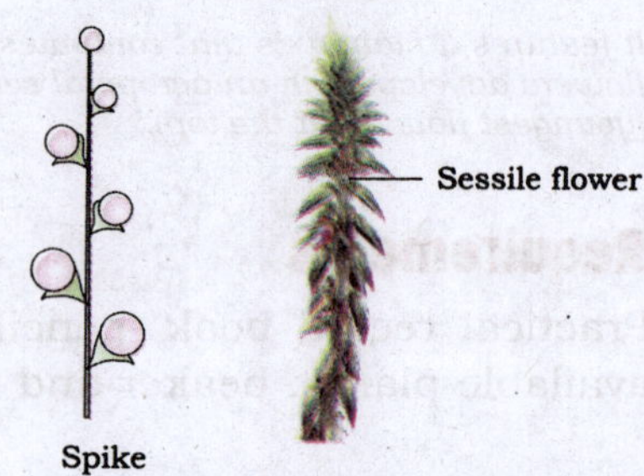

Fig. 5.3 Spike of *Achyranthes*

iv. Catkin : Mulberry (Morus)

Identification Characteristic

Pendunce unbranched, grows indefinitely and bears unisexual, sessile flowers.

General Characteristics

1. The inflorescence is compact with a short peduncle that are often hanging.
2. Flowers arise in an acropetal succession/ manner.
3. On maturity the spike falls as a single unit.
4. *Betula* (birch) and *Quercus* (oak) are the other examples of catkin inflorescence.

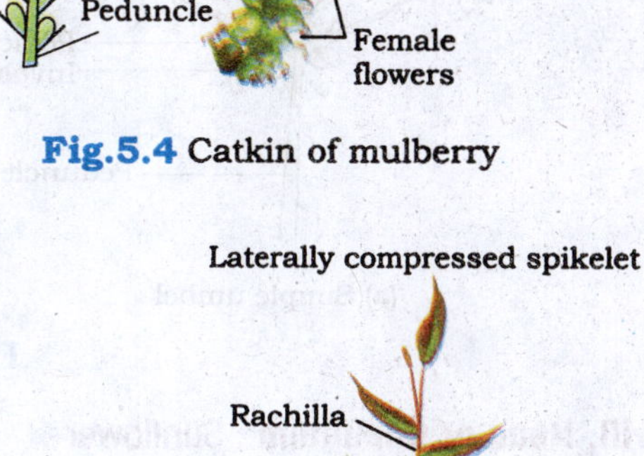

Fig.5.4 Catkin of mulberry

v. Spikelets : Wheat

Identification Characteristics

1. It consists of one or more flowers.
2. Axis of the spikelet called rachilla contain bracts in the axil of which sessile flowers are borne.
3. Flower bears bracts called glumes.

Laterally compressed spikelet
Rachilla
First floret
Upper glume
Pedicel
Lower glume

Fig. 5.5 Spikelet of wheat

General Characteristics

1. It is a very small spike with one or few small flowers or florets.
2. Opposite to lemma there is a small bract-like organs called **palea**. So, the flower is enclosed by lemma and palea.
3. Rice is an another example of spikelet inflorescence.

vi. Spadix : *Colocasia*

Identification Characteristics

1. Peduncle is fleshy and unbranched and grows indefinitely.
2. Presence of spathe with spike inflorescence.

General Characteristics

1. The peduncle bears sessile and unisexual flowers. Upper flowers are male and lower flowers are female.
2. The entire inflorescence is covered by one or more, green or often brightly coloured bracts called **spathe**.
3. Banana is an another example of spadix inflorescence with bright red bracts.

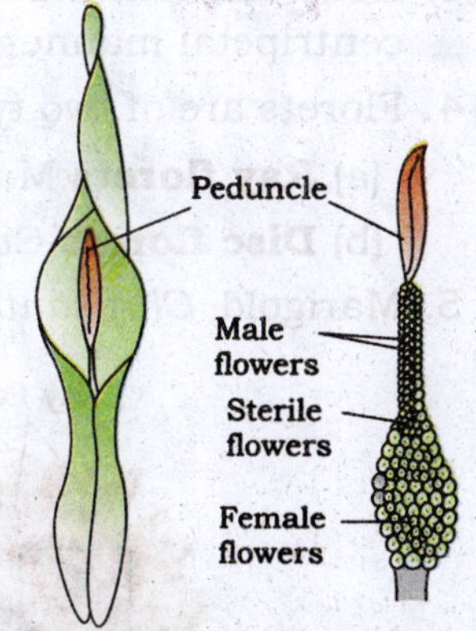

Fig. 5.6 Spadix of *Colocasia*

vii. Umbel : Coriander

Identification Characteristics

1. In this peduncle is often unbranched and reduced significantly.
2. Flowers are mainly arranged in acropetal sequence.

General Characteristics

1. The main axis or peduncle bears, a group of flowers which have pedicels of more or less equal lengths, so that flowers seem to spread out from a common point.

2. In the umbel, there is a whorl of bracts or an **involucre** at the base of flower and each flower develops from the axil of a bract.
3. Sometimes umbel becomes branched and is called as **compound umbel**.
4. The flowers arise in centripetal succession.
5. Carrot, fennel, parsley, etc., are the other examples of umbel inflorescence.

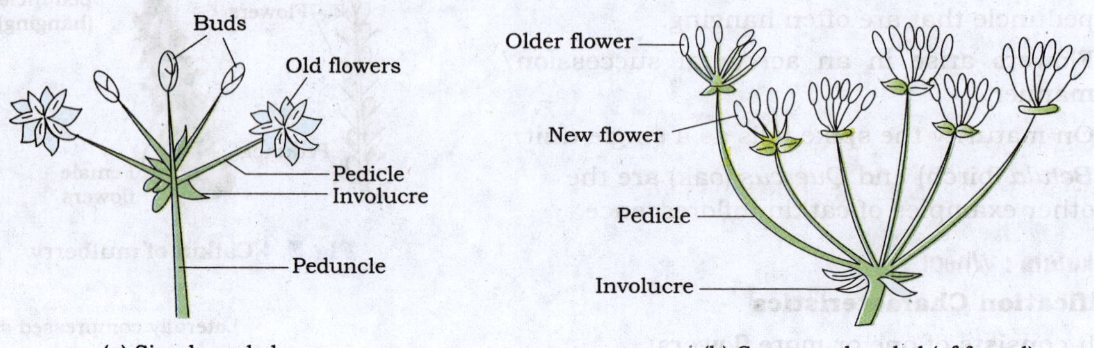

Fig. 5.7 Umbel inflorescence

viii. Head or Capitulum : Sunflower

Identification Characteristics

1. The peduncle is highly condensed and is discoid.
2. Many sessile flowers called florets are attached to the disc-shaped receptacles.

General Characteristics

1. Main axis is flattened into a more or less convex structure which is called **receptacle**.
2. Receptacle bears mass of small sessile flowers called **florets** on its surface, with one or more whorls of prominent bracts at base forming **involucre**.
3. Head contains older outer flowers and younger inner flowers, i.e. flowers are arranged in a centripetal manner.
4. Florets are of two types
   (a) **Ray florets** Marginal, strap-shaped, sterile florets which are always zygomorphic.
   (b) **Disc florets** Central, tubular, bisexual florets that are usually actinomorphic.
5. Marigold, *Chrysanthemum* and *Cosmos* also show head or capitulum type of inflorescence.

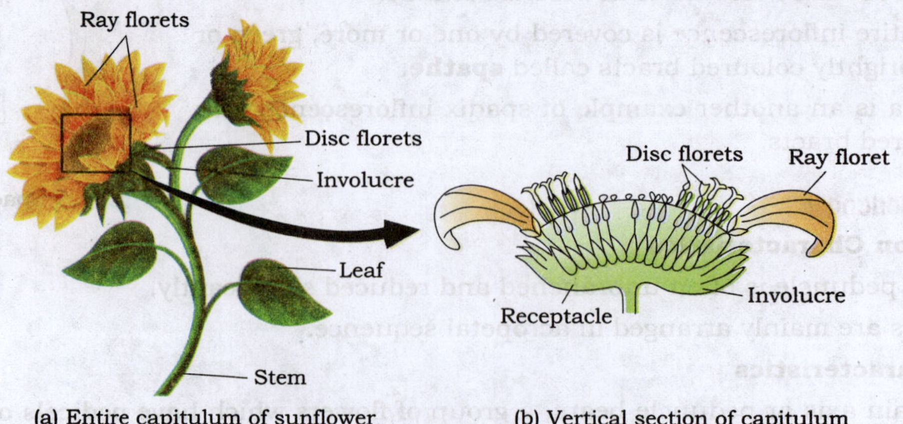

Fig. 5.8 Capitulum inflorescence

Cymose Inflorescence

i. Monochasial or Uniparous Cyme : *Begonia*

Identification Characteristics

1. In this inflorescence, peduncle terminates into flower.
2. It produces only one lateral branch at a time which ends into a single flower.

General Characteristics

1. Lateral and succeeding branches again produce only one branch at a time like the primary one. This pattern is repeated and the peduncle is formed by the fusion of bases of axillary branches and the main axis. This type of axis is called **sympodial**.
2. Monochasial cyme is of two types:
   (a) **Helicoid cyme** When all the lateral branches develop on the same side of peduncle, forming a sort of helix, the arrangement is called helicoid cyme, e.g. *Begonia*.
   (b) **Scorpioid cyme** When the lateral branches develop on alternate sides forming a zig-zag pattern, the arrangement is called scorpioid cyme, e.g. cotton.

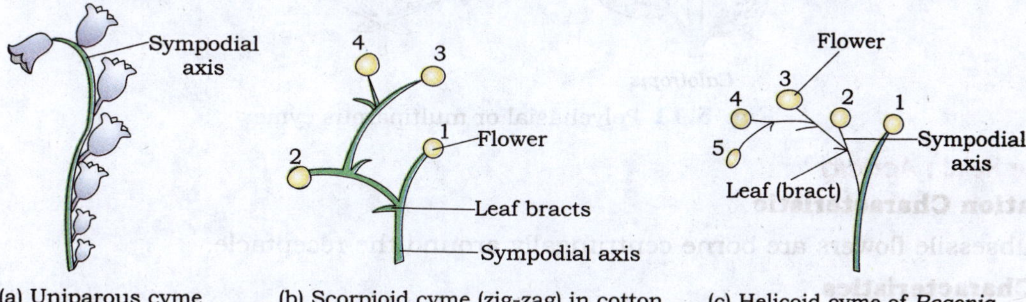

Fig. 5.9 Monochasial or uniparous cyme

ii. Dichasial or Biparous Cyme : Jasmine

Identification Characteristic

The main axis terminates in a flower.

General Characteristics

1. Dichasial cyme inflorescence consists of only three flowers, out of which the central one is the oldest and the two lateral ones arising in the axils of bracts below the older flower are the youngest.
2. *Dianthus* is the other example of biparous cyme.

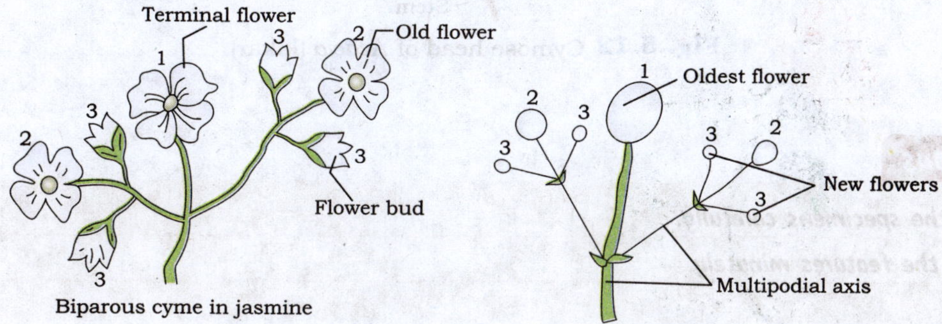

Fig. 5.10 Biparous or dichasial cyme

iii. Polychasial or Multiparous Cyme : *Calotropis*

Identification Characteristic

Peduncle terminates into flower, below which more than two laterally branches develop from the base of terminal flower.

General Characteristics

1. The lateral branches repeat main axis growth.
2. As a number of lateral flowers develop more or less simultaneously, so it looks like an umbel.
3. *Asclepias* also have polychasial or multiparous cyme.

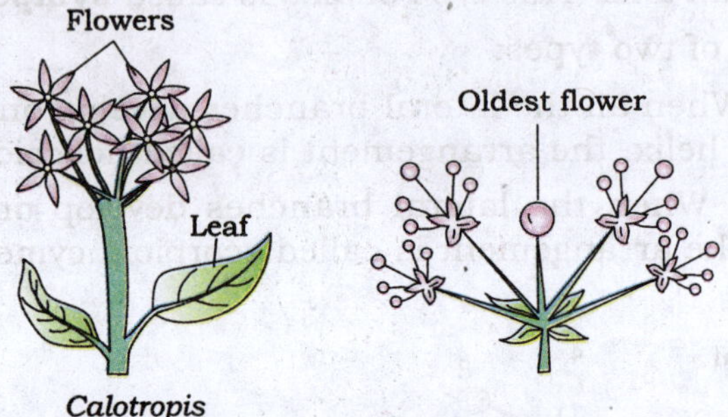

Fig. 5.11 Polychasial or multiparous cyme

iv. Cymose Head : *Acacia*

Identification Characteristic

Sessile/subsessile flowers are borne centrifugally around the receptacle.

General Characteristics

1. In this type of inflorescence, the axis is reduced into a globular receptacle.
2. *Albizia* is an another example of cymose head.

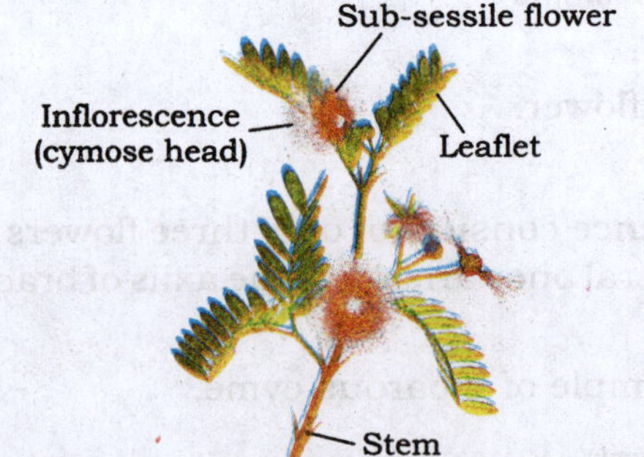

Fig. 5.12 Cymose head of *Acacia* (kikar)

PRECAUTIONS

- *Handle the specimens carefully.*
- *Observe the features minutely.*

Viva-Voce

Q.1 Define the term 'inflorescence'.

Ans The arrangement of flowers on the shoot system of a plant is called **inflorescence**.

Q.2 Give the scientific term used for the stalk of a flower.

Ans The stalk of a flower is called pedicel.

Q.3 List the main types of inflorescences that have been observed in plants.

Ans Inflorescence are of following main types:

(i) Racemose

(ii) Cymose

Q.4 Differentiate between racemose and cymose inflorescences.

Ans In racemose inflorescence, the main axis is elongated and does not terminate into a flower. The flowers are arranged in acropetal succession.

In cymose inflorescence, the growth of main axis is checked and it terminates into a flower. The flowers are arranged in basipetal succession.

Q.5 Give one word for the following terms:

(i) Flower that occurs singly.

(ii) Whorl of bract.

Ans (i) Flower that occurs singly – Solitary flower

(ii) Whorl of bract – Involucre

Q.6 What is capitulum?

Ans The inflorescence, where receptacle or main axis is flat and bears a number of sessile flowers with one or more whorls of bracts is called capitulum.

Q.7 Give one example that shows capitulum inflorescence.

Ans Sunflower shows capitulum type of inflorescence that have two types of florets, i.e. ray florets and disc florets.

Q.8 How are raceme and spike different from each other?

Ans Raceme inflorescence has pedicellate flower while spike has sessile flower.

Q.9 Name a feature that separates a spike from catkin.

Ans A spike has long peduncle that bears bisexual flowers while catkin has a pedulous peduncle that bears unisexual flowers.

Q.10 Cite an importance of studying inflorescences of different plants. NCERT

Ans Studying inflorescences and flower characteristics is important for taxonomic classification and plant identification.

Q.11 Flowers are borne in the form of inflorescence. Why?

Ans The presence of flowers in the form of inflorescence makes them more prominent to the pollinators or pollinating agents.

Q.12 What is the other name for racemose inflorescence? Also give a reason as a justification to this other name.

Ans It is also called as the indefinite inflorescence, because floral axis grows continuously and does not ends in a flower.

Q.13 Give the advantage of capitulum.

Ans In capitulum, the head as a whole becomes more showy and attractive as florets are close together. Therefore, these get pollinated by one or few insects within a short time.

Q.14 Which type of inflorescence is found in tulsi plant?

Ans In tulsi (family–Lamiaceae) verticillaster type of inflorescence is found.

Q.15 Give reason as to why hypanthodium and cyathium are called special type of inflorescences?

Ans Hypanthodium and cyathium are called special type of inflorescences because the main axis of hypanthodium is in the form of cup, while in cyathium the main axis is also in the form of cup having nectar secreting glands that attract pollinators.

Q.16 How is floret different from a flower? NCERT

Ans A flower is a complete reproductive unit in plants, while a floret is a small flower part of a larger inflorescence, commonly found in grasses.

Q.17 Observe a pomegranate fruit and note whether it has developed from a solitary flower or an inflorescence. NCERT

Ans A pomegranate fruit develops from a solitary flower, not from an inflorescence. This means each pomegranate fruit originates from a single flower.

Q.18 Give one example of a flower which occurs singly on the axis.

Ans Shoe flower (*Hibiscus*) is a solitary flower.

Q.19 How can you differentiate between perianth and involucre?

Ans Perianth is a whorl where calyx and corolla cannot be distinguished, while involucre is a whorl of bracts.

Experiment 6.a

AIM

To study the human skeleton with the help of virtual images/models only.

Theory/Principle

The hard, supportive and protective elements of the animal body constitute the **skeleton** or **skeletal system**. The skeleton consists of a framework of bones and few cartilages. Bone and cartilage both are specialised connective tissue.

The human skeletal system in adults is composed of 206 bones. Out of these, 80 bones make up the axial skeleton, while 126 bones form the appendicular skeleton. The axial skeleton consists of the bones of the skull, vertebral column, sternum and ribs. The appendicular skeleton consists of the bones of the limbs along with their girdles.

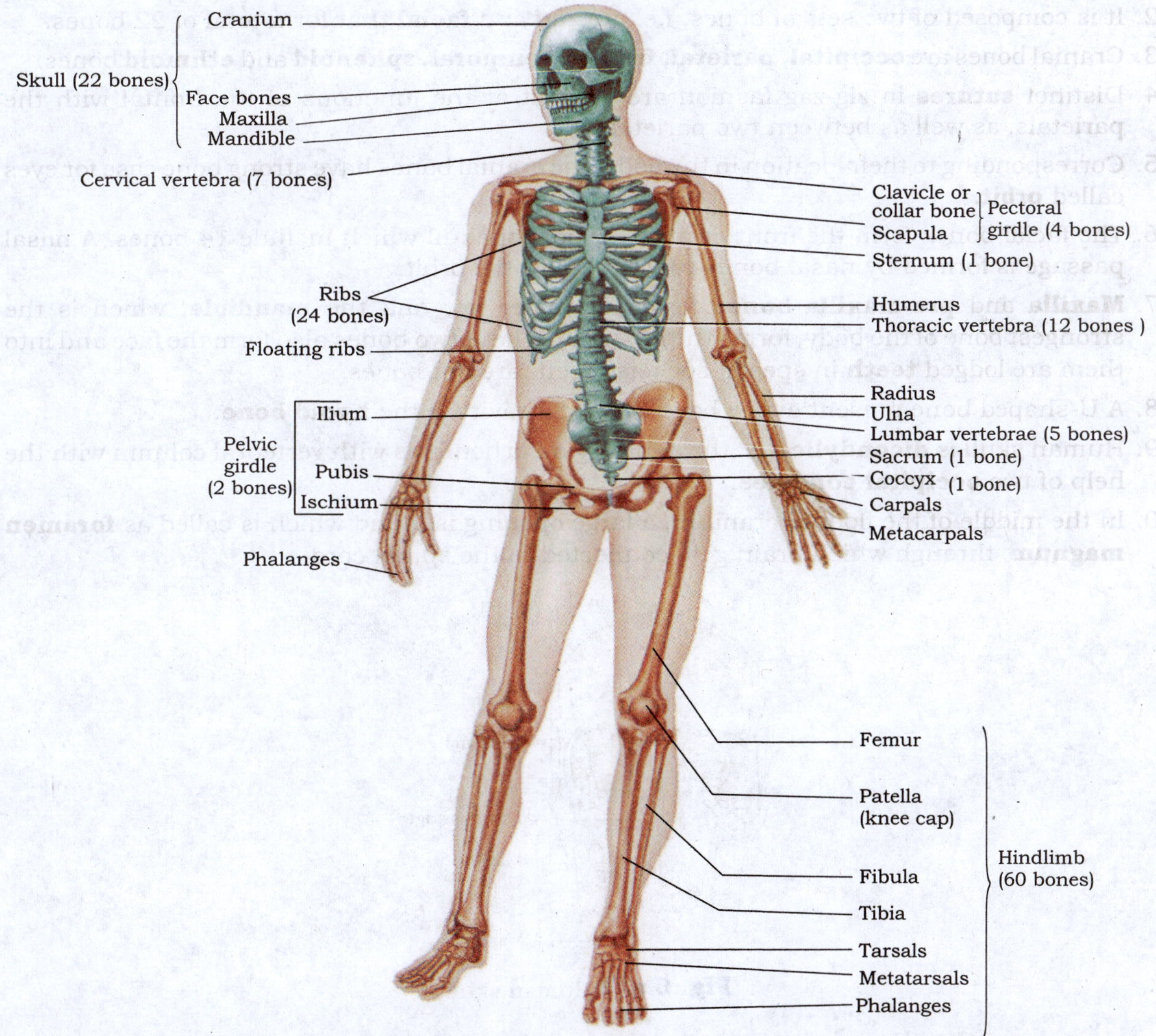

Fig. 6.a. 1 Human skeleton (endoskeleton) showing different types of bones

Skeleton system provides support to softer body parts as well as protects the delicate internal organs like brain, heart, lung, etc. Besides these major functions, skeleton also provides surface for muscle attachment, helps in movement, manufacturing blood corpuscles in bone marrow, etc.

Requirements

Chart or model of human skeleton, pencil, practical record book, eraser and practical guide.

Procedure

1. Observe different types of bones present in human skeleton.
2. Draw well labelled diagram of the bones and write the comments in your notebook.

Observations

A. Human Skull

Characteristics

1. It possesses strong bony case for the protection of brain which is called **cranium**. All of the bones of cranium are articulated by fibrous or fixed or immovable joints.
2. It is composed of two sets of bones, i.e. **cranial** and **facial** that form total of 22 bones.
3. Cranial bones are **occipital, parietal, frontal, temporal, sphenoid** and **ethmoid** bones.
4. Distinct **sutures** in zig-zag fashion are present at the junctions of the frontal with the parietals, as well as between two parietals.
5. Corresponding to their location in the body, the cranial bones have strong bone case for eyes called **orbit.**
6. The facial bones form the front or anterior part of skull which include 14 bones. A nasal passage is formed by nasal bones present below the orbit.
7. **Maxilla** and **pre-maxilla bones** form the upper jaw and the **mandible**, which is the strongest bone of the body, forms the lower jaw. These two bones also form the face and into them are lodged **teeth** in special sockets. Teeth are not bones.
8. A U-shaped bone present at the base of buccal cavity is the **hyoid bone.**
9. Human skull is **dicondylic**, i.e. the skull region articulates with vertebral column with the help of two **occipital condyles**.
10. In the middle of the floor of cranium, a large opening is found which is called as **foramen magnum**, through which brain gets connected to the spinal cord.

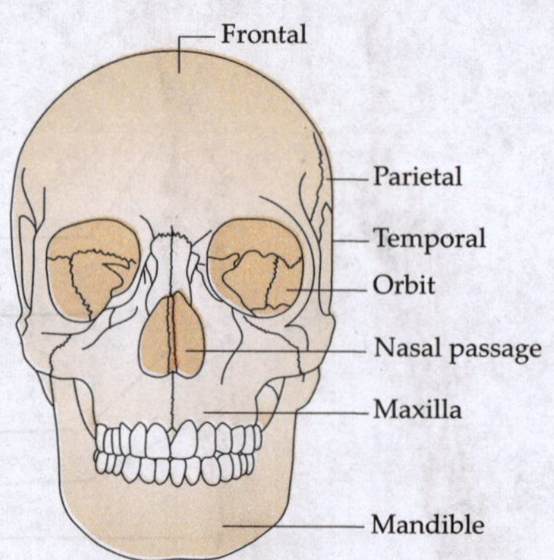

Fig. 6.a. 2 Human skull

B. Vertebral Column

Characteristics

1. It is also called as **spine** or **backbone** and is dorsally placed, extending from the base of the skull to the pelvis and constitutes the main framework of trunk.
2. Vertebral column forms the central axis of the body and helps it to keep it erect.
3. Each vertebra has a central hollow portion called **neural canal** through which the spinal cord passes.
4. It is made up of 26 serially arranged units called **vertebrae** (sing. Vertebra).
5. Vertebrae are of following five types, i.e. **cervical**, **thoracic**, **lumbar**, **sacral** and **coccygeal** or **caudal**.
6. It constitutes four curves that enhance balancing power and firmness for upright posture of the body.

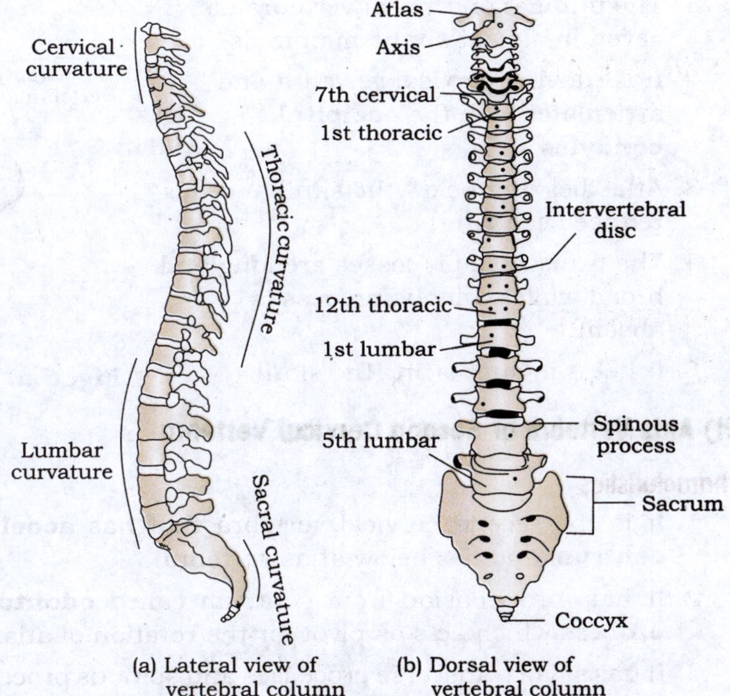

(a) Lateral view of vertebral column (b) Dorsal view of vertebral column

Fig. 6.a. 3 Vertebral column of human

7. The vertebral formula for human is C_7, T_{12}, L_5, $S_{(5)}$, $C_{(4)}$.
8. Five sacral vertebrae are fused into one bone and four coccygeal vertebrae are also fused together to form one bone.
9. Vertebral column supports the head, encloses and protect spinal cord as well as serves as a point of attachment for the skull, ribs, pectoral and pelvic girdles. It also allows flexing and bending of the back and body.

Structure of a Typical Vertebra

Characteristics

1. Typical vertebra has a large, disc-like anterior, flattened portion called **centrum** or **body**, which is modified notochord.
2. These are two laterally projecting transverse processes.
3. There is a cavity in the typical vertebra called **vertebral** or **neural canal**. It provides passage for spinal cord.
4. There is a pointed structure on the dorsal surface called **neural spine** or **spinous process** which provides protection to the spinal cord.

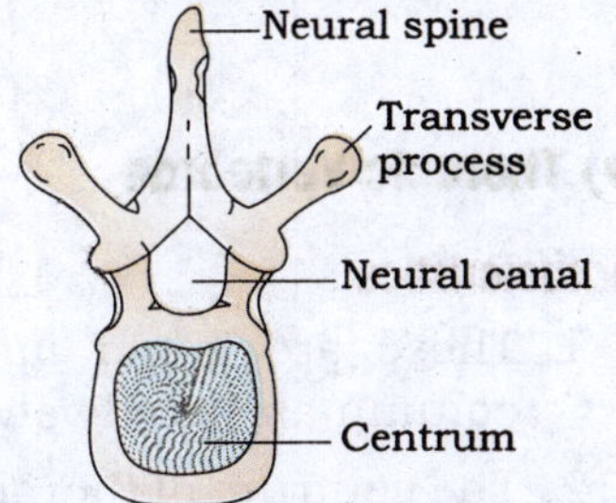

Fig. 6.a. 4 Parts of a typical vertebra

5. The posterior portion of vertebra is called **neural arch** which possesses different processes.
6. **Intervertebral discs** are present between the centre of two neighbouring vertebrae.
7. Two neighbouring vertebrae articulate with each other through their anterior and posterior **zygapophyses**.

(i) Atlas Vertebrae or First Cervical Vertebra

Characteristics

1. The number of cervical vertebrae is seven in almost all the mammals.
2. It is the first cervical vertebra and articulates with the **occipital condyles**.
3. Atlas lies just below the skull and has reduced centrum.
4. The transverse processes are long and broad while, spinous process is absent.
5. It helps in supporting the skull.

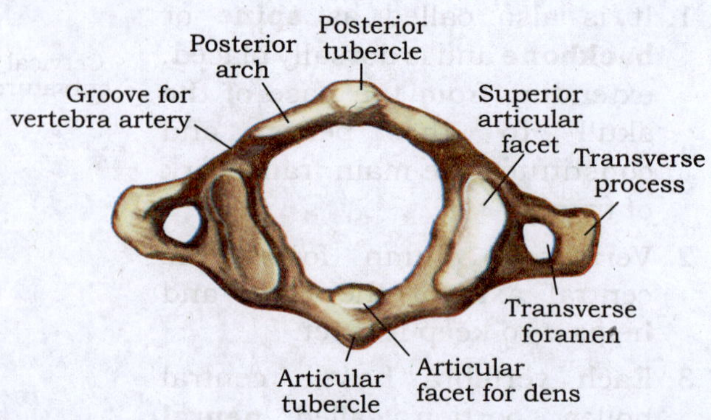

Fig. 6.a. 5 Atlas vertebrae (first cervical vertebrae)

(ii) Axis Vertebra or Second Cervical Vertebra

Characteristics

1. It is the second cervical vertebra that has **acoelus centrum** and lies below atlas vertebra.
2. It has an extension from centrum called **odontoid process** which acts as pivot for the rotation of atlas.
3. It has small transverse processes and spinous process is raised and has bifid-tip.
4. Allowed side to side or turning movements.

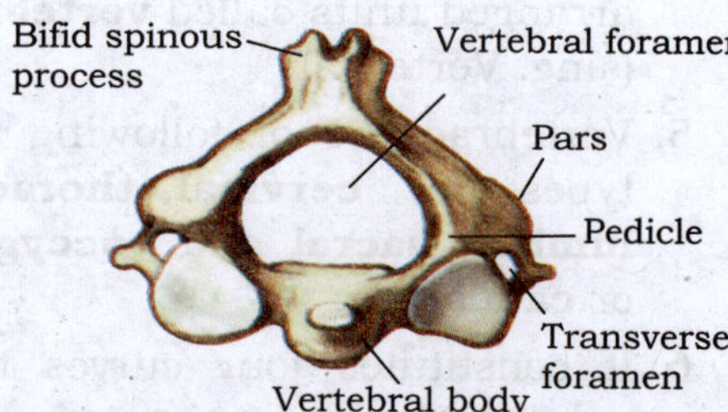

Fig. 6.a. 6 Axis vertebrae (second cervical vertebra)

(iii) Typical Cervical Vertebrae

Characteristics

1. The third, fourth, fifth, sixth and seventh cervical vertebrae are called **typical cervical vertebrae.**
2. They have long bifurcated spines and long transverse processes.

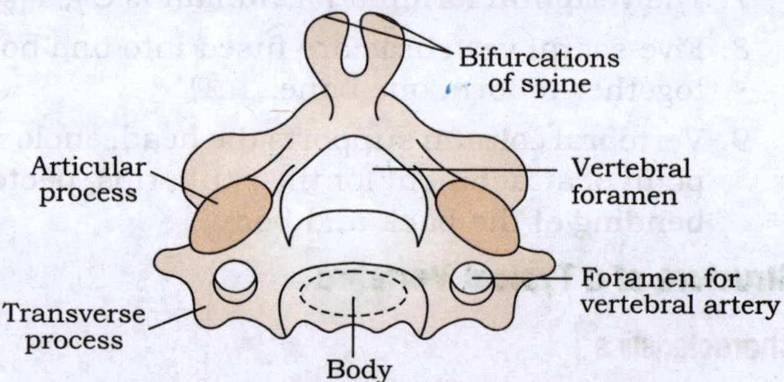

Fig. 6.a. 7 Typical cervical vertebra

(iv) Thoracic Vertebrae

Characteristics

1. These are found in chest region of vertebral column and are twelve in number.
2. The centrum of thoracic vertebrae is acoelus and is flat on the upper as well as lower side, i.e. **amphiplatyon**.
3. Vertebrae articulates with head of ribs at points called **demifacet** (**superior** and **inferior demifacets**).
4. Transverse process is club-shaped or short and **neural spine** is long and backward.

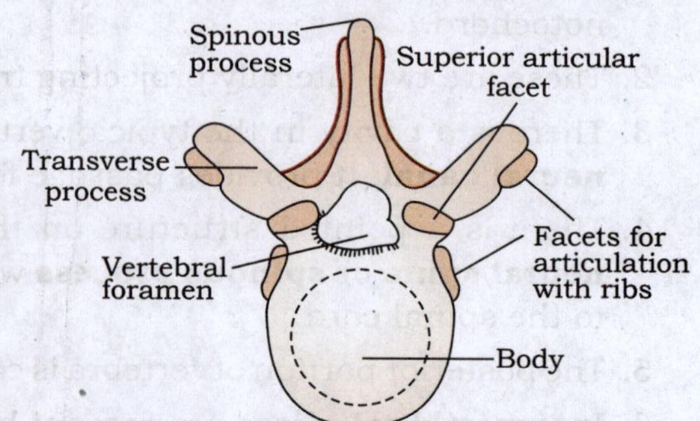

Fig. 6.a. 8 A thoracic vertebra

(v) Lumbar Vertebrae

Characteristics

1. It is the largest and strongest in the vertebral column.
2. These are five in number and are found in abdomen region of the body.
3. Centrum is big, flat and acoelus with well-defined **neural spine.**
4. Transverse process is thin, long, strong and well-developed with a small accessory process near its base.

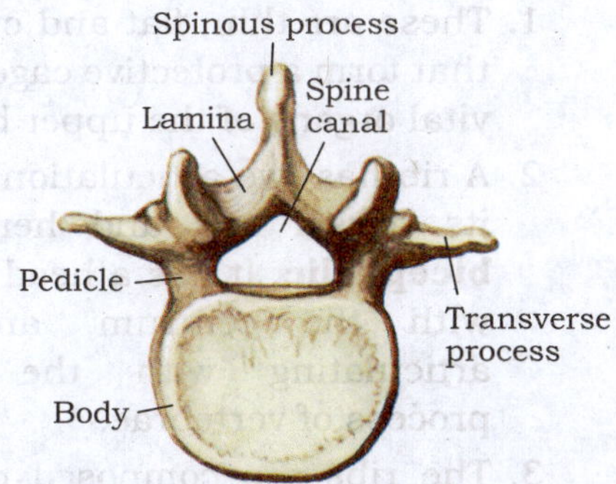

Fig. 6.a. 9 Lumbar vertebrae

(vi) Sacral Vertebrae or Sacrum

Characteristics

1. These are five in number and are present in the pelvic region of the body.
2. These are fused to form a single triangular bone called **sacrum**.
3. Sacrum have extra-articular surface and articulates with ilium of pelvic girdle.
4. The transverse process of sacrum is modified into broad structure that projects laterally from the body.

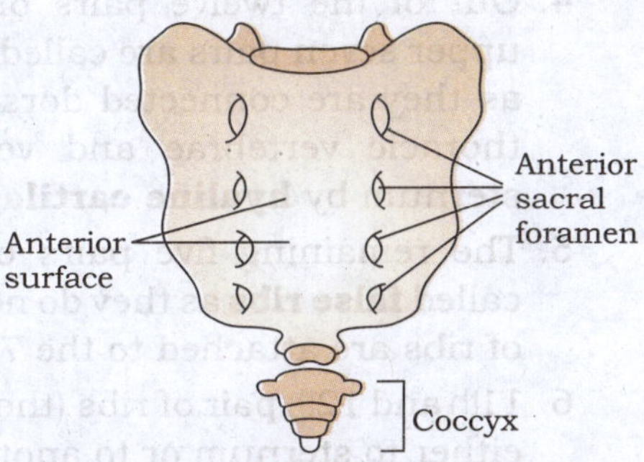

Fig. 6.a. 10 Sacrum and coccyx

(vii) Caudal Vertebrae or Coccyx

Characteristics

1. These are four in number that are fused to form **coccyx**.
2. These are found at the end of backbone and are **vestigial in adult**.
3. Transverse processes of coccyx are rudimentary.

C. Thoracic Cage or Rib Cage

Characteristics

1. It is made up of thoracic vertebrae, sternum and ribs.
2. It is also called as **thoracic basket** that covers and protects the vital organs like lungs and heart.

i. Sternum

Characteristics

1. It is also called **breast bone**.
2. It is a flat, dagger-shaped bone that lies just under the skin.
3. The bone is located on the ventral midline of thorax (in the middle of front chest wall).
4. It consist of three major parts:
   (a) Hexagonal disc present at the top **(manubrium)**.
   (b) Middle portion **(body)**.
   (c) Lower end with reduced bone **(xiphoid process)**.
5. It bears seven notches for the articulation with ribs.
6. Sternum provides surface for muscle attachment and helps in respiratory mechanism.

ii. Ribs

Characteristics

1. These are thin, flat and curved bones that form a protective cage around the vital organs of the upper body.
2. A rib has two articulation surfaces on its dorsal end and hence, called **bicephalic**. It has a head articulating with the centrum, and tubercle articulating with the transverse process of vertebrae.
3. The ribs are composed of 24 bones arranged in 12 pairs.
4. Out of the twelve pairs of ribs, the upper seven pairs are called **true ribs**. as they are connected dorsally to the thoracic vertebrae and ventrally to sternum by **hyaline cartilage**.
5. The remaining five pairs of ribs are called **false ribs** as they do not articulate directly with sternal ribs. The 8th, 9thand 10thpairs of ribs are attached to the 7th pair and indirectly to the sternum.
6. 11th and 12th pair of ribs (the last two pairs) are free as their anterior ends are not attached either to sternum or to another rib hence, they are called as **floating ribs**.
7. Ribs are protective in nature and also help in respiration.

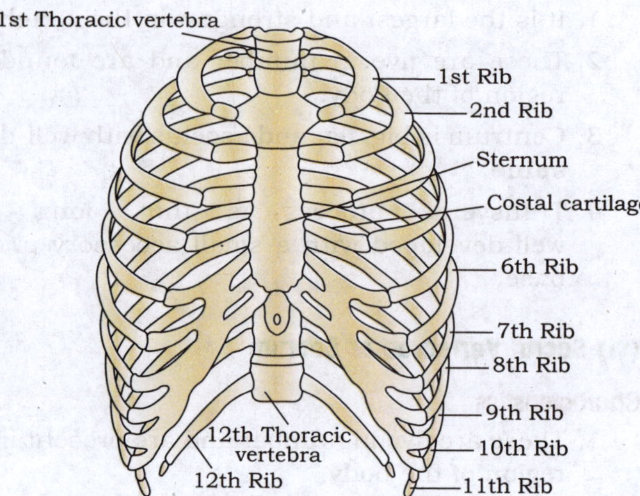

Fig. 6.a. 11 Rib cage (showing ribs and sternum)

iii. Pectoral Girdle

Characteristics

1. It is also called as **shoulder girdle**.
2. It consists of two bones:
   (a) Scapula or shoulder blade. (b) Clavicle or collar bone.

(a) Scapula of Pectoral Girdle

Characteristics

1. It is a large, flat and triangular bone that consists of a slightly elevated ridge called **spine**.
2. The end of each spine projects as a flattened and expanded portion called **acromion process**. It articulates with the clavicle.
3. Another process called **coracoid process** projects upwards from the broad end of scapula near **acromion process**.
4. Scapula below acromion process forms a socket-like cavity or depression (cup-like) called **glenoid cavity**.
5. This cavity articulates with head of humerus bone forming shoulder joint.

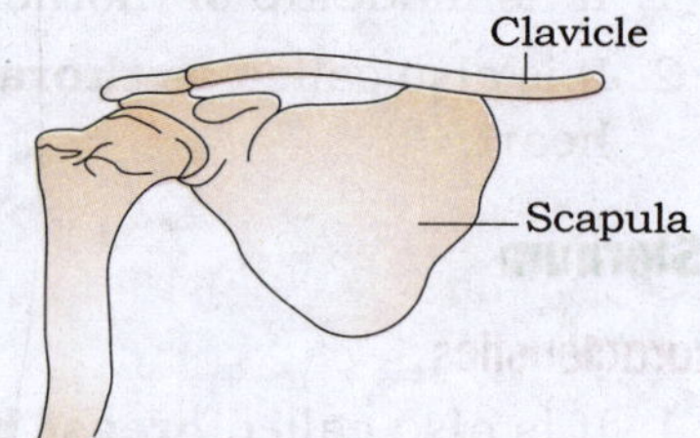

Fig. 6.a. 12 Pectoral girdle

(b) Clavicle of Pectoral Girdle

Characteristics

1. It is a long, slender bone with two curvatures, one at each end.
2. It articulates with the acromion.

D. Pelvic Girdle or Hip Girdle

Characteristics

1. It is located in the lower part of the trunk.
2. It consists of two **coxal or hip bones**, also known as the two halves of the pelvic girdle.
3. Each coxal bone is formed by the fusion of three bones, i.e.
   (i) Upper **ilium** (ii) Lower **ischium**
   (iii) Inner **pubis**

Fig. 6.a. 13 Anterior view of pelvic girdle

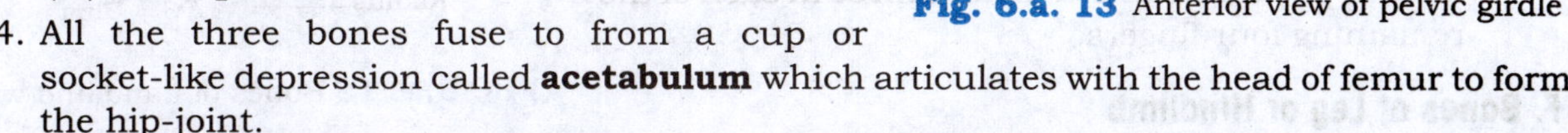

4. All the three bones fuse to from a cup or socket-like depression called **acetabulum** which articulates with the head of femur to form the hip-joint.

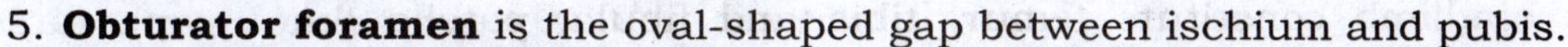

5. **Obturator foramen** is the oval-shaped gap between ischium and pubis.
6. Two halves of pelvic girdle meet ventrally to form **pubic symphysis** that contains **fibro-cartilaginous disc**.
7. Pelvic girdle provides articulation to the bones of leg, supports and protects **abdominal** viscera and provides attachment to leg muscles.

E. Bones of Hand or Forelimb

It is made up of bones consisting of humerus, radius and ulna, carpals, metacarpals and phalanges.

i. Humerus

Characteristics

1. It is the straight bone with a long shaft and forms the upper arm.
2. The rounded upper end or the head of the humerus fits into the glenoid cavity of the pectoral girdle.
3. It has a crest at its proximal end in the form of **deltoid ridge** for the attachment of arm muscles.
4. The distal end has a **foramen** and a **trochlear process**, which forms elbow joint with radius and ulna.

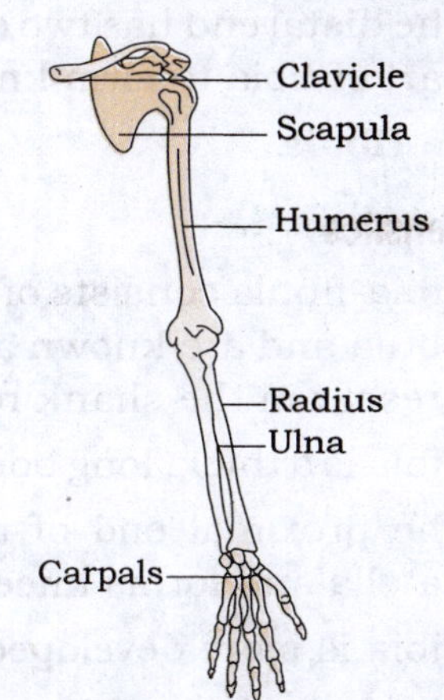

Fig. 6.a. 14 Bones of arms (forelimb) with parts of pectoral girdle attached

ii. Radius - Ulna

Characteristics

1. Radius-ulna consists of two separate bones of the forearm, i.e. **radius** and **ulna.**
2. Ulna is medial, long (longer than radius) and well developed.
3. It has larger **olecranon process**, which articulates with humerus.
4. There are two articular surfaces at the lower end of radius, one for ulna and the other for **wrist bones**.
5. Radius is lateral and contributes to the movement of the wrist.

iii. Carpals, Metacarpals and Phalanges

Characteristics

1. Wrist or carpals are composed of 8 small bones. These are scaphoid, lunate, triquetrum and pisiform (arranged in proximal row) and trapezium, trapezoid, capitate and hamate (arranged in distal row).
2. Five long metacarpals form the palm of hand.
3. 14 phalanges constitute the bones of fingers. There are two phalanges in thumb and three in each of the remaining four fingers.

Fig. 6.a. 15 Bones of hand and wrist

F. Bones of Leg or Hindlimb

Bones of leg or hindlimb constitute femur, tibia and fibula, patella (knee cap), tarsals, metatarsals and phalanges.

i. Femur

Characteristics

1. It is the longest bone of human skeletal system.
2. The upper end has a rounded head that fits into the acetabulum of pelvic girdle.
3. The proximal end has trochanters for attachment of thigh muscles.
4. The distal end has two condyles that articulate with triangular-shaped patella and proximal part of tibia to form knee on the ventral side.

ii. Tibia-fibula

Characteristics

1. Tibia-fibula consists of two separate bones, i.e. tibia and fibula and are known as **bone of the shank** as they are present in the shank region of leg.
2. Tibia is a thick, long bone that lies medially and in front.
3. The proximal end of tibia articulates with femur and patella and forms knee.
4. Tibia is more developed than fibula.
5. Fibula is short, thin and located more laterally.

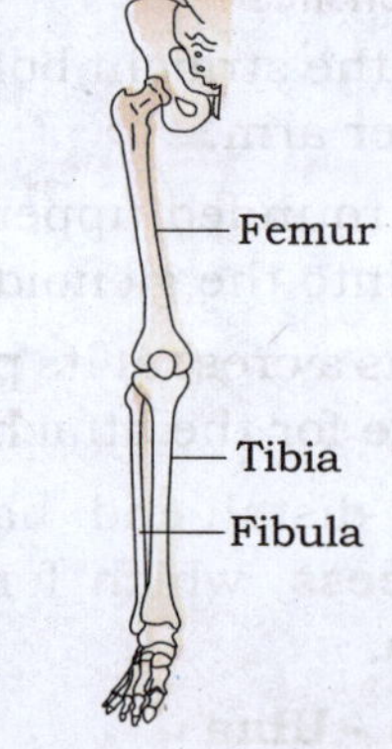

Fig. 6.a. 16 Bones of hindlimb or leg of human

iii. Patella

Characteristics

1. **Patella** is a cup-shaped bone that covers knee ventrally.
2. It is a **sesamoid bone**, i.e. bone embedded within a tendon.
3. These are formed by **ossification of tendons.**

iv. Tarsals, Metatarsals and Phalanges

Characteristics

1. There are 7 tarsal bones which are arranged in two rows to form the ankle.
2. Metatarsals consists of five bones that form foot.

3. The bones of toes are called **phalanges**. It consists of two bones in big toe and three bones in each of the remaining toes. Total number of phalanges are 14.

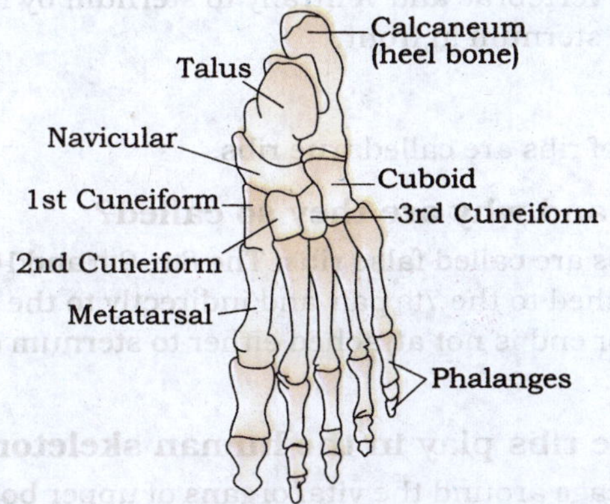

Fig. 6.a.17 Bones of human foot and ankle

PRECAUTIONS

- *The structure of bones should be observed carefully.*
- *The human skeletal model should be handled properly and damage to bones should be prevented.*

Viva-Voce

Q.1 What is the function or role of skeleton system?

Ans Skeleton system provides support to softer body parts as well as protects the delicate internal organs like brain, heart, lung, etc. It also provides surface for muscle attachment, brings movement, helps in manufacturing blood corpuscles in bone marrow, etc.

Q.2 Which is the longest bone of human skeleton?

Ans Femur or thigh bone is the longest bone of human skeleton.

Q.3 Where does the head of femur articulate?

Ans The head of femur articulates in the cavity of the pelvic girdle called acetabulum.

Q.4 Name the first and second cervical vertebrae.

Ans Atlas is the first vertebra while axis is the second cervical vertebra.

Q.5 Which region of vertebrae is the largest and strongest in vertebral column?

Ans Lumbar vertebrae is the largest and strongest region in the vertebral column.

Q.6 Name three major parts of sternum.

Ans The three major parts of sternum are as follows

(i) Hexagonal disc present at the top called manubrium.

(ii) Middle portion called body.

(iii) Lower end with reduced bone, called xiphoid process.

Q.7 Name the different parts of thoracic cage or rib cage.

Ans Thoracic cage or rib cage is made up of thoracic vertebrae, sternum and ribs.

Q.8 How many bones are there in ribs?

Ans The ribs are composed of 24 bones arranged in 12 pairs. Among these, seven pairs are connected dorsally to the thoracic vertebrae and ventrally to sternum by hyaline cartilage, remaining are not directly attached to the sternum in front.

Q.9 What are true ribs?

Ans The upper seven pairs of ribs are called true ribs.

Q.10 What are false ribs and why are they so called?

Ans The last five pairs of ribs are called false ribs. The 8th, 9th and 10th pair of ribs are called so because these are attached to the 7th pair and indirectly to the sternum. 11th and 12th pair of ribs are free as their anterior end is not attached either to sternum or to any other rib, hence these are also called floating ribs.

Q.11 State briefly the role ribs play in the human skeleton.

Ans Ribs form a protective cage around the vital organs of upper body like heart, lungs, etc. and also help in respiration.

Q.12 Which two bones are called bones of shank?

Ans Tibia and fibula are known as bones of shank.

Q.13 Name the flat bone of the pectoral girdle.

Ans Scapula is the large, flat and triangular bone of pectoral girdle that consists of a sharp ridge called spine.

Q.14 Name the three bones that fuse to form pelvic girdle.

Ans The pelvic girdle is formed by the fusion of three bones, i.e.

(i) upper ilium

(ii) lower ischium

(iii) anterior pubis

Q.15 Give the names of bones that form forelimb.

Ans The forelimb consists of humerus, radius-ulna, carpals (8 bones), metacarpals (5 bones) and phalanges (14 bones).

Q.16 Differentiate between bone and cartilage.

Ans Bone has a very hard matrix due to the calcium salts (calcium phosphate) and are made up of a protein called ossein. Cartilage has slightly pliable matrix due to the chondroitin salt and there is no inorganic deposition. It is made up of protein called chondrin.

Q.17 Name the smallest bone of human skeleton. Where is it found and also give the sequence of bones?

Ans Stapes is the smallest bone of human skeleton which is found in ear. The sequence of the three bones found in ear are malleus, incus and stapes.

Q.18 Study of skeleton system is termed as.

Ans Study of skeleton system is termed as osteology.

Q.19 What is the other name of bone stapes?

Ans Stirrup is the other name of stapes.

Q.20 In which bones the bone marrow is present?

Ans Long bones have bone marrow which is capable of manufacturing red blood corpuscles.

Q.21 Name the chemical constituent of bones.

Ans Bones are made up of collagen and calcium phosphate.

Experiment 6.b

AIM

To study of different types of joints in human skeleton with the help of virtual images/models only.

Theory/ Principle

The regions of articulation between two or more bones or between a bone and a cartilage are called **joint**, which are essential for all types of movements and make the body flexible. Force generated by muscles is used to carry out movement through joints, where the joints acts as a fulcrum.

Types of Joints

Bones may be movable, slightly movable or immovable depending upon the nature of joints.

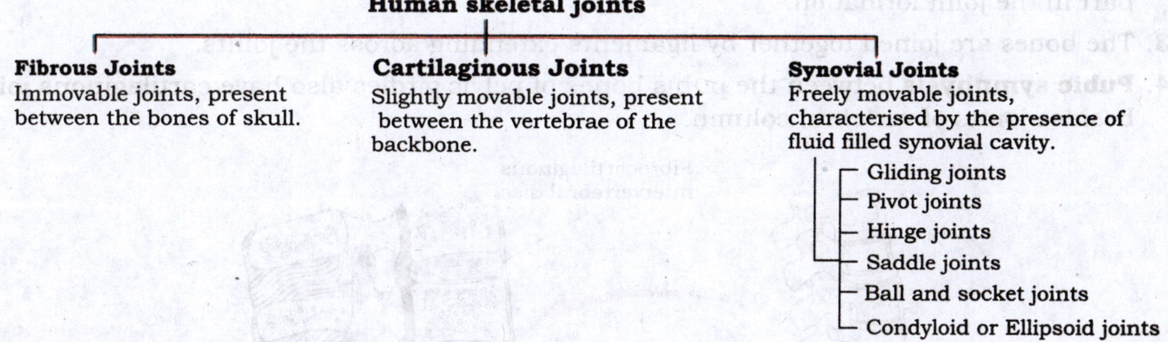

Requirements

Specimen of human skeleton, charts and models of skeleton, pencil, eraser, practical record book and laboratory guide.

Procedure

1. Observe the different types of bones and joints present in a human skeleton.
2. Draw well labelled diagrams of the joints and write the comments in your practical record book.

Observations

A. Fibrous Joints

Characteristics

1. These are immovable joints which do not allow the movement of bones.
2. Bones are held firmly by bundles of **white fibrous collagen**.
3. The place of immovable joints are often called as **sutures**.

4. Syndesmosis or joint between tibia and fibula is also a fibrous joint besides skull joints.

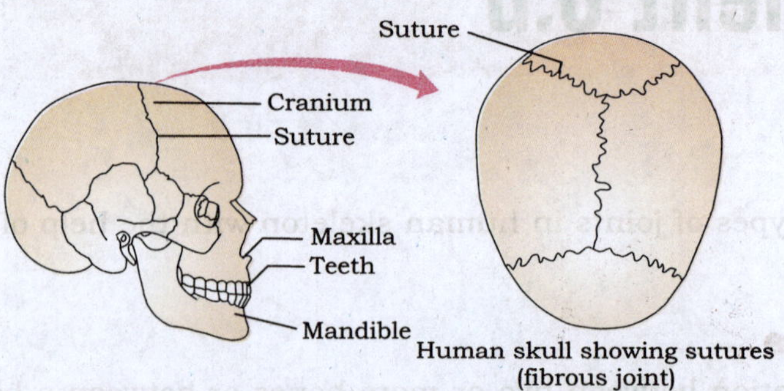

Fig. 6.b.1 Fibrous joint in skull of human

B. Cartilaginous Joints

Characteristics

1. These are slightly movable joints, also called as **symphysis**.
2. **Fibro-cartilage** or **white fibrous** cartilage is present between the ends of the bones taking part in the joint formation.
3. The bones are joined together by ligaments extending across the joints.
4. **Pubic symphysis** between the pubis bones of pelvic girdles also have cartilaginous joints besides joints of vertebral column.

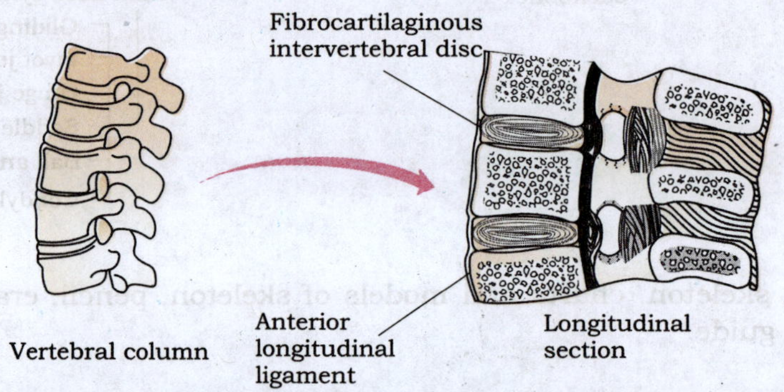

Fig. 6.b.2 Cartilaginous joint

C. Synovial Joints

Characteristics

1. These are freely movable joints.
2. The enlargement of one bone fits into a depression of another, allowing for a wide range of motion.
3. **Synovial cavity** (space between two bones) is lined by fibrous **synovial membrane. Synovial fluid** is present between the joints and acts as a cushion to prevent friction between the joints. It is gelatinous in nature.

4. **Articular cartilage** (a layer of hyaline cartilage) covers the ends of the bones which provides smooth and elastic surface as well as reduces friction.

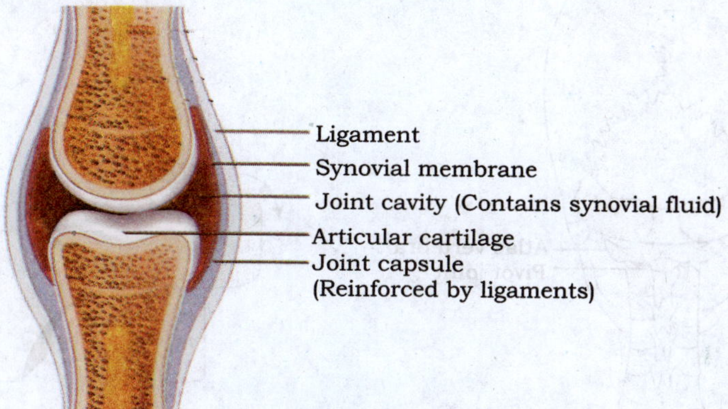

Fig. 6.b.3 Synovial joint

Types of Synovial Joints

i. Gliding Joints

Characteristics

1. This joint allows limited movement as the bones are closely packed together or held in place by ligaments.
2. No twisting is allowed as articular surfaces of gliding bones are **flat**. Back and forth and side to side movements are allowed, but only for a few joining elements.
3. Joints found in carpals of wrist and tarsals of ankle are gliding joints.

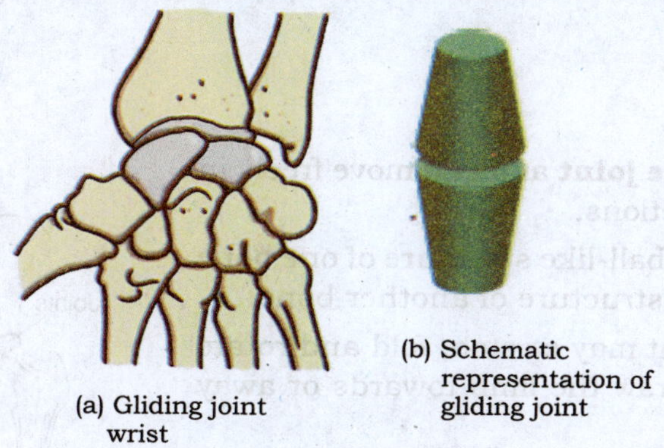

Fig. 6.b.4 Gliding joint

ii. Pivot Joints

Characteristics

1. These joints are responsible for **rotational movement** between bones.
2. In this type of joint, rounded end of one bone fits into a shallow pit of another bone which remains stationary.
3. These joints are found between the atlas and axis vertebrae of backbone. It is the odontoid process of the axis vertebra over which the atlas along with skull rotate.

4. This joint is also present between upper end of radius and ulna.

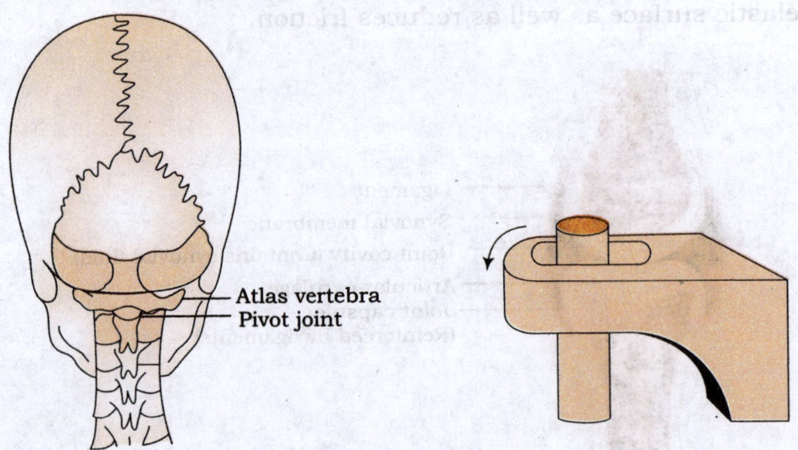

(a) Pivot joint between atlas and axis vertebrae (b) Schematic representation of pivot joint

Fig. 6.b.5 Pivot joint

iii. Hinge Joints

Characteristics

1. This joint allows the **movement in one plane only** and is held intact by ligament.
2. In this type of joint, one edge of the socket is extended to limit the movement of bone in that direction, ensuring controlled movement.
3. This type of joint is found in knee joint, elbow joint, ankle joint and joints between phalanges or interphalangeal joints.

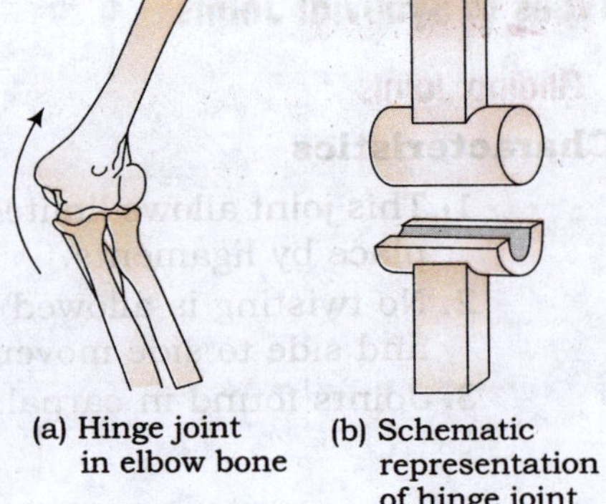

(a) Hinge joint in elbow bone (b) Schematic representation of hinge joint

Fig. 6.b.6 Hinge joint

iv. Ball and Socket Joints

Characteristics

1. It is the **most movable joint** and can move freely in all the planes or directions.
2. In this type of joint, a ball-like structure of one bone fits into a socket-like structure of another bone.
3. Movement at this joint may stretch, fold and rotate limbs and also can draw the limb towards or away from the body.
4. These joints are present between humerus with pectoral girdle, femur with pelvic girdle, and maleus with incus (in ear ossicles).

(a) Ball and socket joint between femur and pelvic girdle (b) Schematic representation of socket joint

Fig. 6.b.7 Ball and socket joint

v. Saddle Joints

Characteristics

1. These joints allow **movement in two planes**.
2. These resemble ball and socket joints but are less developed than the latter.
3. The ball in this joint is a small projection of one bone which fits into a saddle-like depression of another bone.

4. These joints are found in bones of metacarpals and carpals of thumb.

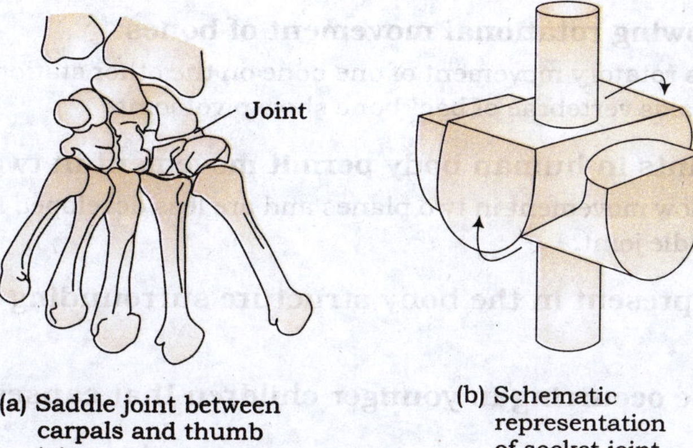

(a) Saddle joint between carpals and thumb joint

(b) Schematic representation of socket joint

Fig. 6.b.8 Saddle joint

PRECAUTIONS

- *Specimen should be handled carefully.*
- *The joints must be observed and drawn carefully.*

Viva-Voce

Q.1 Where are the sutures or fibrous joints found?

Ans Sutures or fibrous joints are found in skull of human beings.

Q.2 Name the joints present between the vertebrae in vertebral column.

Ans Cartilaginous joints are present between vertebrae. They allow slight movement because of cartilage pads present between the ends of bones.

Q.3 Give an example of cartilaginous joints.

Ans Pubic symphysis or joints between the vertebrae of backbone are examples of cartilaginous joints.

Q.4 Name the joint that can move freely.

Ans Synovial joints are freely movable joints that allow considerable movement.

Q.5 Which substance is responsible for lubricating the freely movable joints?

Ans Synovial fluid is the thick sticky fluid that acts as a cushion to prevent friction between the joints by lubricating them.

Q.6 Which joint allows the movement of bone only in a single plane?

Ans Hinge joint present in elbow and knee shows or permits movement in a single plane only.

Q.7 Which type of joint is found in hip or pelvic bones that makes it movable?

Ans Ball and socket joint is present in hip or pelvic bones that makes it movable.

Q.8 Name a joint allowing rotational movement of bones.

Ans The joint that allows rotatory movement of one bone on the other stationary bone is called pivot joint, e.g. atlas and axis vertebrae of backbone show pivot joint.

Q.9 Which type of joints in human body permit movement in two planes?

Ans Those joints that allow movement in two planes and are less developed form of ball and socket joints are called saddle joint.

Q.10 Name the joints present in the bony structure surrounding brain?

Ans Sutures.

Q.11 Name the disease occurring in younger children that causes inflammation of joints.

Ans Still's diseases is a kind of rheumatoid arthritis that occurs in younger people.

Q.12 Name a disease of joints occurring in old age people. How is it caused?

Ans Osteoarthritis or degenerative joint disease is characterised by progressive erosion of articular cartilage. It is commonly seen in old age people because the secretion of synovial fluid in the joints decreases with age.

Q.13 Why is the stiffness of joints seen in old age?

Ans In old age, the stiffness of joints is due to the decrease in synovial fluid.

Q.14 Name some common injuries of joints.

Ans Dislocation and cartilage tears are common injuries of joints.

Experiment/Activity No.________ Date ________ Page No. ________

Teacher Signature ________________

Experiment/Activity No.________ Date ________ Page No. ________

Teacher Signature ____________________

Experiment/Activity No.________ Date ________ Page No. ________

Teacher Signature ________

Experiment/Activity No.________ Date ________ Page No. ________

Teacher Signature ________________

Experiment/Activity No.________ Date ________ Page No. ________

Teacher Signature ________________

Experiment/Activity No.________ Date ________ Page No. ________

Teacher Signature ________________

Experiment/Activity No.________ Date ________ Page No. ________

Teacher Signature________________

Experiment/Activity No.________ Date ________ Page No. ________

Teacher Signature ________

Experiment/Activity No.________ Date ________ Page No. ________

Teacher Signature ________________

Experiment/Activity No.________ Date ________ Page No. ________

Teacher Signature ________

Experiment/Activity No.________ Date ________ Page No. ________

Teacher Signature ________________

Experiment/Activity No. ________ Date ________ Page No. ________

Teacher Signature ________

Experiment/Activity No.________ Date ________ Page No. ________

Teacher Signature ________

Experiment/Activity No.________ Date ________ Page No. ________

Teacher Signature ________________

Experiment/Activity No.________ Date ________ Page No. ________

Teacher Signature ________________

Experiment/Activity No.________ Date ________ Page No. ________

Teacher Signature ________

Experiment/Activity No.________ Date ________ Page No. ________

Teacher Signature ________________

Experiment/Activity No.________ Date ________ Page No. ________

Teacher Signature ____________

Experiment/Activity No.________ Date ________ Page No. ________

Teacher Signature ________________

Experiment/Activity No.________ Date ________ Page No. ________

Teacher Signature ________________

Experiment/Activity No.________ Date ________ Page No. ________

Teacher Signature ________

Experiment/Activity No.________ Date ________ Page No. ________

Teacher Signature ________________

Experiment/Activity No.________ Date ________ Page No. ________

Teacher Signature ________________

Experiment/Activity No.________ Date ________ Page No. ________

Teacher Signature ________

Experiment/Activity No.________ Date ________ Page No. ________

Teacher Signature ________________

Experiment/Activity No.________ Date ________ Page No. ________

Teacher Signature ________

Experiment/Activity No.________ Date ________ Page No. ________

Teacher Signature ________________

Experiment/Activity No.________ Date ________ Page No. ________

Teacher Signature ________________

Experiment/Activity No.________ Date ________ Page No. ________

Teacher Signature ________

Experiment/Activity No.________ Date ________ Page No. ________

Teacher Signature ________________

Experiment/Activity No.________ Date ________ Page No. ________

Teacher Signature ________________

Experiment/Activity No.________ Date ________ Page No. ________

Teacher Signature________________

Experiment/Activity No.________ Date ________ Page No. ________

Teacher Signature________________

Experiment/Activity No.________ Date ________ Page No. ________

Teacher Signature ________________

Experiment/Activity No.________ Date ________ Page No. ________

Teacher Signature____________

Experiment/Activity No.________ Date ________ Page No. ________

Teacher Signature ________________

Experiment/Activity No.________ Date ________ Page No. ________

Teacher Signature ________________

Experiment/Activity No.________ Date ________ Page No. ________

Teacher Signature ________________

Experiment/Activity No.________ Date ________ Page No. ________

Teacher Signature ____________

Experiment/Activity No.________ Date ________ Page No. ________

Teacher Signature ____________

Experiment/Activity No.________ Date ________ Page No. ________

Teacher Signature ____________

Experiment/Activity No.________ Date ________ Page No. ________

Teacher Signature ________

Experiment/Activity No.________ Date ________ Page No. ________

Teacher Signature ____________

Experiment/Activity No.________ Date ________ Page No. ________

Teacher Signature ________________

Experiment/Activity No.________ Date ________ Page No. ________

Teacher Signature ________________

Experiment/Activity No.________ Date ________ Page No. ________

Teacher Signature ________________

Experiment/Activity No.________ Date ________ Page No. ________

Teacher Signature ________

Experiment/Activity No.________ Date ________ Page No. ________

Teacher Signature ________________

Experiment/Activity No.________ Date ________ Page No. ________

Teacher Signature ________________

Experiment/Activity No.________ Date ________ Page No. ________

Teacher Signature ________

Experiment/Activity No.________ Date ________ Page No. ________

Teacher Signature ________________

Experiment/Activity No.________ Date ________ Page No. ________

Teacher Signature ________

Experiment/Activity No.________ Date ________ Page No. ________

Teacher Signature ________________

Experiment/Activity No.________ Date ________ Page No. ________

Teacher Signature____________

Experiment/Activity No.________ Date ________ Page No. ________

Teacher Signature ____________

Experiment/Activity No.________ Date ________ Page No. ________

Teacher Signature ________________

Experiment/Activity No.________ Date ________ Page No. ________

Teacher Signature ________

Experiment/Activity No.________ Date ________ Page No. ________

Teacher Signature ________________

Experiment/Activity No.________ Date ________ Page No. ________

Teacher Signature ________________

Experiment/Activity No.________ Date ________ Page No. ________

Teacher Signature ________________

Experiment/Activity No.________ Date ________ Page No. ________

Teacher Signature ________________

Experiment/Activity No.________ Date ________ Page No. ________

Teacher Signature ________________

Experiment/Activity No.________ Date ________ Page No. ________

Teacher Signature ____________

Experiment/Activity No.________ Date ________ Page No. ________

Teacher Signature ________________

Experiment/Activity No.________ Date ________ Page No. ________

Teacher Signature ________________

Experiment/Activity No.________ Date ________ Page No. ________

Teacher Signature ________

Experiment/Activity No.________ Date ________ Page No. ________

Teacher Signature ________________

Experiment/Activity No.________ Date ________ Page No. ________

Teacher Signature ________________

Experiment/Activity No.________ Date ________ Page No. ________

Teacher Signature ________________

Experiment/Activity No.________ Date ________ Page No. ________

Teacher Signature ________

Experiment/Activity No.________ Date ________ Page No. ________

Teacher Signature ____________

Experiment/Activity No.________ Date ________ Page No. ________

Teacher Signature __________

Experiment/Activity No.________ Date ________ Page No. ________

Teacher Signature ________

Experiment/Activity No.________ Date ________ Page No. ________

Teacher Signature ________

Experiment/Activity No.________ Date ________ Page No. ________

Teacher Signature ________

Experiment/Activity No.________ Date ________ Page No. ________

Teacher Signature ________

Experiment/Activity No.________ Date ________ Page No. ________

Teacher Signature ________